Surviving Andersonville

Surviving Andersonville

One Prisoner's Recollections of the Civil War's Most Notorious Camp

ED GLENNAN

Edited by David A. Ranzan

McFarland & Company, Inc., Publishers
Jefferson, North Carolina, and London

LIBRARY OF CONGRESS CATALOGUING-IN-PUBLICATION DATA

Glennan, Ed, 1840–1924.
    Surviving Andersonville : one prisoner's recollections
of the Civil War's most notorious camp / Ed Glennan ;
edited by David A. Ranzan.
      p.   cm.
    Includes bibliographical references and index.

    ISBN 978-0-7864-7361-8
    softcover : acid free paper ∞

    1. Glennan, Ed, 1840–1924.   2. Andersonville Prison —
Biography.   3. United States — History — Civil War, 1861–
1865 — Personal narratives.   4. United States — History —
Civil War, 1861–1865 — Prisoners and prisons.
5. United States. Army. Illinois Infantry Regiment, 42nd
(1861–1865)   6. Prisoners of war — Georgia —
Andersonville — Biography.   7. Andersonville (Ga.) —
Biography.   I. Ranzan, David, A., editor.   II. Title.
E612.A5G55 2013
973.7'8 — dc23   2013016075

BRITISH LIBRARY CATALOGUING DATA ARE AVAILABLE

Cover art: Bird's-eye view of Andersonville Prison from
the south-east with the vast prison area surrounded by
stockade fences and several banks of cannons, by J.W.
Morton, Jr., 1890 (Library of Congress).

Manufactured in the United States of America

*McFarland & Company, Inc., Publishers
  Box 611, Jefferson, North Carolina 28640
    www.mcfarlandpub.com*

Table of Contents

Preface

In the summer of 2008, I began my employment as the university archivist at Salisbury University, managing the University Archives and the archives at the Edward H. Nabb Research Center for Delmarva History and Culture. While performing my initial inventory of the Nabb Research Center's archival holdings, I came across the Rose Embry Carey Collection that contained photocopies of a Union soldier's reminiscence. After several days of reading the soldier's prose, I was hooked. His narrative illustrated the hardships typical of prisoners of war but with a personable flair that quickly drew me in to his story. Laden with humor, cynicism, honesty, desperation and hatred, I was engaged with his struggle to remain human in a place shrouded in inhumanity and horror.

I decided to do some background research on the author. An Irish immigrant, Edward Glennan enlisted in Company F of the Forty-second Illinois Infantry Regiment in 1861. Rising to the rank of first sergeant, he participated in the Western Theater of the American Civil War. Wounded twice, he was captured during the battle of Chickamauga and spent the next fourteen months in various prisons in Virginia and Georgia. What made his experiences so special was that he survived Andersonville.

In 1891, while a patient at the Leavenworth National Home, Glennan began to write down his experiences in vivid detail, describing the daily adversity of a Union soldier while a prisoner of war. His journal, comprised of three volumes, bears the hand-lettered title "Reminiscence of A Prisoner of War." He filled close to three hundred, closely written pages reminiscing his life from 20 September 1863 to 4 June 1865. The Glennan Reminiscence has been handed down from generation to generation and was in the possession of Ed Glennan's grandnephew,

Charles Embry. Unfortunately, a family member requested to photo-copy the pages and kept the original. He or she instead gave Charles the photocopies. These photocopies were handed down to his daughter (Ed's great-grandniece) Rose Embry Carey of Salisbury, Maryland, and she allowed the Edward H. Nabb Research Center for Delmarva History and Culture at Salisbury University to photocopy her photocopied mate-rial.

With my experience working for two documentary editing projects, the Papers of the War Department, 1784–1800, at East Stroudsburg Uni-versity and the Thomas A. Edison Papers at Rutgers University, I began the task of transcribing Glennan's remarkable story and identifying the people he encountered, places he visited and events he observed. The project took a year to complete.

Although Ed Glennan is the focus of the publication, the significance of his writings goes beyond the man himself. The reader can gain a detailed understanding of the prisons of the South. The depth of the publication makes it of long-term value not only to Civil War enthusiasts but also to a range of scholars and students, including general historians, social scientists, and political scientists. In addition, this book's value lies in its ability to enhance other publications for researchers and enthu-siasts with never-before-published eyewitness accounts of the key events and places during this period.

A Note on the Editorial Policy

Good or bad, Ed Glennan possesses a unique voice. His stream-of-consciousness writing style paints a vivid picture of his tour of duty during the Civil War. However, his stylistic approach can hinder the reading experience for the audience. As a reader, we are taught punctu-ation, sentence and paragraph structure and the rules of capitalization. This does not occur in Glennan's text, which in turn creates an editorial dilemma. First, how does one meet the criteria of a scholarly documen-tary edition while still allowing for the fact that a human being wrote the text? Second, how would one make his narrative into a readable manuscript? It is unclear if Glennan was thinking of a possible publica-tion but if he did pursue it, the editor would have been forced to set sev-eral rules or emendations to standardize the text for improved readability as the manuscript is littered with numerous eccentricities and idiosyncrasies.

With this in mind, an editorial policy was developed. Other scholarly editions were reviewed and through these examinations, C. Vann Woodward's *Mary Chestnut's Civil War* closely paralleled the issues in Glennan's manuscript. Because of the similarities, the editor adopted that publication's editorial policy with a few modifications.

The text is transcribed as accurately and literally as possible in the hope of preserving the style of the nineteenth century writing. Because the transcription retains the spelling inconsistencies of the originals, this may cause potential problems for the reader. Where there is any doubt about the interpretation of a particular word that conjectured word is followed by a question mark and enclosed in square brackets. It is the editor's intention to literally transcribe what the individual wrote, not to suggest the author's intent. Only in a few cases are words corrected. If the word is confusingly misspelled, so that sense is uncertain, either the missing letter is properly inserted or the corrected word will appear after the misspelling. In both cases, the correction is enclosed in square brackets. Interlineations are brought down to the line of the text at the place indicated as well as addition in the margins. Omitted text is indicated with a dash enclosed in square brackets [—] and crossed-out words and phrases are retained when legible with the deleted passage placed in the text with a strike-through bar. Except for regularizing the capitalization, punctuation and in several incidents the spelling, attention has been taken not to alter the author's writing or its content.

Pronunciation was a major concern throughout the narrative. Glennan's constant use of dashes of varying length and placement above, amid and below the line level makes it difficult to comprehend his intent. The editor has silently interpreted those dashes as periods when they serve to separate sentences. The writer's overuse of commas defies the rules of modern writing. Therefore, the editor has silently imposed some restriction upon Glennan's use of commas. If the commas have no place in the text, they were silently removed or changed to the correct punctuation.

While writing down his memories, Glennan was oblivious to demarcating paragraphs, therefore the editor has inserted paragraph breaks where he thought appropriate. The editor imposed a modern form of capitalization in those cases where the first word in the new paragraph was lowercased. The editor also exercises rules of capitalization consistent with intelligibility. Unintentional repetitions are silently corrected, whereas obvious slips of the pen were ignored. All names of ships have been italicized. Explanatory insertions by the editor to indicate, for example, a missing or torn page are similarly bracketed and italicized. All ellipses are the editor's and are not placed in brackets.

Introduction by David A. Ranzan

Never while our Mercifull Creator Lets me Live & retain my Sences,
Can I forget that date, the 20th of March 1864. No, if I wanted to,
I Could not Forget it For I am Reminded of it Every time I See my
Features & Hair in a Glass. Yes, Everytime I receive a twinge of Pain
& think to myself where did thats Come From, the answer is Ander-
sonville. Everytime I Have to Sit down from Weakness while walking
for Exercise & I wonder to my self what makes me So weak & again
I Answer Andersonville— Ed Glennan

At the same time tensions between the North and South were increasing, Irish immigrants were arriving in droves in search for a better life in America. As the Potato Famine devastated the Irish countryside throughout the late 1840s, Edward Glennan, his wife Alice, and their eight children emigrated from County Roscommon to Manchester, England, in 1846.[1] Residing at 7 Newgates Drive, Edward and Alice added two more children to their clan. After accumulating enough money for passage, they decided to uproot the family for America circa 1857. When this Irish clan arrived in the United States, they headed west and settled for a short time in Kankakee County, Illinois, and Mount Pleasant, Henry County, Iowa, in pursue of the American dream.[2] By the fall of 1860, the family had laid down roots in Reeder Township, Anderson County, Kansas.

Upon hearing of the Southern secession, many Irish-Americans enlisted in the federal army. Likewise, in the Glennan clan, patriotic feelings ran strong. The third eldest son, the younger Edward Glennan, born in Ireland on 14 April 1840, headed north from Kankakee County for Camp Douglas in Chicago, Illinois, and enlisted with the Drummond Guard on 14 August 1861. His desire to serve stemmed from two incidents in his life. While living in England for eleven years, he would overhear the British soldiers romanticize their experiences while under fire in close engagements.[3] In addition, while he worked in the South during the winter of 1860–61, he formed a not-so-favorable opinion of the men he would be fighting against throughout the war.

Camp Douglas, named after Senator Stephen A. Douglas, was situated on a tract of land owned by Henry Graves at 60th Street and Cottage Grove Avenue. (Later in the war it became known as the North's "Andersonville" for its inhumane conditions, earning the nickname "the eighty acres of Hell."[4]) Captain Charles Phillips of Chicago organized the company and Captain William. A. Webb was the mustering officer for the brigade. Standing 5'11½" tall, the light-haired blue-eyed twenty-one-year-old Irishman was assigned to Company F of the Forty-second Illinois Infantry Regiment and thus his military service in the Civil War began. The men composing Glennan's regiment were from the midwestern states of Illinois, Indiana, Ohio and Michigan. The men of his company resided principally around Chicago and Hillsdale, Michigan.

Considered a Black Irish due to his dark complexion, Glennan spent the first five weeks drilling. Glennan's first practical military experience occurred when he volunteered for night picket duty. Stationed one half mile northwest from the company's quarters, he was ordered to keep new recruits from deserting. To keep himself company, he brought out a companion. The companion was a bottle of firewater, given to him by his brother, Patrick, when he and his family visited for an afternoon. Glennan "thought it was a good time to In[i]tiate it to a Soldiers Life & [he] often Consulted it in Regard to the Weather & So Forth."[5] Unfortunately, under the influence of his "friend," he wandered from his post in search of water and was arrested.

This was an interesting underlying obsession throughout Glennan's service. Glennan would search for the forbidden elixir, known to him as "medicine," Tennessee mountain dew, moonshine or whiskey, while in camp, on reconnaissance, during a battle or as a prisoner of war. He acquired it from Jewish storeowners, saloons, ambulance wagons and hospitals. The "medicine" assisted the healing process while recuperating from wounds received or to pass the time away between battles.

During the first week of October, the regiment received orders to travel to St. Louis. They boarded passenger coaches and traveled along the Illinois Central Railroad. At St. Louis, they spent four more weeks at Benton Barracks continuing to drill. The regiment relocated to Warsaw, Missouri, on the Osage River. While there, they lost the first man in the regiment by death. While standing in line, a soldier carelessly placed his foot on the hammer of his gun. His foot slipped. The gun went off, sending the ball up through his chin and out through the top of his head, killing him instantly.

The regiment was on the march again. While marching to Springfield, Missouri, to reinforce Major General John C. Freemont against Rebel General Sterling Price, Glennan was selected for a special duty. Men from various regiments in the division were stealing horses, mules and cattle from neighboring towns and selling them on the road. Ordered to the town of Tipton, Missouri, to arrest them, Glennan quickly search the town and found them hiding in the saloon. But instead of arresting them, Glennan designed a scheme. Every evening he reported to the Provost Marshal that he was still searching for them and in the morning, he would return to the saloon and remained all day partaking in the local libations. After spending a "jolly good time" for ten days, he returned to his company.[6]

While in winter quarters at Smithton, Missouri, Glennan received a letter from his father advising him to do his duty for "our Gallant Stars & Stripes." Glennan promised, with God's help, he "would do it while there was danger to it" or he "would never show [his] face to [his father] at home, who so bravely told [him] to stick to [his] colors & do [his] duty."[7] In addition, while at Smithton, he was promoted to rank of corporal. Glennan participated in the battles of Island Number Ten, Corinth, Farmington, Columbia, Nashville, Stone River, Hoover's Gap, Liberty Gap, Tullahoma, and Chickamauga of the Western Theater. Of his 768 days of active service, he was under artillery fire and not engaged by the enemy thirty-seven days and under fire and engaged only nine days.

Before the battle of Island Number Ten, Glennan befriended Percy St. Clair, a mischievous Sergeant Major of his regiment. Through his connections, Glennan received an appointment as a color bearer in charge of carrying the right wing or the National Flag for his regiment. Reminiscing he declared, "This, my friend, was one of the proudest position I could wish for to be thought worthy of carrying our Glorious Emblem of Liberty — the Stars & Stripes & I pledged myself that while I lived to carry it, I should never disgrace it or the confidence reposed in me & I do not think my friends I ever did."[8] Shortly after the appointment, his military service was almost cut short. While performing reconnaissance on Island Number Ten, after the battle of Fort Donelson, Glennan received a face full of powder specks when an old Rebel magazine blew up "like a thousand thunders or a First Class Earth quake." His hair and whiskers were all burnt and he felt like he had been "t[h]rough a Thrashing Machine or a Sausage Mills."[9]

As the Forty-second Illinois Infantry gallantly participated during the Western Theater, the horrific imagery of war stained the countryside. Glennan described one such scene as he arrived just two weeks after the battle of Shiloh. "It was like being in a butcher or slaughter yard. The air was foul with the smell coming from the battle field all around us in the air from the half decayed & half burnt horses & from the buried dead & the blood of both dead & wounded. This soaked in the Earth & of course infesting the air all around. For in a heavy battle it is always so in the hurry, the dead are buried in pits sometimes & often dug shallow & into it are put all the dead so that after a rain, which usually comes after a heavy engagement on account of the concussion caused in the atmosphere by the firing of artillery, the bodys are often exposed & the smell from them faints the air."[10]

Of all the engagements that he participated in, the battle of Farmington, in his recollection, had the hardest and most desperate fighting than in any battle he was in during his time of service. The battle of Farmington was the "first step up the Ladder that this Gallant Irishman climbed." The opinion of the old soldiers was that "if a man could hold himself to the scratch and go through without running away, he would be all right." Glennan felt proud of himself that he "did not run from [his] First Battle for it was [the] First Worst Engagement" and he had the "Satisfaction of Knowing that [he] did not Desert Either Colors or Comrades in their Hour of Danger."[11]

The next step gave him his "first star." On 4 June 1862, during the battle of Boonville, while the actions were halted, he sat down when, "zip," his left knee felt "like a long needle had been run into it" and his next feeling was that the whole knee was "blown of[f]" as soon as air struck the wound.[12] A Minie ball had entered on the inside of his left knee and about a quarter of an inch above the joint. The surgeon, while probing for the ball, suggested he might have to amputate Glennan's leg.

It was more than probable that the jagged ball would cut the artery and he may bleed to death. Glennan told him: "no, that Leg Left Home with me & I would take it Back with me."[13]

Glennan was transported to Keokuk, Iowa, to recuperate. While there, he learned about a Rebel raiding party in the town of Alexandria, Missouri. With the assistance of a crutch, he volunteered to go with a rescue party and successfully chased the marauders out of the town. After spending two and a half months in Iowa, he avoided being discharged from service. The day he heard they were going to send some convalescents to their regiments and he decided to go with them. He was not really able for duty but his discharge paper was made out and was sent to St. Louis. If he waited for the paper to return, he would be obliged to take it and go home after only eleven months of service. Instead, he rejoined his regiment at the town of Tuscumbia, Alabama, on its way to Nashville, Tennessee.

During his second stint with the regiment, he rose through the ranks. In November 1862, while in Nashville, he was promoted to the rank of third sergeant and in January 1863, after the battle of Stone's River, to first sergeant. On 20 September 1863, Glennan received his "second star." During a heated firefight on the second day of the battle of Chickamauga, he felt a sting in his right foot. The "Jonny" had made a close call for Glennan's head but missed it and hit his foot.

Hitching a ride on an ambulance, Glennan traveled three miles and a half from the battlefield, arriving at the hospital at Crawfish Springs about three o'clock in the afternoon. This would be his last engagement. "Now my friends, I will have to bid you farewell. Bid farewell to my comrades & I bid farewell to you for I am now a Prisoner of War & this ends my reminiscence of the War from 61–65."[14]

On 20 September 1863, Glennan ended his service as a soldier of the United States and became a prisoner of war of the Confederate States. Along with three hundred comrades, he was stranded behind enemy lines during the battle of Chickamauga. For the next fourteen months, he endured the horrors of malnutrition, exposure, disease and self-doubt. The first prison camp Glennan was kept in was in Richmond, Virginia. Glennan was placed in a large brick tobacco manufacturing building called the Smith Building. Following this containment, the prisoners were sent to Danville, Virginia, where they were kept in even worse conditions. In fact, the prisoners were given "vaccines" for smallpox that killed many and rafters were torn down off the roof in order to obtain firewood. An escape was even attempted. The prisoners had sawed through the hinges of a double door that led to a side street. On the appointed night, Glennan stood in line on the stairs to make a break for it. Unfortunately, a traitor was amongst them and informed the prison guards of the planned escape.

Six months into his imprisonment, Glennan was transported to Camp Sumter near Andersonville, Georgia. He recalled the events that occurred throughout his imprisonment, such as the hanging of the Raider Six, escape tunnels, gambling, trading, ration wagons, diseases and their deadly vaccines. Glennan came down with scurvy during his time in Andersonville, and nearly lost the ability to walk. To increase the chances of survival, Glennan skillfully befriended other prisoners, sharing resources acquired through trade, theft and trickery. Unfortunately, his friends left him either by being paroled or succumbing to death.

On 14 November 1864, Glennan left Andersonville. He was among ten thousand prisoners who were selected for special exchange. After being transferred to Camp Lawton in Millen, Georgia, he was crammed into a boxcar for Savannah, Georgia. There, on 20 November 1864, he signed a parole not to serve in the United States army against the South until he was regularly exchanged. He weighed approximately seventy pounds. He boarded a steamer, sailed north into the Chesapeake Bay, and arrived at Annapolis, Maryland, on 25 November. He was led into the parole camp and received a complete new uniform and two months pay of forty-eight dollars. For the first couple of weeks, he dined on oysters, crackers and porter.

On 16 December, by Order of the Secretary of War, all paroled prisoners were allowed a thirty-day furlough. On the trek home, the train he was on jumped the tracks and crashed, pinning Glennan inside. "Pinning [his] left leg; the same left leg that had an ounce of Rebel lead still in it and the surgeon tried to amputate, thinking it was useless; the same left leg while in prison that scurvy had doubled up like a jack knife and now the Hannibal & St. Joe Rail Road Company wanted to make sausage meat of it, bones & all." After his rescue from the train and spending time in Kansas, visiting family, he returned to the parole camp in March of 1865 and was sent to the hospital with a bout of diphtheria two days later.

He remained nearly three weeks in the hospital when he was ordered to Chicago to be mustered out. While en route, at some Ohio station, Glennan learned about Lincoln's assassination, which occurred on 14 April 1865. The next day he arrived in Chicago. While visiting his brother, Patrick, he paid his respect to the fallen president. Lincoln's body was lying in state at the Old Chicago Court House from May 1–2.

On 4 June 1865, First Sergeant Edward Glennan mustered out of Company F of the Forty-second Illinois Infantry Regiment and moved to Anderson County, Kansas to live with his family, who had relocated during the early stages of the war.[15] On 22 February 1870, Glennan married an Irish woman from Iowa named Jane Caveger (1839–1879) with Reverend Father J. F. Cunningham officiating. The newlyweds resided in Wakarusa, Douglas County, Kansas, with his sister Ann and brother-in-law John Christy.[16] By 1875, Edward and Jane had moved back to Reeder Township, Anderson County, Kansas. After his wife's death, Glennan resided with his nephew, C. W. Embry, in Harrison, Franklin County, Kansas in 1880.

On 24 January 1889, Glennan checked into the U.S. National Home for Disabled Volunteer Soldiers in Leavenworth, Kansas.[17] On his official record, he suffered from multiple ailments; such as a gunshot wound in his left knee, lumbago, discharge from the lungs, cataracts of the eyes, chronic gastritis and arteriosclerosis. Glennan left the National Home in 1893 and according to the 1895 Kansas State Census, was a farmer in the town of Pottawatomie in Coffey County. Starting in 1912, his health started failing again as he spent more time in the National Home. According to the 1920 Federal Census, Glennan resided in the Saint Francis Hospital in Topeka City, Shawnee County, Kansas. Edward Glennan died on 19 May 1924 at the age of 84 in Leavenworth, Kansas, and was buried beside his wife in St. Patrick's Cemetery of Emerald-Williamsburg, Kansas.[18]

ONE

September 1863 to March 1864

About three or Between three & Four Oclock on Sunday afternoon Sept 20th 1863, I with about Three Hundred Prisoners of My Devision at Craw Fish Springs Georgia & Laying around Fires Built outside in the open air for our Comfort, the more serious of the wounded occupying the Few Tents we Had. The springs was about one Hundred Rods from us to the south with the Pike Road Running right by us to Chattanooga. Just across the Road & on the West of us was Heavy Timber. To the North of us & in the Direction of the Battle Feild of Chickamauga which was about Three Miles distant, there was open Ground for a distance of about 60 Rods, which then descended out of sight of us. The Ground we were on was High with Double Log House by which we were & to the East of us was a Heavy timbered Bottom Land but very clear of under Brush. The House had been occupyed but now contained I should Judge about 75 Bushels of Wheat.

I think there was about 100 of us outside Laying around & at the time three or Four Oclock, one of My Comrades with an Exclamation drew our attention to a Body of Rebel Cavalry Just Coming in View From the Battle Feild & about 80 Rods distant, they were coming in Line of Battle & appeared to be about 3 or 400 of them. My First thought was they were going to charge us & my next thought was that we could not stop them with the Few cripples in Sight but we could make them pay dearly For the Pleasure of charging us.

With these thoughts in my mind I called out to the Boys that Every man able to sit or stand to get His Rifle & Help at Least Protect His Comrades who were unable to Protect Himself. They all Cheefully Complyed & arranged themselves in a Body, the most of them being unable to stand up, sat down on the Ground & all Prepared there Rifles. We formed our selves as I Have stated on open Ground between the tents & the Enemy, our right resting on the log House. The Rebel Officers seeing our Demonstration Halted their men.

I Had sent word inside the tents to our surgeons & they now Came out & saw us Preparing a Reception for our Visitors & also them awaiting in Line about 40 Rods from us. I told the Surgeon what my opinion was of them charging us but he said not to Fire untill they made the first Demonstration. The Rebel Officers seeing ours out & not Knowing what to make of us Halted their men & Advanced to us with a white HandKercheif as a Flag. When they came close Enough, they asked what the men meant by being drawn up so & the surgeon told them what we Thought that they meant to charge us & that we were Prepared to Resist them.

The Rebel Commanding officer Said they Had no intention of charg-

Ed Glennan, ca. 1870 (courtesy Rose Embry Carey).

ing us as we were then inside their Lines & therefore Prisoners for that. Our Troops had Retreated to Chattanooga & their whole army was between us & our men but He said He would not be Responsible for His men if we Fired. The Surgeon then said under them Conditions, he would Surrender & Ordered us to dispose of our Arms as we were Prisoners. The Rebel officers went back to Bring their men up & we, who were able, smashed the stocks of our Rifles against the Ends of the Log House So the Rebs would not get any use of them & that was the way I bid my Little Whitney Gun & leaving it in such Condition that no Jonnie should Ever draw a Bead on any of my Brave Companions in Blue.

Soon the Rebel Cavalry Came up, they were the 8th Texas & Called Gerrys Texas Rangers[1] & Rangers they were For they Ranged all through the Hospital taking what they wanted & also Ranged through the men taking from us what they pleased. One Big Galoot of a Ya-hoo rode up to me & sweetly said, Hello Yank. Oh-Get-out-you,-that's not my name. But He insisted & Followed me saying, Look Here, I want no Foolishness but Just Hand over your Pock[et]book & other trinkets. I told Him I Had no trinkets but a Pocket Knife, which I gave Him. He then took my Cap & gave me His old Rusty Grey one with the 8th Texas on the Front of it & that was all He got From me. I Had some money but He did not get it.

All the others were treated the same way. They did now search us but [—] tried to Bluff out of us all they could. They Left us. Soon about sun down, there was about a Pint of Boiled wheat Issued to us for supper. There was nothing Else to give us. My Regimental Surgeon Came to me & told me I would Have to do the Best I Could. There was no Possible room For me in the tents but He would have Large Fires Built outside for us & he said He would try & get me some Blankets to sleep on. After dark he Came & gave me two Blankets & I prepared to Lay down for the night.

There was very Few of us outside with any Blankets so I Called to me one of the 88th Ills. It was Called the Chicago Board of Trade Regiment & was organized in Chicago. This man I Saw was a Country man of mine. His name was William Best[2] & He was a Brother in Law of Taylor the Pork Pastier of Chicago at the time. Best was wounded in the Knee by a Buck shot. It was a Flesh wound & not Dangerous. I invited Bill as I Called Him to share my Blanket & we Layed down & in spite of the Pain I was Suffering from, I went to sleep. How long, I dont Know but I woke up & When I woke, I was sitting upon my Blankets apparently Comfortable & Just sitting there. Now I Knew when I went to sleep I was Laying down so what the Dickens Woke me up & put me Sitting up? It Certainly was not the Pain of my Foot. That was my first Thought. No, my wound was not very Painfull, at Least not Enough to wake me & Certainly not Enough to Put me a sitting up on My — My — Oh My Blankets!

I looked around thinking some Fellow woke me up but no, Every man was sleeping around me. I spoke to Bill, no answer. He was sound asleep. Not a Wakefull soul in sight, I now felt my Blankets, Both very Stiff. I Had not noticed them when I Lays down but now I saw they were stiff from the Effects of Blood drying on them. I Supposed they Had been taken from some Poor wounded Comrade before the Surgeon Had Brought them to me. I again Layed down. I slept & again awoke sitting up still. I Could not account for it For my Wound was not troublesome & the Feeling I Knew it was no use for me to Lay down again for my sleep was all gone.

I thought of the Poor Fellow that Had last Lain on them. It was a Kind of lonesome sitting there with all the other sleeping so I gave Bill a Punch that woke Him. He asked me what I woke Him for & I told Him I could not Sleep telling Him How I Had twice been woke up sitting & about the Blood on the Blankets. That Raised Him & He sat up Looked at the Blankets & Wanted to crawl out away from them but I told Him to remain & if we could not sleep, we Could stay awake & talk. We done so & I then Found out who He was as I have Mentioned. While we were talking, I looked to my right & north in the direction of the springs. There was Probably 12 or 15 other Fires as ours was, with a Body of men Laying around them as we were sleeping but as I looked, I saw Just Coming in view of the Light of the Farthest Fire a man in Grey Uniform.

He did not look very Plain to me at First but as He Came nearer to the Fire nearest Him, he walked around it & seemed to be Examining the men. My thought was that He was looking for something to steal or for some one to do some mischeif to. I called Bills attention to Him & we Both watched Him Come From Fire to Fire Examining all as He came along untill He got to our Fire when he saw us Sitting up. He Came directly to us & Spoke. I saw he was a Countryman of mine, asked Him to sit down which He did & remained about one Hour with us talking Sociably. I asked Him how He came to be in the Rebel army. He said He Belonged, when the War Broke out, to the First U. S. Dragoons then stationed at New Orleans. That the most of His Co. was Irishman & that from there at that time, they Could not get north so they Joined the First Confederate cavalry & were then Halted at the Springs & He thought as He Could not Sleep, He would take a walk over & See us. He asked what we Had to Eat, I told Him Nothing but wheat. He said in the Morning about 8 Oclock when you Hear the crack of a Carbine down there in the Bottom & He Pointed in the direction East of us, tell your Surgeon to send some of the Nurses down there. They will Find a Beef shot & tell Him to Have it brought up for Food for you. He Bid us Good by.

We did not Lay down any more that night & in the morning, I told the Surgeon of our night visitor & what He Said & sure Enough, we Heard the Crack of a Carbine & 3 or 4 nurses with the Front Wheels of an old Buggy went down & soon Returned with a two-year-old Heiffer on it. The[y] Found Her Killed but did not see any one so my Rebel Friend was as good as His word & that Beef was very acceptable & Badly needed. The meat was used for those that were the worst wounded & the wheat Boiled in the water & given to us & for the 5 or 6 days we remained there, that was all the Food we Had, about a Pint of wheat three times a day Cooked in the Water the Beef was Boiled in.

Monday the 21st passed without anything unusual Happening. Tuesday, some of our Nurses went to the Battle Feild & Returned in the afternoon & told me there was a lot of my Regiment yet on the Feild wounded & in a Bad Condition. Thunderation! My Gallant Comrades three days Laying on that Bloody Feild without Care or attendance. If I Have to crawl there, I will go to them in the morning. It is now too late to go this Evening so in the morning, I told Bill I was going. He Said He would go with me & Help me so He got another of His Regiment that was not wounded to go along. His name was Pete Nolan[3] from Milwaukee, Wis.

Bill & Pete got on Each Side of me & we started right after Breakfast. It was slow tedious Travelling that three or three & a Half Miles. We Passed the Ground Where we saved the Battery on the afternoon of the 19th & My God, Can I Ever Forget the Sight that now met My Eyes. Bear With me My Kind Friends, I Promise you the truth in what I saw & Felt in these my Long weary months of Captivity & also told you, you would have to see Hor[r]ible Sights with my Eyes & they have not Commenced & now For a description of the Battle Feild of Chickamauga or at Least the part of it that I had Fought over on the 19th & 20th & now visited under the Circumstances as stated.

It is a common & usual thing in a Heavy Battle when Grass & Leaves are dry, for them to take Fire from the Firing & Especially from the artillery Firing. The Powder, I suppose you Know, that is Fixed for Cannon are Put up in Heavy Flann[e]ll Cartridges & When the Gun is Fired, that Flannell retains the Fire & sets fire to the grass & leaves & often where there is Heavy Infantry Firing, the grass take Fire from the Paper Cartridges we used. A single Rifle Cartridge does not give much Danger of Firing the Grass [—] Out where there is Thousands of them Firing at once, it Formed a mass of small sparks that in dry grass is Certain to set it a fire. That will account for what I am now about to describe as we Came to the Battle Feild of the 19th.

Men Lay in all shapes Dead, all without a single Exception Had been stripped of their Clothing, some More some Less but all Every one Had been stripped of their Uniforms or outer Garments & Left Shame on the Brutes who Had done it. Some were Partly Burnt, Roasted by the Fire of Burning grass & leaves, some their arms Crisped, some with their Legs or Bodys Partly so. A Sickening Horrible Sight even For such a Hardenend Wretch as I to see, what a sight then For Ladys to see. {For Ladys, you say, oh no, Lady would Look or go near such a sight.} Excuse me, Look there & you will see Wagon Load of them coming along through that mass of Burnt Human Bodys driving around so as to avoid the Wheels running over the Bodys. Yes, see them Coming looking around at the sights of that Battle Feild & apparently unmoved by the Sights of Human Misery Depicted by those Features, who some of them at least from Their Positions in Death must Have been yet alive when the Fire Struck them For their Positions & Expressions show it the Look of Agony & Contracted Features show they Died after the Fire Found them unable to move from the Effects of their wounds. They Had to remain & be slowley Roasted to Death.

See that Load of Southern Ladys, 6 or 7 of them, Come nearer, all apparently Pleased from their Expressions that their Southern Friends had Layed so many of the Hated Yankees low. The Death of so many of My Gallant Comrades did not affect me what so ever for that is the Fortune of war & what we all Expected but the sign of my stript, Burnt & Mutilated Brave Gallant Companions in Arms did affect me deeply then & does yet. When I think of their unburied Body Four days after they Fell Fighting Bravely for our dear old Flag. For Except those Women in the wagon, it would be an injustice to the sex to call them Ladys, & our three selves, Bill, Pete & myself, there was not another Living Being on that Feild of death. No nor neither a dead or wounded Rebel, it was Literally a Feild of Northern dead & Here let me say, the sight of those women there on that Feild done more to Lower My Estimation of the Female Sex than all I Had Ever seen before that or since. It Left a Bitter Feeling at the time & does yet when I think of them but away from them.

I am tired of speaking of them if you, my Friends, are not my Comrades assisted me along. I wanted to get to the Feild of the 20th as it was there my Regimental Comrades were Reported to be Lying, so on we went slowley Passing occasionally a sight such as I have described. We are now in sight of the Hill we charged down from on Sunday Morning & also in sight of the Widow Glens House.[4] We get to it & then turn to our right in the track our Regiment took in the Charge. I see where our Battery was placed, a Few Dead Men & Horses. A few Rods more & I then Come to where the Brush is a little Thinner. I Know I am near where we Halted under that Terrific Fire of Musketry. Yes, there is the little Log where I Layed when I got my B[u]llet & there a few feet in Front is where my Rebel Friend stood when he gave it to me & received His own from me in return.

I look along to my left where my Regiment stood & I Can trace the Line of Battle by the Bodys of my dead Gallant Comrades of the 42nd but you, my Brave Lads, are gone & Beyond all Earthly Care, I must Find my wounded ones. I see none. I call & am Answered from my left & rear & go there when I see 15 of My Poor Comrades Gathered in groups of 2, 3, or 4 together with a little Awning formed by Broken Twigs of the brush over their Heads to Protect them from the Suns Burning Heat. It is now about Noon & Has taken us about Four Hours & a Half to come that three miles & a Half. The Sight I saw of my Poor Poor Regimental Comrades May God grant that I may never see a Sight of Such Woe Begone Misery & Suffering again.

Amongst them was one of my Company, Frank Hewitt[5] of Hillsdale, Mechigan & one of the Best Boys of my Company. I went to Frank; there was two of my regt with Him. I asked Frank where He was wounded & He Said in the Leg. I wanted to See His Wound & Found He was Hit by a Minnie Ball in the Thigh. It was a bad Flesh wound but the Bone was untouched. I told Him if He Could have got to the Hospital, He would be all right in a Few days that the Bone was not Injured but that now His prospects were very bad as His Leg was Terribly swollen & the maggots were as thick in the wound as they Could be, they were Crawling out of it Big white ones.

Bear with me Friends, I shall often now have to speak unpleasant sounding words but not unnessasarily only when it is nessasary to give you a true Idea of what I am describing. Franks Condition was Critical on account of His wound & if He Could get immediate ambulance, it was Barely Possible His Life might be saved if He Could get rid of those

Maggots out of His wound & if not, nothing Earthly Could save Him & told Him so & also that if He would try, we would Help take Him back with us. Pete & Bill said they would take Him back if they had to Carry Him all the way but no, Poor Frank Had lost all intirest in Life & said he could not bear to move. He was about 19 or 20 years of age.

Bill & Pete seeing Frank was not willing to try & go with us, they left me with Him & they Broke off Brush and placed it as a Better shade over the groups of my Poor Comrades. Frank told me in a[n]swers to me that He Had nothing to Eat Since the Battle but some salt Pork He got from a Rebel Surgeon on Monday afternoon. He got it in Exchange for a gold Pen & Pencil He Had given the Rebel Surgeon for the Peice of Pork & then He said after Eating that Pork, He got Crazy for Water. The Surgeon gave none of them any attendance to their wounds & when they asked Him to, He Said He Had not time afterwards a Rebel Soldier Came near them & Frank Bribed Him with His Pocket Knife to go & get Him a Canteen of Water. That was all the Food & Water they Had. I told Frank How we were at the Hospital for Food or we would Have brought them some, that it was through the Nurses who Came to them yesterday that I Had Learnt of them being there. He said yes, they Had found them & Gathered them up in little Squads as I Saw them & Broke the Brush to make a Shelter for them. I asked Him why they did not get water for them & if he thought there was any near. He said He did not think there was any Water near for the Rebels that got the water for Him was gone a long time & it was Rather Riskey for the nurses to be found Prowling around For any Straggling Jonny was Liable to shoot them on Sight. I asked Him How it came that they Rebels when they moved their own wounded did not take them & care for them as we always did for theirs without any Distinction. He said He did not Know only they Had not for Immediately after the Fight, they Came through & Picked out their own wounded & would not touch them & that night, the night of the 20th, He said, after dark, He could hear them going around picking up their Dead & Burying them. He could Hear them all that night & Part of the next fore noon, the 21st, but they never Buried a Single Yankee Boy.

No, the Bodys of my Gallant Comrades yet Lay where they Fell, Bloating, Rotting in that Hot Southern Clime 4 days after Death a mass of Human Putrefaction. Any Further description of my dead Companions is Unnessesary. There Within 8 feet of Frank is the Body of my true

Gallant Comrade, Jake Dingman,[6] already Half Buried in a Hole of His own making. His Position in Death was Peculiar as I saw Him; He was sitting in a Hole about 15 or 18 inches deep. His Hands clasped in Front of His Knees & in that Position was sitting upright Dead. Frank told me Jake died in great agony. He had been shot through the groin & in His Sufferings Had Sat up & Whirled Himself around & round until He had worn that Hole in the ground & Died in it as I saw Him. Poor Gallant Jake at last you are gone & never more will you, my Brave Comrade, Jake with me, a true Gallant Brave Comrade Good By.

There were others Plenty of my Regimental Comrades dead there & Laying around in all Positions but Here none of them were Burnt on account of the Brush, the grass did not take Fire Just there but all Except the wounded were more or less Deprived of their Clothing. I visited the other groups but could not do any thing more For them than Bill & Pete were doing. The most of them were seriously wounded Even if the[y] could Have got immediate Help after the Battle but all without a Single Exception were in a Critical Condition on account of the Long absence Without Help & the Maggots were as thick as the[y] Could Possibly be in all their wounds, which were in a Horrible Condition. The first or Orderly Sergeant of Co. A[7] was under the same covering with Frank Hewitt. He was shot in one shoulder & through Both Hands & when He Held up His Hands for me to see the Maggots Literally Rolled out in a stream. But Enough of Such descriptions, those I Have given will give you some Idea of that Feild of Death & an Idea is all I Can Convey to you.

Frank would not Come with us Back & it being now about two Oclock, nothing to Eat since our Pint of Wheat for Breakfast & Expect nothing untill we get to Hospital, not Even a drink of water. With a Possibility of getting shot on our way back, I bid Frank & my Comrades good By, Promising if I got back Safe to try & get some water sent to them the next day & if I Could get some of the Surgeons to Come to them. So casting a Farewell look over my Living & Dead Comrades, I turned away & with the Help of these my good Comrades, Bill & Pete, Headed back for the Hospital.

I may as well Here state that amply, Nobly, Bravely was those Comrades avenged on their Brutal in Human Beings act to my Living & Dead Comrades of the Battle of Sept 19 & 20th. In Leaving the Living without Care or attendance & the Dead Unburied & Stripping them, at the Second

Battle Fought over some of the same ground & By the Same Men, who were in the First Battle. When they saw the Bleached Bones of their Former Comrades Laying still on the top of the ground Unburied, the[y] became Wild at the Sight & dearly made the Rebels Pay for the Act. After the Battle, they gathered up the Bones & Buried them. This was told to me afterwards in Andersonville by a Co. Comrade & I speak of it now Lest I forget it while in that Hell Hole of the Southern Confederacy.

We arrived safe after dark at the Hospital, Passing on the road to it, several small Partys of Rebel Cavalry, who did not molest us in any way more than asking where we Had been. I Reported to the Surgeon the Condition of my wounded Comrades & He said in the morning, He would try & get them in. So in the morning, He Had some Boards Fastened to the Fore or Front Wheels of that old Buggie already Mentioned & sent men out to Bring my Comrades in. The Rebels Had taken all the Horses & Ambulances so it was the only Possible Conveyance Could be Fixed up. It was slow work they Could only bring one or two at a time & it took them that day & the next to get them all in. Some of them died soon after they got to the Hospital but all, Every one died. After the[y] Came, their Flesh was so corrupted that the Surgeons with the strongest Turpentine could not drive those maggots out of their Wounds & not one Lived.

Bill Best & Peter Nolan stuck to me after our Expedition to the Battle Feild & untill I mention diffirent of them, you may Consider them with me from now on, no matter where I am or what [I am] doing, they are with me sleeping or waking. So I will resume, I think it was the 6th or 7th day of my stay there when Early in the morning, some Rebel officers came & told us that all who were Possibly able to walk to the Rail Road 4 or 5 Miles distant, to Fall in & go as they were going to send us to City Point Va to be Exchanged. We all Knew that City Point was the Place of regular Exchange of Prisoners & all who could Possibly & Even some who were seriously wounded were ankious to go & the sooner to get again amongst our own Comrades.

Our Forces then were at Chattanooga only about 18 or 20 Miles From us but we were willing to go around the Confederacy to get to them. I did not feel well able to go but Bill & Pete did not want to leave me & said [they] would help me get along or Carry me if I gave out & we are Filt so Elated at the Prospect of getting back that several who started died on the way. So we started & Gathered up some the same

22

way From other Hospitals they did not attempt to Hurry us but allowed us take our time. We Passed through a Portion of the Battle Feild of the 19th & there again saw the Sights I described & many were the remarks the men made amongst themselves at the inhumanity of the Rebels Leaving the Bodys of our Dead Comrades to rot on the Surface & Pick out & Bury their own.

About 5 Oclock, we arrived at Ringold, Georgia, a station on the Rail Road & the[y] placed us in an old store two Storys High. I wish others were put in the second story & I think that Evening they Issued to Each of us one or two Crackers that was the only Food we Had since we left the Hospital & we Had come about 7 Miles. Bill or Pete, one of them, had Brought a Blanket & one Half a Pup tent with them so we Slept. Next morning when we got up, I Beleive the[y] Issued another Cracker to us. We Had no water & were not allowed to go out & the only way to leave the second story was by the stairs. So a lot of us to get out of the croud in the room went down Part way on the stairs until we were Halted by the Rebel Guard who told us to remain there as He was Ordered to allow no one to go by Him. So we sat there talking to Him, He appeared Sociable & told us His Regiment Brigade & Devision. He was one of Braggs men. While we were talking to Him, another Jonnie Passing along the Side walk saw us on the stairs & stopped & Commenced using abusive Language to us. We were Prisoners & therefore were deprived of one Privilage of giving Him as good as He gave us & there were men there Crippled that would gladly have gone down in their Condition & throttled that Foul Mouthed Corn Fed. My Irish was getting up as well as others of my Comrades sitting there.

I asked our Guard if it was Customary for them to allow their Prisoners to be abused as He was allowing us to be. The Reb on the Side walk drew His Revolver & Pointed it at us but before he Could Fire our Guard Covered Him with His Rifle telling Him if He Fired at us, He would Kill Him on the spot then the two Rebs had some unpleasant words. It appeared the side Walk Jonnie was one of Longstreets Corp & He was mad because His Corp had Suffered so severely in the Battle but our Guard made Him go away. I Supposed the Fellow was drinking & His fight was up. It was a Pity, he did not see us a few days sooner when any of us could have accomadated Him. That man was a Coward at Heart.

I think we remained at Ringold three or Four days when we were all put on Flat or Coal Cars. There was Either 57 or 67, I Forget which on Each Cars with a Guard placed at Each End of the Cars. The whole made one train of about 700 of wounded men, all Loaded in Flat Cars. None of us was well able to stand up so we Had to remain in a Sitting Position & when sitting down, we were wedged in Pretty Close but at night that was when the Circus Commenced. Now I will Explain Lying down for one night & that will answer for all the 6 or 7 we were on that southern Excursion Train.

It is about Dark, some one of us says Boys Lets down all right in our car. We arranged that the man in the Front End of our car should Lay down First so Here He goes, Hugging up to the End of the Car as tight as He Can. His breast Touching the Car as also His Knees, which are drawn up. There is not room for Him to stretch out for on the opposite side of the car, there is another man Laying down Just as He is, for we Have to sleep in two Lines, the Heads of Each Line against the side of the car. Now place a man sitting in a chair, His Legs drawn up Close to the rounds of it & then Lay Him down to sleep Just in that Position & you Have our Position as we occupied our Berths in our sleeper. On that trip, now Spooned as we Called it, the next man Lays down the same way & so on until one side are all down but the last man on that side, there is no room for Him. He calls out spoon up you Fellows & give me room to Lay down then each man squeeses Closer untill He finally Squeeses Himself down. The other side then does the same & then we are packed as tight as Sardines— A Fact & to Illusterate suppose some Poor Fellow on account of Him being squeesed so tight or His wound is Painfull, He cannot sleep & wants to get out of that squeese & stand up well.

He tries to get up so as not to wake the others but no, by George, He is Held in there tight from the pressure on both sides of Him so He has to Exert some stren[g]th to do so but Finally, He squeeses out & snap. His Feet is Caught in between the men sleeping on Each Side of Him. The Line Has Expanded & Closed [—] risen From of it is near morning remains standing For He cannot Sit down without sitting on a Comrade & He Cannot move for there is not a place two inches square unoccupied but if He cannot stand up untill morning in Order for Him to Lay down again, he has to get the Guard at the End of the Cars to wake up the man in the Corner & He wakes the next up & so on untill the whole side is again awake when the same thing is gone over spooning untill we are again down & sometimes that would Happen three or Four times a night. With very Few Exceptions, the Boys would Cheerfully Comply & some would Joke about it saying it was a Cold night that we Could not spoon over Five or Six times a night to accomadate a Comrade again.

Some Poor Fellow would get tired Lyeng so long on one side & would want to turn over on the other side so He would call out spoon over when all would have to again wake up & turn over. Fun, Oh Thunder, yes, Lots of Fun. Why it got to be a part of our night Exercise or drill & some of the Boys got so used to it that they would spoon over in their sleep & not Know it. Each man Had His own spot & there Had to stay what Ever place we occupyed when we Came on the car that we retained untill we arrived at our Journeys End.

I Cannot give any General description of the country or towns I passed through so I will Commence as I remember it. We started From Ringold, the men were very Kind to Each other as also the Guards. They were all Braggs men & men that Had Fought us on every Battle Feild & treated us Kindly. [—] Lieutenant in Charge of the Guard when we would come to any City where we Had to remain an Hour or two, He would Come Himself along by Each Car & ask us if we wanted to Buy anything. If so, we would give Him our Money telling Him what we wanted & He would take some of His men along to Carry what He Purchased Bringing to Each man his change & the Articles He had Bought. He was a youn[g] Man about 26 or 28 years old. I asked Him one day why He was so Kind to us & went to so much trouble. He said He Had Fought us from the Beginning of the war & Had Ever Found us Brave Enemys & that now we were wounded & under His Care, He would treat us as He Had Himself been treated while in our Hands. He said He Had been a Prisoner in our Hands several times & Had always received Kind treatment for us & as long as we were with Him, He would do the same for us. He said you are all right while under my Care & the Care of my Guards, who Have Fought you & Know what you are but God Help you when you get to Richmond & under the Home Guards then look out For yourselfes.

I did not think much of that Remark at the time but many times during the weary months of my Captivity Have I thought of them & How well He Knew the Hell Hounds into whose Care we were going. We are on the Road Remember going south. We Have Passed Rome, Ga.

where the People, Principally women & children with a Few old men, were waiting to see the Yanks go through as Prisoners. On we Passed severall smaller Towns & Stations untill we came into Atlanta, there we remained some time side tracked & Had Lots of Visitors. Some were allowed to sell to us by the Guards & Few I could see by their Expressive Features were Union at Heart but Dare not Express themselves openly.

They stood Back in the Crowd & Looked on & many a tear I saw Linger in the Eye of a Kind Hearted Lady or young Girl. May God Bless them for their silent sympathy Expressed For us. On again nothing of any note occurring untill we got to Columbia, the Capital of South Carolina, there we Had to unload on one side of the City & march through it to go on another Rail Road.

The City was Beautifully Situated, nice wide clean streets well shaded with Large Silver Maple trees. It was slow Painfull Walking after being Cramped up for three or four days but we Hobbled along Amidst the same scowling countenances of the People Lined along the side walks. Amongst all, I saw none that Looked as though there was any Pity for us, the First Yanks they Had seen. We got to the Center of the City, a very wide Road or street running I think North & south & if so, then we came in from the west. The street must Have been a least about 20 rods wide with a wide Carriage drive on both sides of it & a Beautifull wide Promenade in the center of the street with seats Here & there at intervals all well shaded by very fine trees.

We were Halted for a few moments just as we Came to this avenue of Beauty when the Rebel Lieut[enant] Ordered the Prisoners to Close up in a compact a Body as Possible & ordered His Guards to close in on the Prisoners & Hold themselves in Readiness to Fire on the First Person that Molested the Prisoners. Hello, are they going to Mob us Poor Devils Crippled & unable to Help ourselves. By Thunder, if they do, some of them will Pay dear For it For Cripples as we are, we can yet in a Mob do a Little work before we Cave in to them.

I Look around me all Black scowling Countenances a Few old men all the rest women, Their aprons Gathered up with one Hand. I see the shape of some thing it looks like apples— apples— Thunder, no, there is one old Hag with one of them in Her Hand & its a Rock— Ho— them are Rocks in your aprons. Then all right before you can throw the second one, we will be amongst you.

Ah—there is one old Grey Headed Sinner Looking at me or in my direction as though He would Like to get acquainted with me. Yes, you old Z-a-u-p, Ill introduce myself to you first thing if there is any Fun Here. Those Thoughts Quickly passed th[r]ough my Head as also Bill & Pete & others near me. We Had Picked our object to go for first If we Had to make a Break but we also Knew it would be certain death to us in our Condition Even amongst those women for there was Enough of them to Eat us up.

It seemed as though all the women in the south was there. It was but a Few Moments when the Lieut[enant] saw that all the Prisoners, we in Close Compact Order & His men Ready & with the Order for the mob to make way & Let us Pass through. We marched on without any Further trouble & got to where we were to get on our other train. The Mob Following & using some rather Loud Epithets, which are Better Left in [—] Reminiscence. This is the Columbia that was destroyed by Fire when Sherman Passed through it a year afterwards when on His March to the sea.[8]

We again were Piled in Flat Cars as before & on we went. The Rail Road now ran through a more uneven Country in which there was several Cuts over these Rail Road. Cuts were Wagon Bridges, the first one of those Bridges we came in Sight of was Crowded with Women & Children Leaning over the rails of the Bridge Watching us Come & as our train was Passing under them, they Saluted us with a shower of Stones, a good many of the Boys were Hit by them but the distance was too Close to injure much although it showed their Better Feeling against us & Provoked the Lieut[enant] & Guards to think that their Southern women should show such Unlady like Qualitys. But Look out Boys, Here is another Bridge & Loaded for us a lot of us that had the use of our Hands stood up as we came near the Bridge & as the[y] threw the stones, we Caught them & after passing under the Bridge, threw them Back at them & there were several Little screams in the Femenine Voice with—Oh—you—mean—nasty—Yankees—you Nasty—Northern Mud—Sills—O—Oh—you—you—Oh—My.

That operation we repeated at Each Bridge & it Pleased the Guards as much as it did us. By Evening we got away from that rough section of Country & were troubled no more with a Shower of stones. On we went & at the End of 6 or 7 days we arrived in Richmond, the Rebel

Capital & unloaded from the Cars. I do not Know what Part of the City we came into but we came in from the South. I walked but Know that I felt very tired & sore & also a little Hungry.

The Ration we got Issued to us on the Road was not Sufficient. I think it was about Four Hard Tack[9] a day with a small Peice of Bacon. We Formed in Line & marched Forward & taken to a Brick Building. I do not Know for Certain but think it was what they Called Libby Prison[10] although I saw no Prisoners there. We were taken in in squads of 15 or 20 & ordered to give up all our valuables Money, Watches, Jewellry, Knives or any thing of value we Had. If we gave it Freely, the officer told us they would give a Receipt for it & we would Have it all returned to us when we were Exchanged but if they Had to search us, what Ever they found would be Confiscated & lost to us. Some of the Boys gave Part of their Money & Risked Being searched.

I Had Either 18 or 28 dollars, I forget which, but I gave it & what Ever I Had in my Pockets. They were Satisfied with what they got from the squad I was with & did not search us so they sent us out, got

Libby Prison, Richmond, Virginia, photograph by Alexander Gardner, 1864 (courtesy Library of Congress).

Libby Prison, north side, Richmond, Virginia, ca. 1865 (courtesy Library of Congress).

in another squad & soon untill they were through with all of us then marched us of[f] & around a Corner on our Left & Put us in a Brick Building two storys High. I with others was placed on the first Floor. The Building was about 100 Feet Long & about 30 or 35 Feet Wide & Had been used For a Tobacco Building. I Beleive it was Called the Smith Building[11] & now my Friends Commences my actual Imprisonment & the Hardest Part For me to describe in Order to give you a true Idea of the Sufferings of the Prisoners of War. To describe is all I Can do, For I give you the Remotest Idea of our Feelings would be an Impossibility so I will begin by giving a Description of the Room or floor I am in as out of it I never went untill removed, which Came after about 6 Weeks.

I Have given the sise of the Building & that I was on the first Floor of it. In the Center of the Floor running Lenthwise was a row of Tobacco Presses & with the frames attached to them reached from the Floor to the Ceiling & took up about 8 or 10 feet of the space on the Floor. The space Left between the Presses & the wall on Each side was used by us to Sleep on & when we Laied down to sleep, there was Just Barely space Enough to do so as there are four Rows of us, one Line with their Heads to the wall & along by it another with their Heads to the Tobacco Presses. The feet of Both these Lines of men Came within about two feet

29

of Each other & that two Feet of space was the only free place for all to walk on. What Ever spot we took when first Entering that out retained Permanently. The opposite side of the Floor was arranged the same way & the place I with Bill & Pete took was in a Corner away from my window.

There was about 350 or 400 of us on the Floor. We appointed a Sergeant to take char[g]e of our rations & draw them for us. Then for conveinence of issuing to the men, we devided into messes of 16 men & Each mess of 16 appointed a man to draw their Rations From the Floor Sergeant for them & Issue to them. My mess appointed me to draw for them & in my mess was Bill & Pete. Back in the rear of the Room was a small office but was now used by the Floor Sergeant to divide the Rations amongst the mess sergeants. In this way, there was we will say 25 mess sergeants Each one of Course representing 16 men.

The Rations are Brought in to this little office or room, the Floor sergeant devides the whole in to 25 Piles then when He thinks all the Piles are Equal, He Picks out any of us, the 25 Mess Sergeants, for no one Else is allowed in that room while the issuing or devideing is in Progress. So He Picks out one, any one, He Happens to think of & says turn your Back. We will say my Back is turned, the Floor Sergeant then says with His Hand on a Pile, whose is this? I answer No. 10. The sergeant Representing or drawing for the 16 men by number mess 10, He takes the Pile. His number is Called for & goes & devides it Amongst His men & so on. The Floor Sergeant goes untill all are Issued, Each times He says Whose is this, I Call the number of some Mess for it is by numbers we are Called while Issuing rations.

It is Issued to the 16 men the same way, I make 16 little Piles of it then tell some of my mess to turn His Back, Call whose is this & so on untill all were issued. My Corner was on the south side of the room & the only windows giving Light to us was on that side. The window is about the center of the room Looked out on a vacant Lot.

It was up in to this Vacant Lot that Col Straighter[12] & His Party of officers Came From Libby Prison after tunnelling out. They are the Party the Rebel Government were Holding as Hostages For the Rebel General Morgon,[13] which Government was Holding in the Columbia, Ohio Penotentiary. Just across this vacant Lot & South was the Famous or Infamous Libby Prison. The whole side or Front of Libby was facing me as I looked from the window & a sign with Libby and some tallow Chandlers was

Fastenend on or near one Corner of the Building. I Have now Endeavored to give you a description of my Prison Exterior & interior as I remember them so I will now try to give our manner of Living with such incidents of Prison Life as I Can remember.

The next morning after our Arrival in the Smith Building & about 10 Oclock or rather about 7 Oclock, a Rebel officer & sergeant Came in & ordered all in Line. We all stood up. He called the Roll every man answered to His name as it was Called. This was done Every morning so as to Know if any Had Escaped through the night. In Fact, it was done in all the Prisons I was in So Hereafter I shall not mention it only when it becomes nessesary to do so.

About 10 oclock on our first morning, the Floor Sergeant took out about 20 or 22 men to draw our Rations. They Had to go some distance & when they returned, I think 14 of them were Carrying Each two Buckets & the other 6 or 8 were Carrying Bread, I Beleive it was Flour Bread. Those men Carried what they Brought into this Little room, in the Buckets was rice & some Beef. The rations was Devided as I described. I took mine I think my mess was Either No. 15 or 16. I divided mine to my mess & I now Have my Portion of it [—].

The Quantity & Quality of one, the Bread is Good Bakers Bread & will weight from 8 to 10 ounces. My Rice is about Half Cooked & in Quantity about three or Four table spoons Full. My Beef is Fairly Cooked but of a Peculiar Flavor or taste & in Quantity From one to two ounces. That is my food for the next 24 Hours for we only drew once a day about the same to time Each Forenoon & Can truthfully say in Quantity, it is more than a Four Average for Each days Rations while I was in Richmond but the Quality I Can not Say the Same For but Later on, I will give you a sample of the Quality for Remember, this is our First days Ration so it will not do to run it down on the start, we Have plenty of time yet. Water for drinking Purposes we got from a Fawcet in a Corner on the opposite Side of the room, it was Hydrant water.

The men were all strangers to me Except Bill & Pete & few of those I am now Amongst are wounded. My own wound is still Painfull & the only treatment I Can give it is to take the Bandage of[f] & wet it at the Fawcet then put it on again. Still I manage to Limp around on our Promenade two feet wide & 100 feet Long, a Brave walk but very few uses it for walking Purposes. No, we sit down on or in our alotted places & use that Promenade to spit in. Its the only place we Have as they did not Furnish us with spittoons & we did not bring ours with us. Oh no, it was a great oversight in us not to have done so & we were nearly all Tobacco users so you may Imagine what kind of a Promenade that was with about 300 or 400 men spitting in it. {But I Hear you say you dirty things you did you never sweep or Have it out?} Why certainly we did, oh yes, there was a man for Each Side appointed for that purpose.

The Rebels Furnished us or them two men a Broom, Brush or Bundle of Brush. Those men Each morning would loosely run that non descript Broom Lightly over our Promenade & Presto, its done — swept & Garnished untill next morning. O yes, that Promenade was Kept in a Splendid Condition but I will not say as much for its appearance after they had gone over it.

After I Had been 4 or 5 days there, I begun to feel — Well, How did I feel — I felt Like a very Small Sun Flower or a very, very tweeney twing Kling Morning Star. Oh yes, I felt very much that way only if I Had about 5 times more to Eat & Eat 10 times a day, I would feel Bigger & Better. As I said after 4 or 5 days, Bill, Pete & myself got our Heads together to ruminate, Pick our teeth, oh no, there was nothing in them to pick out. No but we got to speaking of our present prospects & Future Look out & got to Figuring the number of men on our Floor & when we came to compare the number of men Actually Present & the number of Sergean[t]s drawing rations for — 16 men. Each Sergeant we found there was one Sergeant more than there was Sixteen men for. Ho — Ho — so some Galoot of a Yankee was playin[g] Yankee on us & drawing for 16 men, who Had no Existence amongst us & was Living High on 16 mens rations while us poor Poor Devills were Sucking our Gums. Now for the difference it would make in our Rations individually, it would not amount to a toothfull to Each of us but the Principal of it, one man stealing from His Starving Comrades.

I told Pete & Bill to say nothing & as I drew for our mess, I said I would Hunt the theif up. Now about Half way along the wall or the side of the Building I was on & between me & the Little ration Room was two men, one Big Chuckle Headed Fellow & one smaller man about my own age named Warner[14]. Warner I think Belonged to the 2nd Mechigan Cavalry the same as the Sergeant of the Floor or the one who Issued rations to us. He was a 2nd Mich[igan] man too & in the few days we Had been there, I noticed this Warner & His Chuckle Headed Friend, who slept with Him, Eating at diffirent times through the day & wondered at the time where or How they Could get their Grub but did not think anything more of it untill now.

This Warner was acting & drawing rations as a mess Sergeant & I told Pete my Suspicious of Him so next morning when we all went in to get our rations, I Kept my Eye on Warner & told the Floor Serg[ean]t, He was Issuing rations to a mess of 16 men more than He Had. He asked me How I Knew & I told Him the number of men he Had & there was one more Sergeant amongst us than was required for that number of men. He asked if I Knew who it was & told Him I suspected Him Pointing to Warner. He Had the Piles all made so He said let it go & I will see about it.

Warner Denied my charge but I Knew From His actions, He was guilty so I took my Rations & Quickly Issued them to my mess & told Bill to remain & watch Petes Rations & mine & told Pete to come with me. I walked up to where Warner & His Friend was. They were Eating their Rations but Behind them, their Blanket was Bulged out as though there was some thing under it. I asked Warner what He Had under His Blanket. He said it was none of my Business & Jumped to His feet.

I was well Satisfied from His actions. I was right. I told Pete to attend to the Blanket & I Pitched in to attend to Warner & give Him an appetite for His next days Rations & I Beleive I did too, only the next day He only got one, His own ration, instead of 16. While Warner & I was Having our Little Exercise, Pete grabbed Blanket & Rations & Hustled them down to Bill in the Corner & told Him for His Life to allow no one to touch them & Hustled back to me. By this time, the Boys Had made a Ring for the Performance. Warner & I was giving Free & Warners Chuckle Headed Friend Had Climbed up on top of the Tobacco Presses to Encourage Warner but Pete soon stopped His non sense & Warner & I Had a Clear ring & no Favors. It did not Last very long, I suppose Warner Had Eat too much or was too Fat or something or maybe he was out of Wind. I dont Know what His reason was for not Continuing the Circus but He Said He Had Enough & of Course Pete & I went back to Bill, who was Guarding the Plunder.

I took Warners Blanket back to Him & then Sat down to my well Earned Breakfast, Dinner or Supper. Call it as you please but that Broke up [—] Begrudged me what Extra Grub that day. We Fared so well on that say that Pete wanted me to Hunt up an other Fraud of a Sergeant & He would Wipe Him out as He said it was His turn next.

About this time or soon after, Smith, the owner of the Building,[15] Came in, I suppose to see if we were destroying anything. He was a man about 55 or 60 years of age, Stout & of Medium Sise. I Heard He was a Union man at Heart but Had that & other Buildings with Property in Richmond & remained to try & save it from being Confiscated while in the North, Baltimore I think, He Had other Property & His son was there to save it from our Government so that He was Playing Double but spoke very Kindly to us telling us not to destroy anything, Particularly the Tobacco Presses, as there was no tobacco in them. It Had all been taken out before we came — & if He was allowed to He would willingly bring us some tobacco but that he was not allowed to do so. I Beleived Him for we really did need Tobacco, the only way we could get it was from the Rebel Guards Buying it which we could any night after dark.

It was always cheap Enough Considering Money value there but we will get to that after a while. Now as soon as Smith Left, the Boys got to Examining the Presses. They Could Raise all of them but one & Yankee like the one they could not raise was just the one the[y] wanted so some of them tore a Board up from the Floor & made a Hand Spike of it to raise that Press & the[y] done so when, Jerusalem, what a nice Pile of tobacco it was, those small [—] & Packed as tight together as the[y] Could be Pressed. Then such a scrambling, pulling & Climbing over Each other Like a Hive of Bees at a sugar Cask.

I wanted to be in the Fun but Pete Said on account of my Foot I Had Better stay out & He would try His Luck. I Saw Him go to that Crowd, it was on the opposite Side from me. I saw Pete get down on His Knees on the outside of that Mass of Heaving Humanity & work Himself in Amongst them under their Legs, Himself on His Hands & Knees & He is out of sight. Thunder! They will smother Him, squeese Him, Tramp Him to Death.

Bill is afraid to tackle the Crowd & I Begin to think it is time to see about Pete when I see Him backing out the same way He went in & straightening up. He came over to me with a smile & He commence Pulling out of His Pockets, His Breast & clothing Plug after Plug untill He counted I Beleive it was 23 Plugs. I asked Him How He Happened to be so lucky in so short a time. He said there was a Particular Friend of His Just ahead of Him as He went in & also on His Hands & Knees as He was but His Friend Had a Knife & with the Knife would pry of[f] Plug after Plug & Stick the Plug in His Pocket & while His Friend was digging of[f] another Plug, He Pete would take the other Plug out & Put it in His own Pocket & So He Had Kept on Supplying His own from the other Fellows Pocket untill He thought it was time to go with what He Had.

I Suppose it is what you Call Subtraction. Well thats Just what Pete done, He Subtracted that Tobacco from that Fellows Pocket into His own so it Could [—] Studying Substraction at sc[h]ool & suppose they teach it yet in sc[h]ools so Pete was only Practising an old Lessons which was taught Him at sc[h]ool & He was yet a good Hand at it. For that Tobacco Came very Handy Just then as it Enabled us to Help swell the Stream on our Promenade.

We are now about two weeks in Limbo & begin to be Very Uneasy about something. {You may say well whats the matter with you now, aint you satisfied?} Well, to tell the truth, no. I am not Satisfied & you may Judge by my actions that I am not For you may see by me shrugging my shoulder with My inclination to Rub my self against something that I am getting uneasy, yes, very uneasy.

Ha — there is some Fellow Back Biting <u>me</u>. {How do I Know it?} Gosh, dont I feel Him? There He goes again. Ha, you [—] now I am going to Catch you So I reach my Hand Back & down my Back Bone. Ha! Ive got Him between my Thumb & Fore finger. I Haul Him out Kicking & Biting me He is ashamed to Show His dirty face to me after the way He Has treated me, Back Biting me, Living of[f] my Poor Bones. Goodness, nows How Long but Ive got you at Last, my Fine Fat Southern Fellow & I take Him by the nape of the neck & walk Him to a window where I Can see the Color of His Eyes & the Len[g]th of His teeth for it was too dark in my corner.

So Here we Have Him in the light & I dont Like the Looks of Him a Bit. He is small of medium sise but must Have Powerfull Jaws from the way He Bites. He is Bashfull or ashamed to Look at me for I Cannot see the color of His Eyes but His Body Color is [—] General Color in Grey inclined to drab with a Dark Blue Black Stripe running Len[g]thwise north & south & Ending at the south west Corner of His Ear. Oh them Ears of His, I forgot to describe them but it is now too late

35

so I will Finish by giving Him a Name by which you may Her[e]after Know Him by as the Line Backed Grey Back.

There is another name for Him but I Have not time to look for it in the dictionary but He or others Like it was the Cause of Many — Many — Many — of My Poor Comrades Death in them Southern Slaughter Pens. I will not Hereafter Mention them only when I shall be oblidged to in this narrative but you will Ever Bear in Mind that during the rest of my Imprisonment, they are on me in Scores, Hundreds & I have no Hesitation, yes in thousands of it Had been Possible for me to Have Counted them. For they did not Confine themselves to Back biting but would fully as often act as Bo[s]om Friends & Even now while writing, I Imagine they are within reach of my Fingers — Ouch — Quit — that so to continue.

In Richmond, the diffirence in value of the No[r]thern Greenback & the Southern Paper Money was at this time about one to Ten in Favor of the gree[n]back & we could Buy 10 Loaves of Bread for one dollar in Green Back, where for the same number of Loaves we Had to Pay 10 dollars in Confederate money or a dollar a Loaf & Everything Else we Bought in the same Proportion of one dollar to ten — & we could Buy anything the[y] Had to sell For they were Ankious for Northern Money.

As the windows were all on the side of the Floor all the [—] through them windows the outside them on the Lower Half were secured by a Heavy Wire Screens Securely Fastened but the Corner of one of those screenes was Pulled Loose by the Rebel Guard for the Conveinence of trading by Passing through to us the articles Bought of them & receiving the value Promised from us. Oh yes, they got good very good Yankee value from us & I think you will agree with me Pretty soon, the Rebels would trade Bread at the Price stated, Rice 75cts Per Pound Confederate money Salt, 5 dollars Per Pound, Same value Tobacco From one to two dollars Per Pound Confederate Money. That was about the Principal articles the[y] Had to sell & what we most required but always if we gave them green Backs.

They woul[d] allows us ten of Confederate in value to one of ours Greenbacks now as they, the Jonnies, always Preffered greenbacks & they were getting scarce. For them, they got some nice clean white Paper & also some nice green Paint on some green something that answered for green Paint & Painted some green Backs to make a ten dollar Bill. They would Cut out the ten out of a Ten Cent Paper Peice such as the Government Issued them & Paste it on their Manufactured Bill & as our trading Had all to be done after dark, that nice new green Back would if it Had a ten on the Face of it get 100 Loaves of Bread or its value in Tobacco, Rice or Salt & For about two weeks, there was Lively Business done in the Green back & Baker Business but the Jonnys tumbled to the Gre[e]nBack Racket & then we Had to Look sharp For ther[e] would For Tricks on [—] window or they would shoot & if one of us wanted to trade with them, he would go to the trading window rap on it & if the Reb on Guard outside did not want to trade, He would shake His Head in Answer to the Rap on the Window. But if He did want to trade He would Come up close to the window. The Yank would ~~slighgtly~~ slightly raise it & say want to trade Jonnie? Yes Yank, whats yer got? Ive got a ten dollar Green Back, Ill trade for Bread. Oh no, you dont, a Pardner of Mine got stuck on one of them Thare no account green Backs the other night & I want trade for any, you Yanks are too slick for wee uns so sir, I wont trade. I Cant trust you uns & the Jonnie would start away but the Yank would Say Here you Jonnie, Ive got a nice Knife, Ill trade & He would show it to Him or what Ever article He Had to trade & they would then agree on their trade & the time of night to Exchange the[i]r Properties. It would usually be about 10 or 11 oclock at night for it was strictly against Orders for the Guards to trade with us or Have Any Communication with us whatever.

About this time a Regimental Comrade of Bills, who slept near us Had a watch that He wanted to trade for Bread. He was one of those Quiet Easy going no Push in Him Fellows Like my Self. For instance He Had Formed no Friendship with any one. He was afraid some one would steal His watch & trade it of[f] & He Knew they would Steal His Bread from Him as He Had no Friends to Help Him Protect after He Had it. So He asked Bill what He could do, Bill Brought Him to me & He asked me if we would Help Him. I told Him yes, we would [—] get it to the sleeping Place but after that, He would Have to protect it Himself as he slept too Far from us.

I Promised for all Bill & Pete for I Knew they would do as I done. This mans Reason for wanting our Help was that he Knew if He went alone to trade His watch for Bread, the Boys would make a raid on Him & take His Bread from Him if He Had no one to Protect Him & some times Even Help did not save some of them if the attacking Party thought themselves the strongest. But I Suppose He thought Bill & Pete & myself sufficient to Protect Him from our actions in Breaking up that Extra Mess a few weeks before So I told Him to make His trade with the Guard & Let us know the time we were wanted & we would be Ready. He traded the watch for 120 Loaves of Bread & at 10 oclock that night, we were on Hand & Brought Him back all safe. We left Him at His place & returned to ours but He soon Came again to us & said He was afraid they would Come & take His Bread befor[e] Morning & asked us if we would Buy some of it. I told Him yes & we Bought 27 Loaves for 10 dollars & were to Pay Him when we were Exchanged.

Now we Had 27 Loaves between three of us & a good chance & the first one to fill up the Corners in our in — our — Oh Well in our Bread Baskets so we sat up & before we Layed down to sleep the three us Had Eat 20 of the Loaves well washed down with the Hydrant Water — Well to tell the truth I did not sleep much for that Bread was so awfull dry that I Had to Keep wetting it all night I Really dont Beleive the Baker put any water at all in it when He made it or if He Had it would not Certainly Have been so dry & them too.

I was so uneasy about those 7 Loaves we Had left & could not Eat that night because we actually Had no spare room for them. That you Know I Had to Keep watch of them[16] so that between the Loaves outside & the Loaves inside that required so much water to Keep them moistened so they would digest Easy, I realy did not get much sleep that night & Bill & Pete was no Better. So between the three of us, them seven Loaves was well watched.

The first thing in the morning, them Loaves realy looked so Lonesome that we Put them with the other 20 & Please Bring me a Bucket of water for I dont feel very well & my Corporation is of such Dimensions that I am afraid its not my own but some other Fellows Ive got. But I could always Bear a great deal of stretching that way, it did not Hurt me much & by the time our rations Came, I was again ready for them. Our Rations by this time were getting a Kind of Misalaneous [Miscellaneous] & that is the men were Bringing more in in the Buckets than they were getting at the cook House for us. Very often the Rice would be rather thin & on the top of the Pails would be a Kind of a Surface of Greasy water. Now when those Buckets would be set down in the deviding Room & the Men go out of it who Had Brought them in, there would be on the top of the Rice & Floating or rather swimming around Thick on the water, those Southern Grey Backs Back Biting Bosom Friends of ours, who Had gone out with our Fellows to get a little Fresh air & draw rations to us & getting out from the inside of their Clothing so as to get a better view of the City. They would drop of[f] their Clothing into the Buckets in Order to try our rice I suppose but any way, the[y] remained there & were Carried in often always. In Fact those Buckets would be covered with them on the surface of the rice or soup x what Ever you or I may Call it. They would be devided Equally as Fair as the other rations & no Favors shown. This is the Positive truth, we got so used to seeing them that it did not make much diffirence but when I went to Eat my rations, I always shut my Eyes for what the Eyes dont see — mm.

This Rebel officer, who comes Each morning to Count us or Call the Roll, one morning Brought in with Him a little Dog, I think it was a scot[tis]h Terrier. The Little Fellow Had often Came in before but this morning He Forgot to go out for in about an Hour after the Officer Came back to us, Called His dog but no Doggie Answered. Then He offered a Reward for Him but that did not find Him so He went away & that afternoon one of the men Brought me a Bone Finger Ring that He said was made out of the shin Bone of that little Terrier. It was of a Kind Bluish or slatish Color. What Ever became of it, I do not now remember but I Have an Idea that I Brought it Home with me & gave it to my Sister Mary.[17] The Boys Had Caught the dog, Killed Him & Eat Him & the[y] must Have been sly about it for I Knew nothing of it untill as I Have Said the Comrade Brought me that ring & told me oh no, it was not Healthy for Even Dogs around there.

The men would often get the Richmond Examiner, a Rebel newspaper Printed there of that name, in which we would see the movements of our Army & other General news from a Rebel Stand point. One day in Looking through the advertisements, I saw an notice from the Rebel Quarter Master General offering the Highest Price Paid for all Dead Horses, mules, Cattle, sheep & Hogs Paid by Him when delivered to Him stating where it or they were to be delivered Whew — thinks my Confederate Q, M Has a Particular use for Dead animals or He would not advertise for them but what the Dickens use Can He make of Carrion For it is Supposed that all animals die Either from Disease or old age & of what use are the[y].

My Next thought was that they might mean to use them as Food For us but Thunderation, no, Certainly the Rebel Authoritys are not that in human as to give us diseased Decayed Flesh to Eat. No, it Can not be Possibly but what other use Can the[y] Have for that advertisement, there it is & the[y] did not Put it in for Fun. Oh <u>no</u> & I could not get rid of that Idea. Neither could I think it Possible they would use it for our use as Food but we shall see, for I changed my mind in regard to their Possibility or Impossibilitys before Long & I think you will also if you Follow me through those Southern death Traps Called Military Prisons.

In a few days after Reading that advertisement, I drew for My Mess a Ration of nice Looking Meat. It was almost Raw. Now I was & am very Fond of Raw Beef & I was glad of my Present chance to satisfy Even on a small scale my appetite for it so I mostly Issued to my man & soon placed that raw Beef where I thought it would do the most good. It was Sweet & nice to Eat But thunderation as soon as I swallowed it, Oh Gee <u>Whiz</u>, whats that my Breath smells as though something Had Crawled into me & died in my Throat or Stomack. It is Sickening now I Always Had a Pretty Strong Stomack but if I Had that Peice of nice Fresh Beef in my Hand again, it should never go into my Bread Basket & as little in Quantity as it was, it was Stronger than me. The Feeling I Had was So Sickening that for some time I could not Eat my Bread but Just sat there. Bill & Pete was about as Bad — & we Came to the Conclusion that it must Have been Mule Meat.

It Certainly was not Beef for it smelled sweet Enough before Eating & ordinary Beef if spoiled would smell. Horse meat is the same, there is no Material diffirence between it & Beef, only in the graine of the Meat. The graine of Horse Beef is coarse while Cattle Beef is Fine so that we thought then at the time & I yet think it was Mule Meat we Had that day & How often Before or after that I do not Know but suppose if they gave it to us then, they Had often done so only that the cooking of it Had taken that smell after Eating of it while this day getting it so raw, the Brute Had retained all its Original Flavor.

I remained about six weeks in Richmond & Have Endeavored to give Such incidents of my Imprisonment in Smith Building as I Can remember & thought would Intirest you but I Have Refrained from giving any description of our Personal appearance or the Interior of our Prison Leaving you to Imagine what it looked like a Room 35 by 100

Feet with 350 or 400 Men Confined there night & day for Six Weeks. In all that time I Beleive I washed My Face 3 or 4 time. We Had no soap; in Fact I may Here State that in no Prison that I was did they Issue to us anything but what I Have stated & will state as I describe my Life in those Hell Holes of Southern Perdition. For Enemys though they were then & a good many of them is yet still in all Truthfullness, I will do them all the Justice I Can by giving them Full credit Either as a Rebel Body or Government or as an Individual Rebel, what Ever they gave or done for me or others as I Saw or <u>Felt</u>. So that My Dear Friends you may Beleive that I will Confine my self to the naked Truth & Facts for Amongst them, I did Find Some Kind Hearted Men & when I meet Such, I will give them their Just dues as I Find them.

Our Bodys are swarming with those Little Back Biters for neither I nor others Had any change of Clothing. In Fact, we Had only Just what were on our Backs & to my Knowledge, no man took them off Even to Sleep for very few Had Even Blankets & there for[e] Had to sleep on Bare Boards & it was Impeasibly to Keep rid of those little Pests so after being about Six weeks there, we were Ordered out they said to go to City Point to be Exchanged.

City Point is about 25 or 30 Miles from Richmond. We all Felt rejoiced as we only Had such a short distance to go & out we went on the street & a Delapidated Crowd we Looked. Starvation was already showing on our Features, Hunger in our Looks & Weakness in our Movements. The most of us were beginning to show a Raggedness in our Clothing, all unshaven our Hair Matted & Long With unwashed Faces. Yes, we would not make a Pretty Picture Either Individually or Collectively but Here we are in the open air again Breathing the Pure air of Heaven after inhaling for six Weeks, the Poisonous air insid[e] of that Pest House called Smiths Building.

We are Formed in Front of The Libby Prison & marched out in the Same direction we Had Come in & that Settled the City Point Exchange. For it was in another direction from the way we were going so we make up our minds to Charge that as another Rebel Lie, which it proved to be. They march us on for a short distance & we are Loaded in Box cars about 55 or 60 men to Each car. It is now I think about the 15th or 20th Nov. & the Weather is getting Cool. We travelled along night & day Passed through several towns. I do not remember the names of any of

View of Danville, Va. Where Union Prisoners Are Confined. Drawn by J. M. Thurston, Company F, 90th Ohio Vols., 1865 (courtesy Library of Congress).

Morning Toilette Union Officers' Prison (Top floor) Danville Va. Winter 64–5. Drawn by Henry Vander Weyde (Tobacco Warehouse used as Confederate Prison, "Sardine" System). Appeared in George Haven Putnam's *A Prisoner of War in Virginia 1864–5* (New York and London: G. P. Putnam's Sons, 1912), page 41.

them or any incident of that Journey but think it was the third day after Leaving Richmond when we were unloaded in Danville, Virginia.

Danville[18] is very Pleasantly situated on High ground & what I saw of it seem[e]d Well Built. The Pee Dee river ran about a Half mile East of the town. I with others were Placed in a Brick tobacco Building. I was put on the Second Floor. There were three Floors in this Prison & Each Floor was occupied by Prisoners. There was Four Building Prison Here in Danville Numbered Prison No. 1, 2, 3 & 4 & all Four of them was occupied by the Chickamauga Prisoners as the Rebels seemed for some Reason to Keep us together. They Had done so in Richmond & again Here in Danville. I Beleive there was about 600 men in Each Building or about 200 on Each Floor.

I was in Prison Number one & on ours, the 2nd Floor, there was no tobacco Presses so we Had a clear Floor & our Sleeping arrangements were Just in the same way as at Richmond, Four rows or Lines of men arranged as described before with a narrow walk between our Feet but Generally we Had more Room to get around & not so crowded. Our Prison arrangements are a Little diffirent, one man Had charge of the whole Building & drew the Rations For all then devided them in three one Part given to Each Floor. The Floor were in charge of a Sergeant, who devided the men into Messes of 10 mens. Again I Had charge of a mess & the Rations were devided Just the same as before. I do not Remember much of this Prison as in a very short time we were moved from it to Prison Number three. This was Just about the same as No. 1 & again I am on the second Floor with my sleeping place by a window on the north side of the Building.

The men on the first Floor Had Pryed up some of the Boards from the Floor & Found a lot of ~~stem~~ Tobacco Stems. We obtained Enough of them to cover the place we slept on 5 or 6 inches Thick in Hopes that by using it to sleep on those Bosom Friend of ours would disap[p]ear. But no, they seemed to Enjoy The Tobacco Stems as well. The[y] Enjoyed the Hard Picking on our Poor Bodys so we make up our minds to Skirmish Them twice Each day. We choosed about 9 or 10 Oclock in the Forenoon & about 3 or 4 in the afternoon & as this Skirmishing is rather new to you, I will try & give you some Kind of an Idea of How it is done For it is an Entirely Diffirent Mode of Extermination from the Skirmishing we used to do with our two Legged Grey Backs in Richmond on account of the dark & crowded Hole in which we were. It was very Little of this Skirmishing we did or could do for it was so dark there that we could not Follow those little Fellows Through all the Highways & Byways of their Haunts but now & From now untill my Release Except while I was unable to do so through sickness or weakness, I twice Each day went through the Exercise I am about to describe & under God I Beleive it & it only saved my Life & the Lives of thousands of others of my Poor Comrades in Prison. You Have to listen to this description some time & as well now as any other time.

I take of[f] my Blouse, turn the Sleeves inside out & commence at the seams a Thumb nail on Each Side of the seam Following it along the whole Len[g]th, closing my nails Tightly on all I find along those seams & when I get to the End of that seam, the Blood is running from of[f]

my nails. {Whose Blood?} Why my own Blood, of Course, I am only Fulfilling scripture. {Now dont say I am not.} For I say I am & I will Prove it
to you, the old or Mosaic Law says a Tooth for a Tooth or an Eye for an
Eye[19] & I am only Taking From those Back Biting Bosom Friends what
they took From me, My own Blood. Those Seams are there Highways &
the Whole Surface of the Cloth or rather Rag, I am Examining is their
By Ways & there I also Find them with what result you may guess.

I repeat the same Operation with my other Clothing & I Have Put
in one Solid Hour of Bloody Work on My Bloody Enemys but in Less
than another Hour, there is as many more Hungry ones Picking & sucking
away. They are on the Floor, in the Wall, on Every thing & in Every Peace
sit down to Eat & you Have to Watch the Bile you are Putting to your
mouth. Lest there is some of them on it, I Can See them Crawling from
the Floor up on the outside of my Pants & take my Hand & Brush them
of[f].

These are Facts & not as strongly Put as I Could truly State, if I
would but will at Least give an Idea of what our Surroundings were. The
Tobacco Stems were useless to us for What Purposes we got them For
so we done away with them. The Rebel officer who Had charge of us,
was of Rank as Major, a Perfect Gentleman who treated us as Humane
as Prison rules would Permit & almost daily would come in talk to us
of the north & often speak of His own Family, who were in Richmond.
I Beleive in His Heart He felt for & sympathised with us for He was all
ways Kind to us.

Our Rations Here were Issued about 10 Oclock Each morning &
were Brought to the Prison door in a wagon when the Men Brought them
in & were more in Quantity & of Better Quality & Better Cooked than
I received in any other Prison. We got Wheat Bread Every other day a
Loaf to two men. The Loaves would weigh about one Pound & a Half
[—] about ¾ of a Pound of Bread to Each man Every other day. We got
a loaf of Corn Bread to two men that made one Pound for Each man
Every day. We got Either about 2 or 2½ ounces of Beef or about 1½ or
2 ouces of Bacon P[r]obably 3 or 4 times Each Week. We got 3 or 4 Table
spoons full of Rice or one or two Spoons full of Little Black Beans but
all was well Cooked, Clean & Eatable & the whole made about one Third
of as much Food as we could Eat or ought to Have to Eat & Just as soon
as I got mine, I sat right down & Eat it then Fasted for 24 Hours untill

next day & Oh My <u>God</u>, Many, <u>Many</u> times Have I got up after Eating My rations—Hungry.

Well, Hunger is not the name for it but I would be Wildly Ravenous. My food would only start my appetite for before I would get my Rations, I would not be Hungry but weak with a Sickening Weakness. I was then Long Enough in Prison to get over the Actual Suffering Pangs of Hunger & it affected me now in Bodily Weakness & I only Felt Hungry after Eating my rations & then that Feeling did not last Long. Our water to drink Had to be carried in Buckets from the River once a day by the mens. There would about 12 or 14 men go from Each floor, Each men Carrying two Buckets & bring back Water. There was none Used only for drinking.

A small yard about 40 feet square was used by the Prisoners for Exercise, it was in rear of the Building. One day near the Head of the Stairs, I Heard some angry words & saw a crowd gather so going down there, I saw one of the Boys with a Bad Cut in His Head. I asked who done it & the crowd Pointed to Warner, The Fellow I Had the little trouble with in Richmond. He stood there with a short Bar of Iron in His Hand with which He Had Hit this Poor fellow with. I started for Warner with the smark. You scoundrel, what did you Hit Him For? But He dropped the Bar & Skipped down stairs, I turned to the man injured. He Had a Long Scalp wound on the Side of His Head. It was only Skin deep & He said it would not amount to much so He went away to the other End of the Room where He Belonged & in two days, He was Dead, Killed with the <u>L-g</u> Grey Backs. They Had Eat in to His Brain & Killed Him. I mention this only to show you How numerous the[y] were as well as Dangerous for the scratch of your Nail or the scratch of a Pin, anything that would draw a drop of Blood on any Part of the Body would attract them in Hundreds, yes, Thousands. If it was Possible for them to get assured one spot & I can Safely say that take the Healthyest strongest man Living place Him in with us make the scratch of a Pin on Him so as to draw Blood & Leave Him in there without Him doing anything to rid Himself of those vermin & I Promise you in less than one week they will Kill Him by Eating in to His Body.

How much sooner then will they Kill one of us, my Poor Starved Comrades Weakened by Long months of starvation. Some of them giving up all Hopes of Ever getting out, nothing in view but Human Misery— Misery & starvation & How Easy to die & rid them selves of it. Easy yes, Very Easy, nothing to do but Lay down inactive & a few days of Suffering

"Flanking the Enemy," sketched by Henry Vander Weyde, ca. 1864 (courtesy Danville Museum of Fine Arts and History).

"Discovery of a new Generation" and "Boots for Sale Price 4 Ration 2 Corn bread,"
drawn by Henry Vander Weyde, ca. 1864 (courtesy Danville Museum of Fine Arts
and History).

"Buckets for Water! Our officers bringing water underground view from East Window," drawn by Henry Vander Weyde, ca. 1864 (courtesy Danville Museum of Fine Arts and History).

will End it. But for a man to Live th[r]ough it, He Had to be Determined to Live if Possible Keep active & be Possessed of Nerves of Steel, a Body of Iron, a Constitution stronger than a Horse & more meanness in His system than there is in the Hind Legs of a Dozen Mules & those are about the only men that did Live th[r]ough & get Home.

Later on I will give you samples of those weak men or men that was not Constitutioned & Built as I Have described above, there is no lack of Subjects Here to write about. No My Friend, there is dozens, scores of them daily around me but the trouble is to Pick out such as may give a General Idea of our Sufferings. No, a Photographic view of us daily, Hourly, Could only give an Idea of us to you. For our Individual Sufferings & misery, none but God alone Can Know & no man Living Can Convey to another How He Felt there or in any other Prison of the South.

The men would Sit around in little groups, some Fellow would Commence by saying, say you Fellows, I Had an awfull good dream Last night. I dreamt I was Home & my Sister Had set out a Bully meal for me & I pitched in, you Bet, Like I was Hungry & I Eat & Eat but Blamed if I Could get Satisfied & there was a mince Pie Just out of my Reach on the Table & Just as I reached for that Pie, I woke up in this Hole. Oh but I was mad I was Having such a good time. That would start some other Fellow on His dream or maybe be the means of getting us a chapter on How Pies were made. One Fellow would say, Oh Gee <u>Whiz</u>, if I only Had one of my wifes Pumpkin Pies, I would be Happy. She used to make the Best Pies in all our Neighbourhood. Then He would tell How She made them & what she Put in them to make them so nice then another Fellow would tell How His Sister would make Custard Pies. Another would tell How His Mother would Make mince Pies & so on untill our teeth would water & we would be so intirested in Listening that before we Knew it, we would be sucking our teeth.

It got to be a <u>daily</u> Conversation with two old Codgers, who slept opposite to us with their feet against ours so that when the[y] sat down, they were not 8 feet from us as we sat with our Backs to the wall. Those two men were from Ohio & Neighbours Farmers when the[y] Enlisted & Both men of about 40 or 45 years of age but this day, they were again in the Pie Business when Pete stood it as Long as He could & He Jumped up with the Exclamation, you Confounded old Buckeyes, if you dont stop that Pie Racket, I will make Pies of Both of you. My Mouth is running Water like a Mill Race & I am as Hungry as a Wolfe any How without you two old Sinners making me worse & that stopped the Pie Factory in our Neighbourhood.

About 9 oclock Every Morning or Just before Rations was Issued, the Rebs Surgeon or Doctor would Come & the guard that came in with

Him would Call out Sick call. If there was any Sick, they went down stairs to Him & Found Him in a Small office on the First Floor where if they required medicine, He gave them what He could, usually Pills— Pills for all ailments. Those Pills were all alike & therefore a cure all but if the man was very sick, He would Have Him taken to Hospital. We Had Heard that the Hospital was carelessly Guarded & that several of the Boys Had Escaped from there but most of them were caught. Pete & I Proposed to Play sick & get to the Hospital. If we could & Keep together & Escape together if Possible, so Pete was to Play dropsy [20] on them & I was to Play Heart Disease.

The next morning at sick call, Pete & I went down. There was only us

Hospital Stewart "fall in you'ens for yer terpentine — how are you sick," drawn by Henry Vander Weyde, ca. 1864 (courtesy Danville Museum of Fine Arts and History).

two that morning & Pete turn Came first. Well my man, whats the matter with you & I co[u]ld see Petes chest swell out & His cheeks. How the dickens He done it I Could not tell but He Swelled Him self out & managed to say Im getting worse, doctor. Yes but what ails you? Whats are you sick of? Whats the matter with you? Pete managed to say dropsy. The doctor asked How long He Had dropsy? Pete said He Had it when

He was Born that it was in the Family & Lately, very lately, it was worse. The doctor gave Him some Pills, told Him How to take them & if He was no better, to Come to Him next morning & Pete was dismissed. Then turning to me, well whats the matter with you? Ive got Heart Disease. How long Have you Had it & How does it affect you? I told him I had been Subject to it for a long time & How it affected me at night & in the day time. He gave me Pills with the same directions as Pete & told me Come in the morning. So back I went, Compared notes with Pete & agreed our chance was good to get out.

The Pills we did not want to throw away & as I Had a Brick Loosened in the wall at my Head, I pulled the Brick out & Put our Pills in then replaced the Brick, a Pretty safe Pill Box that was. I will Explain why I Had Loosened that Brick. There Had been one or two Thorough searches For Case Knives, Pocket Knives or Forks, For valuables of any Kind or any sharp instrument all. Everything they Had Found, they took with them away but I Had a Butcher Knife that I Found when we were at Columbus, Kentucky in March 62 that I thought a great deal of on account of where I got it & the real absolute need I Had of it there in Cutting the rations. Besides it was the only Butcher Knife on our Floor — & was usefull to others as well as me. The first time the searchers Came in, the[y] Cam[e] unexpectedly on us & Found me with my Knife in my Possession & no way to Hide it for my Clothing was to scant to Hide it that way & I Had no Bed. The window Behind me, I raised a little & slipped the Knife out on the Sill, Closed the window. I was not seen do it so my Knife was saved that time. After that Escape, I made that Hole in the wall by Cutting out that Brick & there I Had Kept that Knife all the time only when actually using it & it Had already saved it once & again twice afterwards.

There was Five of us now sleeping together, the other two I will now Introduce to you. One of them is Jim Brett.[21] He Belongs to Bills Regiment I think & is about 28 or 30 years old, a small well Built man with one, I think the Left Lung, Entirely gone, decayed. He was a married man & our Family were or Had been acquainted with His wife before he married Her. Her maiden name, I Beleive was Eaton or Easton, Something like that & the[y] lived in 1858 or 9 on the KanKaKee river in one of the widow Fisher Houses at the Quarry and an old man named Kirk Lived in the other. I think there was two or three girls of them but Jim married the oldest. Jim afterwards died in Andersonville but He was not with me when He died.

The other one of the Five was named Henry <u>Lavalle</u>,[22] a Canadian French Boy about 18 years old & Belonged to the 35th Ills, the Regiment that Killed the Rebel General Ben Mc Cullock[23] in Missouri & the man that said He shot Him I saw in Andersonville. Henry was troubled with the Heart Disease & I got the symptoms of it & Played it on the Rebel Doctors. Next morning when the time for Sick Call Came, I Stood up to the wall & Bumped my Elbows against the Brick to get my Pulse agoing well & I guess I did for when I went down, the doctor said they were going so Fast He Could not Count them & again Pills for Pete & I & again we gave them to the Brick wall. But the next morning, Pete was taken to the Hospital & the morning after Him, I was taken also to the Hospital.

They gave me nice Clean Hospital Clothing & placed me in or on a Clean Cot Bed. Oh boy, it felt good to be again in a Clean Bed with Clean Clothing on & my face & Hands washed. They were Rebel nurses, we Had Men but Fully as Kind to us as we could Expect. There was about 15 or 20 of us in the ward. Next morning the doctor Came Around on His visit, it was not the same who Had taken me From Prison. My Bed steads were Iron so a Little Bumping got my Pulse in splendid Running order For Him & He Pronounced me a bad Case. I Beleived that myself but not in the sence He meant, Pete was not in my ward. The doctor prescribed Pills For me, the nurse Brought them with Some water. I told the nurse I was a Splendid Hand to take Pills so I would take them as directed & He left me but Confound the Pills, its not Pills I want but Pete & Pete I cannot Find. I am not allowed to Leave my Cot. Those are the doctors Orders. My Case is too Critical & the least Excitement may Carry me of[f]. Oh no, I must remain very still & Qu[i]et. My Clothing is all taken away & I Have nothing only those nice clean but very Light & white Hospital clothing, Really they are not, you Know well, Just Suitable this time of year, December 1863, to make a Foot race of two or three Hundred Miles to get into our Lines. In Even if I Could Escape from the Hospital & I Certainly Should have tried it if I Had my own Clothing Even without Pete. But Here are those Pills, what shall I do with them? I am detirmined to remain in Hospital as long as I Can, something may turn up to give me the chance I Came in for but I must get rid of those Pills & I Have no Room for them inside So—Ha—Ive found a Place for them. There is a Wooden Spittoon to my Cot & filled with saw dust. In I put my Pills, Bury them in it & I feel Better after taking them that Way.

Our Food is Clean but not in Quantity Enough. We get it twice a day, Light Broth & Some Kind of a Liquod, they called Tea, in the afternoon. I did not Know anyone there & it was Lonesome for me but I was Still in Hopes something would turn up & so it did for after about two weeks, the nurse took my Spittoon out to Clean it & Put Fresh saw dust in it & in Emptying it, He found a schothecary — Pop — or a Pope,e cary Schoth or a Pothecary — shop — or some that way Especially in the Pill Line for my two weeks, Pills were in it — & when He came Back, He Had in one Hand my Empty Spittoon & in the other Hand my Pill Pile & with Him, the doctor who looked as though He Had to take all them nice Pills of mine Himself but was afraid they would not agree with Him & He made the remark to me that I was a nice specimen of a Yanke[e] to treat His medicine that way & to Play such a Yankee trick on Him. I realy felt sorry for Him but Could not Express it to Him & was sent right Back to Prison but Lucky for me I was sent to my own No. three & got Back with Bill again.

There was no account of Pete but about a month after, I Heard they sent Him to City Point for Exchange & it took Four men to Carry Him out of the Hospital so that was the last I Heard of Him. Now I will Have to settle down again to Business, I was indeed very glad to get Back for Except the Hopes I Had of Escaping & the Clean Bed at the Hospital, I would Rather be with my Comrades in Prison. The Weather is getting very cold. There is often a light snow on the ground. We are allowed no fires in fact there is neither Stoves or Fire places in the Building & If there was, we Have no Wood or Coal. We are actually Suffering with Cold.

It is about Christmas time 1863. We Have been now about three months in Prison without any other Clothing but what we Had on when captured & they are getting Pretty well worn Thin. We are very thin ourselves after those three Months of starvation, Thin Bodily & then in Blood & there fore very Cold for us Four, Bill, Jim, Henry & myself. We Had For Covering the one Blanket getting very thin too & our Half a Pup tent getting very thin also. We were then as you may very well Suppose a very thin outfit all through & we were not the very worst Either for lots of the men Had not a Particle of Covering, only what they Had on their Backs & to get warm or at Least to try to get warm when the sun would shine & at this time of year, it did not shine Eve[r]y day or all day but when it would, a group of 10 or 12 of us would Huddle together by a window the sun was shining through & stand in it so the sun would warm us a little. That was our Mode of getting warm —& we [—] very warm Friends during that time. That is of sticking Close to Each other made warm Friends but it was little Heat we got in that way Either from the sun or our own thin Bodys.

About this time I Heard that our government Had Sent to all Prisoners in the South a Full & Complet[e] Soldiers outfit, a Blanket, overcoat, Blouse, Pants, Cap, Shoes, Stockings & Underwear with Haversack for Each man. That is what I Heard & I will now say what I saw. The Rebel officials Came in & ordered Every man to stand up in Line and as they Came to Each man, the[y] Examined the Condition of His Clothing & Put His name down for what they thought He needed the worst in the shape of Clothing but would ask Him which He would Have a Blanket or overcoat. They gave Him [—] one of [—] Blanket or overcoat but Every thing Else they gave Him what they thought He needed & not what He wanted, no man got a Haversack.

They gave me a cap, shoes, stockings & Lower Underwear. I Choosed a Blanket so also did Bill, Jim & Henry For we Concluded to sleep on a Blanket was Better than an overcoat & Equally as good to Keep warm by wrapping our selves in it & the Majority of the men was of the same opinion, for Nearly all took Blankets. The next day our Clothing was Issued to us & Immediately after, a Rebel Sutler Came in to our Building & on Each Floor Announced that He would Buy of us, those Clothing Just Issued if they were not used or soiled. The Prices He offered in Confederate money was for an overcoat 100 dollars, Blanket 75, shoes 45, Blous[e] 20, drawers 5 & socks 2–50cts or He would trade us to that amount for our Articles, Salt 1 dollars 50 cts a Pound —& Rice at 75 cts Per Pound—& Tobacco, two dollars a Pound. That was His Stock in trade & Figures.

Some of the Boys, in Fact a great many of them, Sold or traded with Him. Oh Gee Whiz—to see those Fellows get their Rice or Salt & Eat, it would do you good to see them but for us to sit there & look on— mmm, Excuse me, Im not there. We could not stand it any Longer so three of us, Bill, Jim & myself, agreed that we Could Spare three Blankets

& with Henrys Blanket & our old one, we Could get along. So the three of us putted Cuts to see who should sell His Blanket, <u>First</u> with the understanding that when we Eat up one Blanket, the others should be sold untill all three were gone & each man should sell or trade His own Blankets. We Pulled Cuts & as usual my Luck, my Blanket Had to go First. The Boys Had rushed in their dry goods to the Sutler so fast the first few days, He Reduced their Cash value but retained His Prices on His goods.

The Guards were doing a little trading on their own Hook now. Those Guards were all on the outside of the Building & the Lower Floor was about ~~three~~ Six Feet Higher than the Side Walk so a man standing on the Side Walk Could Just Reach up to the windows Sill or about seven feet. Those windows were all Screened outside as the Windows at Richmond was & the Lower Corner of the screen Loosened for trading Purposes. I Concluded I Could do Better with the Guard then with the sutler so I went down in the Evening, drew the attention of the Guard & traded with Him. He agreed at ten oclock when He came on duty again to bring me 27 Pounds of Rice & 7 Pounds of salt for my Blanket so I went Back & told the Boys I Had Traded & what I was to get.

They thought I done well & I was in Hopes I would do Better. I told Bill & Jim I wanted them to Help in a little Trick I was going to play to try & save my Blanket & also get that Jonnie Rice & Salt. The[y] agreed to Help so I told them they should come down when the time came & I would Place them on one side of the window out of sight of the guard & when I Had got from Him the rice & salt, they Both Having a good Hold of the Blanket inside they should Pull it Quick & strong & Skip Back up Stairs with it & Leave me to take care of my self. He may said He would get a Coffee Pot, a Large one Holding about a Gallon or over & be Prepared with water & wood to Cook our Supper.

Now I suppose you are wondering where we are going to make our Fire on that second Floor & How we are going to get our wood, both are now Easily Explained. A few days before this, some of the men asked the Major to give us wood to make a Little Fire to warm us by. He Said He would willingly do it if He could but was not allowed to & the Boys were Determined to Have Fire to Cook their Rice by. Several of them Had managed some way to save their Case Knives at the searching & they Had made Saws of them, Saws of a Case Knife, a common Table Knife.

Yes, they Had, to saw up the Bones from our Beef Rations & make Finger rings, tooth Picks & other little trinkets of[f] from those Bones & I Brought some of them Home when I Came in 65.

Laurel was very Plentifull around Danville & the Boys would get it from the Guards & make Rings & Pipes of it & the[y] used those Knives to saw the wood in what Ever sise the[y] wanted to and as saws, they were more usefull than Knives to them. The Roof of our Building was Sealed on the inside with Boards & the Fellows would Climb up to that Ceiling & with those saws, Cut of[f] one End of a Board & then Tare it of[f] & in that way, obtained our wood.

The Tobacco Presses were on the Lower Floor & to Every Tobacco Press was a square Peice of Heavy Sheet Iron about 15 or 18 inches square. We would take one of those Iron Plates as I will call them & Place it on two Bricks Set up Edgewise on the Board Floor & we Build our Fire on the plate within 4 inches of the Floor & as our Cooking or what Ever Else we need the fire. For the Bricks were obtained out of the Wall, we were always Carefull of Fire as also to Keep all traces of it from the Major. The Peices of Boards & Plates we would Hide under our Blankets & the ashes were scattered on our two foot Promenade which was swept as I described while in Richmond. Now Henry Had Promised to get Coffee, Pot Water & Wood & Everything Nessesary to Cook & He done so.

10 Oclock Came, we three, Blanket & Co. went down. I tapped on the window, the Jonny answered me so I raised the Window & asked to pass up the rice & Salt. He Said no, I must give Him the Blanket first as some of wee uns were Cheating His Comrades by Stealing Back what they Had traded to them. I told Him I would not trust Him if He would not trust me & to Prove to Him that I would not Cheat Him, I showed Him the Blanket & also that I was alone. He could not see Bill & Jim as they were out of Sight of Him. He wanted my Blanket & I wanted His Rice & Salt So we [agreed] that I should Hang the Blanket Half out the window, the other Half in. Neither of us were to touch the Blanket untill I Had both Rice & Salt & then He was to take the Blanket. Oh yes, that was a nice Kind Good Hearted Jonnie, I guess. He was a Particular Friend of Mine or thought He was & you Know that is Just as good.

So I Hung out the Blanket as agreed & raised Both my Hands to show I was Honest. I nodded to Bill & Jim & they Grabbed a Hold of the Blanket. The Reb Passed up a small Sack of Rice which I placed on one side then Reached for the Salt & when I got a good Hold of it, I Called out, now. That was the Signal Agreed on Between the Boys & I & in Came Salt & Blanket both Together. It was done Before the Reb Realised it & I Saw Him reach for His Rifle but I was not there. Oh no, I was wanted Just then up Stairs & I Soon got there with my Rice & Salt. The Boys were already there with the Blanket all safe & I really Felt Satisfied With my Nights Trading & Felt Like going down & Explaining to My Friend Jonnie How that Yankee Trick was done but thought that by this time He understood Well Enough How it was done.

Henry set the Pot a Boiling & we soon Had a Pot of Rice Well Thickened with Salt & that salt tasted so good that we Eat some of it while waiting for the rice to Cook. We Eat that Pot Full & Another when I Proposed that we Have a Regular Feast of rice & told Henry to Cook another one. Poor Little Jims was as full as a tick & Said He Had Enough, Bill though[t] His Hide Could Stretch a little more & I wanted to again Feel Happy with all my Wants supplyed. Henry was satisfied Either way So I told Him Fill Her up again, who Cared For Expenses.

It was again ready but Jim tried to do His duty & Failed. Bill nobly stood by it untill He also Bushed & Henry & myself Finished it & towards the last, I think I Could touch the rice in my throat with my Finger. Oh dont Ask me Please How I Felt or Put in that night For I Could not tell you on that I Had a Pretty Good Idea of How a Balloon Felt when inflated. I do not think though that I looked like a Balloon only I felt Like one & Bill was no Better of[f] than me. Henry said He Had no Idea He could stretch So far — & Jim was afraid He was going to Burst.

We Had Eat 27 Pints of Cooked rice or at Partly Cooked Rice & the Confounded Rice, the more water we drank, the more it wanted untill we Had to Quit drinking because, well, because we would Hold no more Water, we were chuck Full & then we Suffered from Thirst. Yes, we were yet actually dry with all that water in us & the Salt we Had Eatin Made us Worse. I Beleive we Eat the Biggest Half of it or about Four Pounds of salt. Rice is a light food so next Fore noon, we were Feeling pretty well & Eat our rations as usual. The Rice Lasted us about 6 or 7 days when I went down again to trade my Blanket, the same one I traded but could only [get] 35 Pounds of Rice & no salt.

Now I do not want to make this trading Business monotonous. We went down as we did Before Prepared the same way & Just as I caught the Rice to draw it up, the Blanket went out the window swish. The Jonny Had Learnt a lesson & was not slow in using it. He Had Fixed Himself By placing some of His Comrades under the window & when the[y] saw I Had the Rice, pulled the Blanket Quick & snatched it from out of the Hands of Bill & Jim, who were unprepared as I Had not yet given the word. We again Had 10 or 12 days Feasting when Bills turn Came, He got only 22 Pounds of Rice & let it go the first time. When that was all used up, Jim did not like to Let His go & we did not urge Him to For He Really needed it for He was not very strong.

We tried to do with our regular Rations but it was tough after Living so Highly on Rice so I Proposed to Bill if He would get me an old Pair of Shoes, I would trade mine of[f]. He said all right. Now Bill did not get Shoes & His pair was getting rather worse for wear so He took them of[f] & went Barefooted around through the Building asking some one to give Him an old Pair of shoes who Had new ones & He got a Pair on the upper Floor & gave me His.

That night I went down & traded them for 25 Pounds of Rice. The Guard refuse to give the rice untill I gave Him the shoes First. I told Him I would give Him one Shoe First & then when I got the rice, I would give Him the other one. He agreed that that was very Fair so I gave Him one shoe & placed the other where He could see it. He Handed up the rice & I started in a Hurry away with the Rice & when I got up stairs, I am Blest if that Shoe [—] place on the Sill Had not come up with me. That was Strange For I Know I placed it there but it could not be Helped now. It was no use to take it back that night but I certainly would take that shoe down stairs some other night as it was no use to me & I suppose the Jonnie that Had the other one thought the same of His For their object in trading with us was speculation & one shoe was useless Except to a one Legged man.

We again Had a good time for a few days & again are depending on our daily Rations so in the afternoon I went down & traded a Pair of Shoes for 20 Pounds of Rice but the Jonny wanted to see my shoes. He said He was not going to be fooled By Wee uns Like Some of His Comrades was so I told all right to Just Wait & I would bring them down & show them to Him, that I was no Yankee to play Yankee tricks on them. No, I was a son of the Emeral Isle & there fore should be Honest but the Reb said He did not Know some of wee uns were pretty Cute. I told Him

59

all right. I went up got my one shoe — & went Back to the window & showed it to Him but He said Why thats only one. Sure Enough why didnt I think of that so I stooped down Like I was Picking the other one up of the Floor & Held up the same shoe to Him. He said all Right Bring them down at 10 Oclock.

I went Back & Bill said my Boy you are Caught now. You worked that single shoe trick good but those Rebs are Learning our Yankee ways & are getting Cute. I told Him I thought I would Pull through. I went to one of the Boys & told Him the Fix I was in & that I wanted one of His new shoes to Finish my trade but that would Bring it Back to [Him all?] Safe. He gave me one as you Know Bill got no new shoes, neither did Jim or Henry so at the time, I went down. There was my Jonnie with the rice. I Passed out My own shoe to Him & told Him to Hand up the rice, the other Shoe was on the window Sill in side So He Could see it but He refused to give the rice untill He got the other shoe & I refused, telling Him one shoe would not do Him Any good without the other & I Positively would not give the other untill I got the Rice. He said all right but Yank, if you play any tricks on me, Ill shoot. Sure, I told Him all right. He reached the Rice up & I took it, snatched it in with the shoe & good By Jonny. That Finished my Stock in trade & I considered we done very well, Luckier than some of our other Fellows for the Jonnies also Had their Backs. Some of them were in this way, they would Promise so many Pounds of rice for what Ever was offered them as trade & trade Fair Enough but when our Fellows would come to open their supposed Sack of Rice, they would find only sand or ashes or Saw dust in it & then those mean Rebs would get Prayers that was not offered as a Prayer for them treating us in such a shame Full way as to cheat us so & it was too bad but then whats sauce for the Goose is Sauce for the [gander].[24] You Know Best so they Had their revenge in their own way & at our Expence.

The men Had taken of[f] all the ceiling from the roof & Burnt it & Had Cut out about three out of Every Four of the Rafters, Leaving but very Few to support the Roof so that, at any time, the weight of it self was Liable to Break it in & we still Had light Snows. It is now I think in the Fore part of Feb[r]uary. The Major now noticed the [—] the Roof & seemed surprised. He looked at the men as much as to say what Kind of Northern Limbs are you any way but said, men, do you Know your danger? Do you Know that if we Have a Heavy Fall of snow, which we are Liable to Have now any time, that the weight of the snow will Break down that roof & then what will Become of you on this Floor besides the men on the next Floor? Some [of] the men answered all right Let it Come. Those that are left will Have plenty of wood for a while & we are not going to Freeze as soon as the roof is done, we will take up the Floor & Burn it & Burn the Building if we dont get wood. The next day there was wood Issued to us not in Plenty but Enough so that we did not destroy anymore of the Building.

Soon after this, the men on the first Floor made any [—] to escape in this way. They Had Kept it very still for Fear of Traitors Amongst ourselves. Yes, I Repeat, traitors, For there was men Amongst us Comrades, who Had Fought Nobly Gallantly for our Flag & would Willingly Have died for it a few moths before but now with Hunger, starvation, suffering, Had driven them so that they would sell us for a loaf of Bread. It is Facts I am stating, they would & were Actually acting as spys on us there & in all Prisons & we Knew it but did not Know the men untill their act revealed Them. It is some thing my Friends that I do not like to say of a Comrade, for those men Had done their duty while in the Ranks. I have no doubt but they Had a Weakness & Hunger, found that weakness, acted on it & made a traitor of them, yes, a Traitor of the Deepest, darkest Dye, a traitor to those Poor Starved & Dieng Companions, a [traitor?] to themselves for they sold the Dearest Sweetest Blessing that man Has to Look Back on, His Honors. They sold it & for what, a Loaf of Bread or a Plug of Tobacco. That was their Reward for being a traitor to their Comrades & Some Times, in Fact, in all Cases where the men in Prison Knew them as traitors, the Rebels took them out & Put them on Parole of Honor — mmm.

The men on the Lower Floor Had got through it By Sawing a Hole in one Corner & a few of them Had made up their minds to try & Tunnell out. They Had worked at it for about three week & Just Had to Completed when some one informed of them & of course that stopped it. The man was suspected but the Rebs took Him out soon, very soon, after that. The Escape Fever got on all of us & the men again on the first floor sawed the Hinges on a double door opening on the side street. This door was Just oppesite and at the Foot of the stairs. It was a Heavy Double Folding door in two Halves, one upper & one Lower. It Had been used to Load

61

& unload Tobacco from the Wagons & was about three feet above the side walk. The Guard Beat was by that door & in Walking His Beat, He would have that door Every 5 or 10 minutes. There was 8 Hinges on it & those were all sawed through with the doors shut for they were never opened while I was there. So you may guess the Patience required with case Knifes as saws to Cut those Hinges but it was done & the time came to make a Break for Liberty.

The Program was for all who were able to make a dash to gather around the Door as Close as Possible & when all Had Gathered at the word now, all who were nearest the door was to Push against [it &?] Push it out on the Side walk then Spring at that Ever Guards were in our way, settle them & away. Every man for Himself, we Knew some would get Killed & a great many recaptured but also there was a Possibility of some of us getting through to our Lines. The time agreed on to make the dash was about 8 oclock in the Evening so that we would Have the whole night to Escape & get as far as we could befor[e] morning so at the time appointed, we met & my Position came about the 4th or 5th step from the Bottom on the Stairs.

The men on the first Floor were all Ready but we were waiting for those up stairs to get down for Except a very Few, no one but few Knew Just when the Break was to be Made, lest the Rebels would Know & be Ready for us so that untill we commenced together, the men did not know the time Had Come. That was our reason for Waiting but the men Commenced to call out, lets Make the Break when a Volley of Musketry was Fired at us through the door. I could Hear the Zip chuck of several Pass over my Head & Hear them strike in the Ceiling above me. We scattered for Knew them, the Rebs, was Posted on our move & our chances gone. There was none Hit but one man above me on the stairs. He got a Peice clipped out of His Ear & all that saved us from getting the Benefit of that Volley was that the Rebels Firing it stood three feet Lower than the door was & Firing from the shoulder making no allowance for us being Higher than they, their Bulletts went too High & done us no damage.

In a few moments, the Rebels Came in side but Every man seemed to be in His place & the officer in Charge of them ordered [all?] the men up above of[f] that floor. The men all came up & devided up the Best they could between our Floor & the third floor. It made as pretty well crowded but it had one good result. It made it more warm for us. The major next morning made a change in the Sergeant of the Building appointing a Man Belonging to the 35th Indiana, A Regiment My Brother James[25] Had belonged to from the name they the 35th Boys & there was about 15 of them on the upper Floor. They all Kept together on one Corner & Knew that I was a brother of Jims so when the new Building Sergeant was appointed, He came down to me asked me if He could do any thing to Help me. I told Him no but if He could Help Bill, I would like it. So He appointed Bill a Floor Sweeper & gave Him an Extra ration for doing it that with our own Four rations done pretty well & He would often send or Bring me something so we Fared a good deal Better.

Green Backs Here with us was very scarce & one dollar in Northern Greenbacks would be Equal to 40 or Sometimes Fifty dollars in Con-Federate Scrip[t]. One of my Comrades & A Country man asked me if I would not Like a drink of Whiskey to Put me in mind of Ancient times. I asked Him if a Duck would Like to swim & He gave me a Canteen, Rebel one & not Quite as Large as ours but Held a full Quart. I took the Canteen. I thought He was Fooling me but I took from Habit & from Habit smelled of it & from Habit Took a drink of it & it was sure Enough Whiskey. I asked Him where He got it & How? He said He gave one of the Guards 65 dollars in Greenbacks for it Just for the Sake of Having it to say that He drink Whiskey in Prison. It was a Big Price for Whiskey & would Have been Death to the Guard if it was Known He done so for That is always a Death offense to sell Whiskey to a Military Prisoner.

The man who gave it to me was a stranger in so Far as I Had Formed no acquaintance with Him & why He Picked me out of so many to devide that Expensive with I do not Know. There was now Rumours of Exchange but we Had no Beleif in them, a good many got Boxes from their Friends in the North. We were allowed to write a one Fourth of a sheet or note Paper [—] three months to our Friends North. Our Letters could not be sealed as the Rebel officials Had to read Them before the[y] were sent to our Lines. If in any Letter was mentioned the Least thing of our Treatment in Prison or any Southern new whatever, that Letter was Burnt or destroyed. It was never sent.

A good many wrote Home for Clothing or Provisions & a good many received them but our Rebel Major, when a Box Came for a man, he Had the Box carried up to the Floor Where the man was & there, in the owners Presence, Have the Box openened & Examine Each Article it Contained & if there was not any Contraband Article in it, he would turn the Box over to the man. It was for a Contraband Article in a Box Coming to a Prisoner would be Powder shot or any arms, money or Liquor. A Letter would be opened [—] if all right given to the owner, if not all right, they would destroy it. Any food or clothing was allowed to be sent & the Honesty of the Major would not allow the Box to be opened, only in the Presence of the man to whom it was addressed. Although it was His Previledge to open it where & when He Please & allow the Prisoner to get what Ever He allowed Him to or in other words, the Major Could Have opened the Box & taken out who He pleased & sent the rest of it to the man that owned it. That is the way it was done in other Prisons but our little Major was too much of a Gentleman to do that way.

I Have seen Him on my Floor open Boxes, the man Standing by & as the[y] would be taking out Each Article, if He so need something He would like to Have. For Instance, A Fine White Shirt or Hand Kercheif or Something that way, He would ask the man if He would sell it. If the man said no, all right but if He said yes, the Major would Pay Him what He asked but of Course always in Confederate money & making allowance for the diffirince in Value of the two, Confederate or Green-back. In all, This officers intercourse with us, He was Kind & considerate. I met a Few such as He was & when I do meet them, I shall Endeavor to do them Justice or I Found I Can also Say For our Guards at Danville, That I did not see any unnessasary Harshness or Cruelty in any of their actions to us.

In February, I think it was, we Heard there was several severe Cases of Small Pox in the Hospital & Amongst the Prisoners in the other Prisons but I [—] of more as yet in our Prison No. 3. A Committee, I Suppose I should call them, of 3 or 4 Rebel Doctors came in & said we should all be vaccinated & they vaccinated the Majority I think on the floor. I Had an Idea that I was well Enough without that operation as I was not & never Had been or am afraid of any Contagious Disease. So before the[y] Came to me, I had Concluded to Bluff them & told my three Comrades, Bill, Henry & Jim Brett I would not be vaccinated so when the doctors came to me & told me to Bare my Arm, I told them I Had been vaccinated in the old Country when very young & did not wish for that operation as I was not afraid of small Pox. But they said it was Compulsory & that

I should be as well as the compulsory word got my Irish up & I thought as Long as I will willing to take my chances of Catching that Disease, they Certainly ought to Leave me alone and Compulsory got me. So I told them no, I would not Have their impure vaccine. Another mixed with my Blood & that if they vaccinated me, they would Have to do it by Force & tie me while they were doing it. They Consulted Amongst themselves Whether to resort to Force in my Case or not but Concluded to let the Wilfull Headed Yank Have His own way & so left me alone [—].

Now Bill when He saw that I Had Bluffed them also refused & they did not insist & I Beleive Jim & Henry also. I am not so Certain of them only that I do not Remember any Effects of Vaccine on them afterwards & if there were, I would Remember it. I think as you will Understand a little Later on up to this time in My Prison, we Had no sickness. Only Such as was to be Expected from our imprisonment but after a Few days, the mens arms that were vaccinated commenced to Fester & swell Badly inflamed & the Men became Sick inside of two Weeks. All the[y] Could accomadate in the Hospital were taken out & the Rest Left there to Rot. Yes, Rot is the only word for it, Left there Scattered out amongst us. Those men of course Had to Lay in their own Places on the floor Rotting, their arm in a Sickening Condition, their Bodys Covered with the Small Pox Blotches, run[n]ing sores, Corruption, a Sickening sight.

Any one who Has seen a small Pox Patient in the worst stages of that Disease will Know what condition those Poor Fellows were in. Only Imagine the Misery, Horrors of those men Layeng there day after day with no Care but Such as we could give them & we Had nothing to give, no, Sometimes not Even a drink of Water. Th[e]y Layed there Rotting in Desease & Filth. A doctor never Came near them but when some Poor Fellow at the Hospital died, they would take one of the men from amongst us to fill His Cot in the Hospital & soon also fill a Hole in their grave yard. You may Imagine also the disease smelling air We Breathed in that room. Packed as we were when we Layed down, our Bodys touched, we were so close & I Could at any place Except Just where I Layed touch on Either Side of me a man Rotting with that Loath some disease small Pox. There were at Least about one third of the men Suffering from that disease & a great many of them in the condition I Have described & all from the Effects of that vaccination.

The description of those men I Have given as Mildly as I Could

Leaving you to Imagine the Effects. A great many of those men Had to Have their arm amputated & of those men, at Least one out of 5 only Lived, for after amputation, Gangrene Set in & that was Certain death in our Condition. For Remember, our Blood was already impure & a very Little Caused Blood Poison & Death. Those men who Had their arm amputated were the men who Had the strongest Constitution. All the weaker ones died without Amputation & I Have yet after 27 years to see the First man who Had Small Pox at Danville Living and Suppose all Died Either there at that of it.

I am now Drawing to a close of my Danville Experience but Cannot Finish it without giving you two of my own Practical Prison tricks & I Can truthfully say they are the only two of that Kind that I done on my Fellow Prisoners during all my Prison Life. I Beleived at the time there was Extematory Circumstances to Each of them so I will give them to you & Let you, My Friends, Judge whether there was or not.

You remember I Have said there was two men, Buck Eyes Neighbours from Ohio, that occupied the space across from my Feet. Well, one of those men Had got a small Box about the sise of a Cracker Box From His Wife North. It Contained Hams, Some Coffee, Sugar & Tea & other Little Notions a Loving Wife Could think of Sending in So Small a Space. Well, this Buckeye openened His Box in the Forenoon at His own sleeping Place & there for opposite to & within 8 feet of where we were sitting, His Friend Naturally was glads that He Had got it & sat down by Him to see what He got from Home & I Suppose the Poor soul thought as that Box Had Come From His Immediate Neighbourhood, that His own Wife might Have put some thing in for them but no, the Box was Emptied out & there was nothing for Him. No, He might be alone on the Face of Gods Earth without Kith or Kin For all the Remembrance there was for Him in that Box.

I Can now as I write see the Features of that man as He Wistfully Looked at the Contents Scattered around Him & He Had no share no intirest in it. It Came from His Home, it came from His nearest Neighbours Wife, they Joined Farms. His Wife & children, they might Have seen it, Helped to Pack it, Handled That Ham, that Package of Coffee or Sugar or tea. Yes, their Dear Hands, My, Have touched any or all of them & there they Lay by Him Within reach of His Hand & He dare not Touch or taste any of them.

Oh, the Wistfull Hungry Longing Look of that man, it was as Much of a Longing Loving Feeling for those Loved ones in the near Neighbour Hood of where that Box Came From. That His Features Expressed as any desire for the food itself although I saw that He Expected & Naturally too that His Friend & Neighbour would devide with Him or at Least give Him some & I certainly thought so as well as Bill, for we Both spoke of it & Expected He would Devide with His Neighbour, the names of those men I do not Know or If I would give them for there is not a single word I am writing Have written or will write but I would be Perfectly willing, the Partys I write about should see & read it for I am writing nothing but truth & Facts as I saw them.

This man who owned the Box replaced the Articles then taking a cracker Spread, some Butter on it & Commeced to Eat. The other Poor fellow Looking on, He Eat for a short time & then turned to His Neighbour & said this Butter is very nice, would you like some & the other one said yes, your wife always made good Butter & I would like to taste it. It would remind me of Home & old times. Home shall I Ever See Home again & the Loved ones. Oh yes, I would Like to taste that Butter all right. The other Fellow said you Have some corn Bread here & I will give you a Peice of Butter For a Peice of your Corn Bread. The man Willingly gave Him the Corn Bread, a Small Peise He Had saved from His Rations & received a small Peice of Butter in Exchange.

The man Looked at the Peice of Butter, the tears started in His Eyes at the Thoughts that Little Peice of Butter brought to His memory & waited Expecting His Friend would give Him a Cracker to Eat with it for He Had given the only Peice of Bread He Had but no, He saw He was not going to get a Cracker so He Eat the Butter alone. The man with the Box put on the Lid & sat on the Box.

You Infernal Stingy scoundrel, the contents of that Box shall never do you any Good if I Can Help it. You Brute, it was Bad Enough to not Devide with your Neighbour under those Circumstances but you — cuss — to take from Him the last & only Peice mouthfull of Bread He Had & give Him a small Peice of Butter for it & you you — Gut — with a Box full of Provisions. If I Live untill dark, Ill take that Box from you or Bust my self [trying]. Yes, if you Have that Box in the morning, if I am Living, I will be a Cripple & unable to take it from you. Just for your Infernal meanness to your Neighbour Friend, you are not, no, a dog

Could not do any more than you did. Those were my thoughts only mildly Expressed at what I saw in the actions of that Buck[e]ye.

I told Bill to come with me & we went away from near there, I asked Bill what He Thoughts of that fellows actions to His Friend & Bill Expressed Him self about as I Felt & I told Him I would take His Box away from Him after dark. Bill said He would Help me but I said no, I did not want Him to get into trouble & for Him to Remain Quiet & I would get what Help I would need. So about 9 oclock that night, I Saw my Friend Lay down with His Head on the Box. He was in about a Half Sitting Position, the men in the floor were all apparently asleep so I went up stairs to the Co. Where the 35th Indiana Boys were & told them what I Had seen & what I wanted to do, take that Box away from that Fellow. I Said Bill would have Helped me but I did not want Him in any trouble. They all were Willing to come with me but I told them If I could I wanted to steal it but if I could not steal it, I would take it by <u>Force</u> so that one man was all I wanted to go with me to get the Box & for the others to Come to the foot of the stairs & remain there to be Handy, in Case we Had a tussle for it & if so then to come & Help but not other wise.

I took with me the Sergeant of the Building, a Big Fellow, Strong but Easy tempered. There was another one of them I would Have preferred to Have taken, He was a Lighter man than the Sergeant but was too Quick tempered & a very imp in a row but I did not want a row if I Could Help it & if there was one He would be Handry so down we went as arranged. I worked my way in Between the men to the Box Leaving the Sergeant standing in the little walk at the fellows Feet. The man as I said was Half sitting with His Head on the Box, I took Him by the Shoulders & Moved over Laying Him down by His Friend.

Now all this was very strange to me, the Fellow did not wake up. I Expected he would Certainly wake from the Handling I was giving Him & also to Have a serious objection from Him at stealing His Box but no, He made no sign, never moved on as I moved Him Bodily from His Position & Layed Him down. I then stooped still watching My sleeping Friend & Picked up the Box. Whew! I thought the Actions of My Friend rather Cingular in allowing Himself to Be Handled So Roughly & not Waking up but Ill be Blamed if I was not more surprised when I Picked up the Box, not at the actions of that Box.

Oh no, the Box was Just as Quiet & still as the man was in Fact that

Box was too Quiet, too still, yes, By Giminy, & too Light also. That Box was Entirely too light For my stren[g]th or Else I Had got as strong as Sampson[26] for when I Braced my self for a good s[t]iff Lift, I Came up Quick & Stiff with a Jerk. Thunder, whats the matter? That Box feels so very light but no matter I Came for the Box & I Have got it. The man Still Lays Motionless & I walk off with it, my Guard Following. I Come to the Bottom of the stairs & there Find my Reserve, we all go up stairs & in to the corner belonging to the 35th Boys, I open that Blamed Box & Find what do you think about three or Four Hands full of Cracker dust sold.

That Buckeye Played Yank on me & they 35th Fellows was mad. They wanted to go right down & make mince meat of That Laverick of a Bucky & would too if I said so but I told them never mind. I would Keep a watch of Him & find out where He Had put it. So I went Back & told Bill of my Luck.

Next day I got a chance to ask the Other old man what His Friend Had done with the contents of the Box & He Said after dark the Evening Before He Said He was afraid some one would make a Raid on His Box so He Carried away a little at a time & gave it to Some of His Friends on the Floor to Keep for Him. I asked the Poor old Fellow if He gave Him any & He said no, that He was always a stingy ol Curmudgeon. I watched the old Codger but did not see Him Eat any thing at His own place & in the after noon, I asked Him where His Box was. He said Some Fellow stole it the night before. I said yes & it was Empty. I then told Him if He did not devide with His neighbour & Partner that the same Parties, who Stole His Box, would Come & take from His Friends, who Had the Provisions He gave them that night & if He wanted to save it, He should devide & if he would not devide, He would lose it all as well as get Himself & His Friends into trouble.

He Knew as well as I did that it was myself, who Stole the Box & also that it was the 35th Boys, who Had Helped me & also that if He did not do as I advised Him, they would Come & do as I Said & the[y] would Have done so & I would Certainly Put them at it & Helped sooner than that Stingy old Ya Hoo should get the Better of me. So it was not Love of His Neighbour but fear of Losing what He Had that made Him devide with His neighbour & He done so but the Poor old Fellow did not die from the Effects of His over Generousity, still he got Enough to satisfied.

That, my Friends, is one of Theiving Tricks Played on my Fellow

69

Prisoners & under those Circumstances as stated I will now give you the other one as I promised. As we Layed on the Floor, the second man to my right was a Michigan Cavalry man I think He belonged to the 2nd. He was an American by Birth, a good Quiet Fellow, Made no trouble what Ever, only the trouble He Caused me & in this way, I Have before said some of the men would not Eat all their Rations when they drew them but some would Eat Half, making two meals of them & some would Eat a little at a time Peicing along or Rather Nib[b]ling & some of those Nib[b]ling Kind would Have a little Nibble in the morning when they got up.

{Now my Friends you may say thats all right, thats good. Those men were very Provident & they always Had some thing to Eat when they wanted it. Yes, those men were good men.} All right, you are welcome to your opinion & that was not my opinion of them at that time & it is my opinion I am writing of, my Friends & not yours so Please dont give your opinion so Freely. Just wait untill I am through. {But you say thats the matter we did not Express any Opinion.} Oh no, I Know you did not but I did & you only want to Bother me so Please let me Continue.

That Mechigan man was one of those who always Had a little left for mornings & the worst of it was He Had a small tin Box like & about the sise of a Coffee Essence Can & when He would draw Bacon, he would Scrape off the Grease of it & Put it in the little can & along through the day or in the morning, He would go to His Haversack which He Still Had & was Hanging up on the wall over His Head & take out a Peice of Corn Bread or Wheat Bread about the sise of the End of His Thumb, dip it in the can of Grease & Eat it.

Oh, it was Sickening to Look at Him, Just Imagine what my Feelings were me sitting there Hungry. Well, Hunger is as good a name for it as any thing Else but I am Sitting there Feeling like the Last Rose of Summer or the Last run of Shad or like the Last of the Mohicans[27] — or the last of any thing you may think of & Imagine How I would Feel to see that out a crumb, dip it in the grease & Presto, its gone, leaving my Mouth full of water. But where the water Came From, I dont Know for I felt as though Even Water Could not stay in me. I Had no Place, no room for it, no Room for any thing. I was Hollow clear through. I felt that way anyhow. Yes, I felt worse than that way but Came not Express it. No, but that Fellow & His Crumb was a Nuisance to me, not the man Himself.

Oh No, He was a Quiet in offensive Fellow like myself & if He would Eat His Rations like I did all as soon as He got them then He would be all right & Just like me. So then you see, it was His Crumbs that was the nuisance to me & must Have been a great Annoyance to Him as He Had to Come so often & taste them so I thought it would be a very great Favor to Him if some Kind Friend would remove them Crumbs & grease some night. That the man would be Happyer & not bothered so often through the day in looking at them.

Now I felt as though no man there could do that Favor better than myself For I was allways rather Conceity that way & I told Bill that I would Examine that Fellows Haversack that night & for Him to not go to sleep. I waited untill the moon went down, Everything was as still as in a grave yard so I stood up, reached over & took that Haver Sack of[f] the wall & Layed down, placed the Haversack between Bill & I. We covered our Heads with the Blanket & Commenced, but Hello, is it Thundering? The noise of them Hard dry Crumbs Cracking under our teeth makes me think so & I give Bill a Punch in the Ribs & whisper to Him to chew them Easy or He will wake up the Town with the noise He is making. He sayd its not Him but me, thats doing it & we then dip those little Bits Crumbs, almost dust in the Grease Can.

We do not chew them much but Get them slip down. They will Have all day the next to soften for we can then Pour Water on them & I am afraid the owner of the Haversack will wake up with the noise our Corn Crackers are making, miss His Haversack & Cause a Rumpus. We finally got the Haversack nice & clean and also well Polished the Little can in side & returned the Haversack to its Proper Place where it Looked Natural again only reduced in <u>sise</u> & I Layed down Feeling Pretty Well Contented with myself & also with the Idea of the Pleasant thoughts that man would Have in the morning when He went to His Haversack for His usual Lunch.

When I woke next morning, the first thing was to see if there was any Crumbs around our Blankets but no, there was no sign that we Had Company the night before & only that I felt a little Better myself from the Effects of the visit. I would Imagine it Had been all a Dream. I was sitting up waiting to see How nicely that man would feel when He found His Larder Empty & sure Enough He soon got up, stretched Himself & reached His Hand For & in that Haversack, He Quickly Pulled His Hand out, Looked at it & then at the Haversack, reached up, took it down, opened & Looked into it. Pulled out that little tin can & looked in it, turned around & looked at me.

I was the only one near Him sitting up & He said Some Fellow Stole my Grub Last night & I Jumped up Looked as Cross as I Could at Him & Said do you mean that I Stole your Grub. Oh no, He Said, I dont mean you but Some Fellow did. Then I said if you dont mean me, dont look at me that way & He said no more, Beleive me Friends if there is a single act of my Life that I regret, I did Truly Regret at that time what I Had done to that Poor Fellow. I Honestly Beleive there was not over two Hands full of Crumbs & dust of Corn Bread & Wheat Bread in that Haversack & what Really made me ashamed for taking it was that He took it so Easy. If He Had got mad & raised a Quarrell with me then I should Have felt Better but no, He never said a word only as I Have Said & if I Could Have returned them Crumbs to Him, I woul[d] Certainly Have done so it taught Him a lesson though & Ever after when He got His Rations, He eat them & at the time, I make no Excuse for my act but give it as it cecured as it is Personal.

The rumorers of Exchange are still in Circulation & we all think there will be a Removal soon. A great many thinks it will be an Exchange, I suppose because they so much wish it & the men who Had Received Boxes were uneasy on account of the [—] Some of them yet Had & they could not carry all with them & if we went to City Point, they would not need so they sold what they did not want to others, they agreeing to Pay them when we got inside our Lines. I Bought a Ham for 20 dollars from some fellow. I do not Remember now but I think it weighed about 9 or 10 Pounds & I agreed to Pay Him when we got to City Point.

From a nother man, George Stewart,[28] He Belonged I think to the 21st Ills {Grants old regiment}. Stewart I think Enlisted from Decatur or around Decatur, Ills but from Him, I bought a <u>Box</u> or <u>Can</u> of Coffee Essence[29] worth in the North about 10 cents but I agreed to Pay Him seven dollars & 50 Cents for it on the usual terms when we got to our Lines. Whew — go — away — from — me — & Let me spread my self Hurrah, Ham, yes, Genuine Northern Fed, Northern Cured Sure Enough Ham — none of your Co[r]n Fed Hams for me, no, give me the Genuine Everytime & Ive got yes & Coffee too.

Here, Henry, go & get your Coffee Pot again, the one we used for the Rice, fill the Pot Full of Water, take this Coffee Box down with you

& make us some Coffee, Skip now & be Lively. The Ham, we will Keep Here. We Can Eat it raw. Skip, Jump you Devill, you but Hurry up & off goes Henry & as you may Have a Curiosity to Know How Henry is going to Make Coffee, let us Follow Him but He Knows His Business. He Had Made Coffee Before for us but never Had any Essence untill now & He Knows I like to Live High when Things are Flush or Business Prospering & Just now our ship Has come [in?] Himself but then you are Ankious to Witness His Patent Process of Making Coffee Without a grain of Coffee & let us Hurry or we may be too late for Henry is no Slouch on a Spread. Only give Him the ingredients & He'll fix them up in grand Stile. So Come on down stairs, out in the little yard there in that Corner, dont you see our Head Cook Henry Lavelle. {Yes, you say I see Him but what is He doing?}

Doing? Why, of Course, making Coffee, dont you see the Coffee Pot on the fire & those nice crust of Corn Bread stick all around the Fire Burning, not toasting But Blazing Burning untill they Look Like a Cinder. There dont you see Him now drop them in the water as they are Burnt Enough. See now, let us get a little closer, look see the water getting Black. Good, thats going to be nice & strong. There see Him Put in a Little Essence. That nice, that will Flavor it good & see Im Blest. If He going to make Toast — Toast. Yes, of Course, Henry is going in Big. He is getting Extravaga. I think He Has a notion that when He get Home, He can run a First Class Hotel. Yes, Henry is a Daisy when He wants to throw Himself Loose on a Big Spread, He must be Expecting Company to day. There now He is all ready, so How Proud He is going through them Half starved Half Clad Hungry Looking Fellows Watching Him as He dodges Here & there to avoid Spilling His Coffee. See, My Friend, How Wistfull they Look at that Coffee & <u>that</u> toast for you Know they Have been Watching Him as Closely as we Have while He was Cooking it.

See that Poor Skinney almost naked Fellow without Hat or Cap, Shirt or Shoes or Stocking, nothing on Gods Earth on Him to Protect Him From this March Wind & Weather but an old Looking Pants, worn of[f] up to His Knees, the Ends of the Legs all Frayed & Fastened at the waist with a peice of a stick run through in place of a Button for the Cloth is too Rotten to Hold a Button Hole. His Blouse, He Has no shirt, is Fastened in front with small Peices of sticks too for He Has Cut the Buttons of[f] & traded them to a Rebel Guard for a little Rice or Some thing to Eat. The arms of the Blouse is worn or Rotted of[f] to above The

Elbows. He is a man from His appearance would Weight when He was Captured about 175 or 180 Pounds but now look at Him with His Pinched, sharp Features, His Face & Hands unwashed & Except For His long Matted Hair & Whiskers, you would Hardly Recognise Him as a Human Being Certainly not as a White man & His Probable Weight as He stands there would not be over 120 Pounds. Look around you, you see he is only a Fair Sample of the Rest of us but Henry is gone out of sight up stairs.

{& you say why did not those men take that food from Him? Henry is only a Boy, Very Light & small of His age & any of those men Could Easily Have taken it from Him.} Very true but the majority and a Large majority of those men would & did die of starvation sooner than touch a thing, even a mouthfull of Food Belonging to a Fellow Prisoners & the Few there that would Have taken it from Him Knew Henry & who He was Cooking For & also Knew if they molested Him, it would not be long untill they would Dearly Pay for it & it would not be nessesary for me to there Either for any or all of the 35th Boys would have taken Henrys Quarrell up as soon as any of their own For the[y] Knew He was with me & that was Enough for the 35th Boys.

Those men standing there well Knew that & therefore did not molest Him but dinner is waiting, Come & take dinner with us. No, dont go. Oh, Come along & Eat dinner. We Have Plenty to day & I want you to try our Coffee. That right, up stairs we go, there step Lightly along our narrow Promenade. Oh yes, it needs a good shower of Rain to Clean it up Thoroughly but we dont have rain Here & we are used to the looks of it & I Know a Person Just Coming in from the outside, it looks like Bad House Keeping but you see the crowded Condition we are in & it is impossibly to Keep Every thing Clean.

Well yes, you might by steering Carefully Float a Flat Bottomed Boat in it. Oh yes, I think myself it looks more like a canal than anything Else. That a snag, oh no, its only an old Quid of Tobacco some Fellow Lost on, threw away & some man Has not yet seen it & Picked it up. {Picked it up? Why? What would He do with that nasty Thing, Picked up out of that dirty Canal?} Oh yes, we are very saving Here, at least some is & wait you will see some man Pick that snag as you Called up. There look see that man Sloop & Pick it up. {What does He do with it?} Why He dries it & Smokes it & the wonder to me is that it Has Layed there so long but come let us go to dinner.

{What is the matter with that man Layeng there?} Oh nothing only is dieng & Has been for a day or two from Small Pox. {Is that what makes the air Smell so Bad?} Yes, thats the way it smel[l]s Here & there so that other Poor Fellow, He is nearly as Bad. {Is there many of us that way?} Well I think there is about 60 Left, all the others who Had the Small Pox Has gone some to the Hospital & others to their long Home & very few if any of those you see will Ever Live take a good look around you now & you will Have a Better Idea of How we Have been Living, no, not Living but dieng by inches, the Last 6 months dieng a slow Lingering Death by Starvation & Vermin & Has been Death.

Death with a Happy release from this Misery For a good Many of those Brave men. Men who Had Left Comfortable Happy Homes & Firesides to give their Life, Limbs or Life Blood for our Dear ol Flag on the Battle Fields. If our Country needed the Sacrafice but never in their Remotest thought, did they think that the Country they Had made Such Sacrifices for would Leave them a Living Dieng Sacrifice in the Hands of the Rebel Hell Hounds but such it really was. We were offered up a Living Holocoust by our nation For the Preservation of our Country & I will Prove it to you If I Live to finish my Prison Experience Here & now, it would be Premature but I will try & remember it when the Proper time comes but Here let us walk around a little & see the others.

{No you do not want to, you are satisfied with what you have already seen & Heard & why do I take such app[ar]ent Pleasure in Explaining those Inhuman Unnatural Sights & Filthy Scenes?} Well, to tell you the truth, I Have wanted to get you in side our Building so you Could see For yourself but I Have been afraid to invite you before & would not now but dinner is waiting so come, Git down. Oh, never mind them little Grey Fellows, they claim the same Previledges Here that we do & make themselves Equ[a]lly at Home & if you dont want to Eat your dinner, they will soon Eat it for you. There Brush them Fellows of[f] your Clothing see them crawling up. Thats right, put your Foot on them. Tame, oh yes, there very tame & very Vicious too. Ha, the[y] are Biting you Well, no matter, sit down & Help yourself. Cups? Oh, we Have only one Amongst us Four, a Quart Cup. I Have managed to save. Yes, it the one I Had when Captured as also this Butcher Knife & this Half Table spoon that we Have Amongst us.

How did I get that Half Canteen? Well, some time ago one of My

Comrades Had no Plate, Cup or Canteen so I Held my Canteen over a Fire untill the saucer [solder] Holding the two Halves together melted them. When they fell apart, I gave one away & you see the other comes very Handy at present as a Platter to Hold our slices of Ham. Take a Peice, try some of that Corn Bread Toast you saw Henry Making in the yard. Now, is not that nice? Here, try some of this nice strong Corneo Coffee. What do you think of it & How do you like our Prison Feast? What? You dont like the taste of our Coffee. Why we think it splendid & this is the first Luxury of that Kind we Have Had in Six months, although when we would want an Extas Feast & Had a little Corn Bread to spare, Henry would make us some Toast Coffee but that was very seldom, maybe 4 or 5 times before but I think that Coffee Essence or Chicory improves the Flavor Greatly.

What do we with the Burnt Crusts? Oh, Eat them of Course, nothing at all Eatable goes to waste Here. No, not Even the Beef Bones for if they are Ribs after Polishing of[f] the out side we split them up fine with our Knife & Henry takes them down stairs & Boils the Peices in a little water untill the Bones are as Soft as He can get them & then while Hot, we soon drink the Broth & tackle the Bones which while Hot are generally a little soft & if Possible for us, we Chew them up & Swallow them but if the Beef Bone is Hard so we Cannot Eat it, we make Finger Rings or Tooth Picks of it & some of these tooth Picks were very ingenous. Some Had from two to Six Little Picks & all Closed up like a Pocket Knife. I saved some but do not Remember what I done with them.

Our Rations of Bacon was Generally thin & from young Porkers & their Ribs for the Ribs were never taken out when Cured & By the By, I must while you are Here tell you How that Bacon was Cured. It was Cured in wood ashes & the ashes was usually Cooked with the Bacon so that we got Bacon & ashes together. The ashes was Extra for they never charged for it but the Ribs, the[y] never Issued a Hams or shoulder meat to us. I suppose that Kind of meat was not Healthy for us so the Ribs we usually Could Eat as we got them but if not, they received the same treatment the Beef Bones did. Now as you have taken dinner with us & I suppose are ankious to Leave our Filthy Prison, I will Bid you good By as in a short time we will be Leaving Danville.

I will be Busy and as I Have a few Remarks yet to make, I Had better send them to you. For about a week after I got the Ham & Coffee Essence, we Lived as I Have Described to you but How shall I describe the Loathsome appearance of our Prison, the Hungry, Starved, woe begone appearance of my Comrades, Poor, Unhappy, Unfortunate But Gallant Companions in the Feild, in the Camp, in the Heat of Battle, in the Face of Death on Many Hard Fought Battle Feilds. You Have Nobly Grandly Gallantly stood By me as a comrade Defending one Principal Freedom, one Flag, old Glory, the Stars & Stripes & For that Principal, That Flag, you & I are Here. Aye, Here Treated worse than Animals, yes treated worse than a Farmer would treat the Lowest of the Brute Creation, the Hog. For a Farmer, a man if for only Self intirest would give His Hogs at Least Sufficient room for Exercise Nessesary for it[s] Health, Sufficient Water for its Wants & Sufficient Food Nessesary at least to sustain Life while we Poor unfortunate Creatures Had the misfortune to be Wounded & Caught Fighting For the Constitution of the United States & against the So Called Confederacy Men of our own Nationality, Creed & Color, who now Treated us as I before Said More than they themselves treated their own Animals. How my Friends when I So Poorly describe My Surroundings so as to give you an Idea of them, How then Can I attempt to describe my Feelings or the Feelings of my Poor Comrades For I Know the Feelings of some of them as well as my own.

We Have often Expressed them to Each other & therefore Know Each others thoughts of our treatment. We do not Cannot Blame our Major in Charge of us for He Has always without a single Exception Shown to us all the Kindness He Could Possibly show & nether can I or we Complain of our Guards for they only done their duty & I Know of none nor never Heard of any of them being unnessesarily Harsh to us.

{Who them you may say do I Blame?} I Blame First Jefferson Davis,[30] the Head & Front of the Rebellion for He had it in His Power if there was any Humanity in Him to give us Better Prison Qu[a]rters with more room. There was plenty of Buildings in Danville & Richmond — & Better Facilities for Cleanliness & therefore for Healthiness, He Could Have given us at least Food at Danville. I never Complained of but the Quantity He, Jeff, while in Life Endeavoured to shift that Responsibility off Himself on to others But Failed to do so for it was Proved directly to <u>Him</u> & He well Knew our Condition. The Officials in other Prisons were often very often Cruel Inhuman to us but Jeff well Knew & allowed it to be so or it could not Have remained so very Long.

Our treatment was well Known in the North but Thousands & thousands did not beleive it Possibly in a Christian Country that men, no matter How Brutal, Could or would treat their Fellow man as we were treated & to this day do not & Cannot yet Beli[e]ve it true. But my Friends, I Could tell you of scenes that I Have seen, Brave gallant men driven to By Hunger & Misery. Yes, actions Beneath Even a Brute except in the Lowest, very Lowest, Extremitys would not do done By Men. Men of good sound Judgement in their Ordinary Condition of Life would no more think of doing no more that taking their own Lives now doing for a single mouthfull of Loathsome food.

What I Can not write & with one or two Exception Have never Spoken of & if I did speak of it Except to those who suffered with me, no one Else would Believe me or Believe it Possible for a Human Being Sane or Insane would stoop so low & next My Friends I Blamed our own Government for leaving us there.

They well Knew at Washington what we were Suffering, what we were Enduring & the Mortality amongst us. Yes, I Blamed them. We Had left Home & the comforts of Home Life to take our Chances of war, to Bare our Breasts between the Bulletts of Rebels & the Bosom of the nation willing to take our chances of Death on the Battle Feild or Come Back maimed for Life & as we Had stepped Forward to save our Country in Her Hour of Need & Danger so also did we Expect our Country to Extend Her Hand to us in our Hour of need. Danger, no, we thought not of Danger, give us our Liberty, give us our Freedom from the Rebell Hell Horde & Place us in the Face of Danger & we ask no Hand but the Hand of God & our Hands with Gallant Comrades to Back & we will Face Danger & take the Consequences. Like men in Danger then we ask no Help but we are in need, yes, Deathly need, Daily, Hourly & where is the strong Hand of our Government in Her need.

I again say we Helped Her but in our need, we are left to Help ourselves but first in a manner, our Hand are tied & then Cast in Prison & Help yourself if you can. I may as well Finish this Subject while I am about it. It would Have to come Some time & as well here as any where. There was some Excuse for our Government actions in Leaving us in Prison. There was Policy in it & I will now give the Reasons as I Heard them in Prison & afterward Heard them Proved by Northern Controversy.

In the Beginning of 1864 about the time General Grant took command of the Armys of the United States, there was a Strong Pressure Brought to bear on our Government in Behalf of the Prisoners of War by their Friends & Relatives. The attention of Congress was Brought to it. General Grants attention was also Brought to it & His opinion asked in Regard to Exchanging Prisoners. He Reply was that it was Better Policy not to Exchange Prisoners at the then Present time & the War would sooner be over as we, the Northern Government, Had more Southern Prisoners than the South Had of ours. The Southern States being Poorly Provided to Provision the Prisoners they Had while the North Had a Plenty of Provisions & Plenty of Fighting Material to draw From & Replace those Captured & in the Enemys Hands Could Well afford to not Exchang[e] Prisoners While the South Had then at that time.

Every Available man in the Feild Could ill afford to lose those then in Prison to the North & by Continuing the War without Exchanging Each Government, North & South, retaining all Prisoners by Captured, the North Having the Most men would Finally wear the South out for the want of men & close the War sooner. Where as if the Prisoners on Both Sides were Exchanged, the Southern Prisoners being well cared For as soon as they were Exchanged were well able to go Immediately in to Battle & we would Have to fight that many more & the Northern men then in Rebel Prisoners being so reduced in Health from Prison treatment & starvation would be unable for months, if ever, able to resume the duties of Soldiers or in other & Plainer Words, Grant was Unwilling to Exchange Sound men for Unsound ones, Even though those or some of those very men who were then if Living Had Fought His Battles & Helped to place Him on the very Pedestal He was then Standing on.

At the time he gave that Opinion or decision For it was actually a Decision For our Government adopted that Policy & untill the close of the War, there was no General Exchange of Prisoners. What Few got out were on a special Exchange of which number I was one which we will Come to in due time. It is neither my Wish or desire my Friends To Pluck a Leaf from the Crown of the Dead Hero. No, I would rather add to it but truth is truth I Have given to you as I & thousands of other Prisoners Heard in Rebel Prisons the cause of our non Exchange.

I afterward while Genl Grant was yet Living Heard that same Subject Publickly discussed in the Press. Grant & His Friends denied it but it was Proven against Him by official Documents in Washington Showing the

Exact words He used & the Substance & Meaning I Have given. That is one cause but there is another Cause for none Exchange that is previous to Grants Reason for Exchange of Prisoners towards the Latter Part of 1863.

About the time I was Captured, The Rebels Had Captured Coloured men who were slaves when the war Broke but Had Escaped & Enlisted in our Army. The Rebels Captured them & Knowing them to Have been Slaves claimed them as Runaway Property & as soon as the[y] captured them sent them Back to Slavery, refusing to Exchange them at all. On any Condition our Government Had received them as Free men Had Enlisted them & therefore was Bound in Honor to Protect them & when the Rebels refused to return them in Exchange — man for man as the rules of Exchange requ[i]red, our Government refused to Exchange at all untill the Rebels were willing to return or Exchange those Coloured Troops.

That was the original Cause of the non Exchange as the Coloured man was Really the original Cause of the war. That was How the matter of Exchange stood when we were captured & when Genl Grant gave that Decision for the first few months after the war Broke out, there was no regular Form of Exchange of Prisoner & a good many was Kept for months in Prison because our Government did not Recognize the Confederates as a Belligerent Power.

A few & Particularly officers were Kept longer in Prison in the Fore Part of the war but were Retained for special Reasons such as Retaliation or other causes but when our Government Recognized the South as Belligerents then the Both Powers agreed on a Cartel of Exchange of Prisoners to Exchange all Prisoners Every Thirty days & some were Exchanged on the Battle Feild. That Form a Rule of Exchange was Kept up Regularly untill [—] with the First Captured Coulored Troops that but a check on the Exchange and Genl Grants Policy Killed the Exchange Entirely.

We did not Know when Captured that the Exchange was stopped & there fore you may Imagine what our Feelings was Each day Each Hour Expecting to be Exchanged & when those Rumours of Exchange would come amongst us, some of the men would almost go wild at the thought of again getting to Gods Country, as we called the North, For we never could call the South by that name but always considered there was only a Paper Wall between our Prisons & Hell & if so, then the inHabitants of the Country must be Devils & Beleive me I often thought that we Had very good Reason to think that some of them at Least were so & I think so get From the Continued Ill Treatment & which they gave us while in their Hands.

My Friends, I do not Consider this digression from My Prison Expeireince out of Place Here as it is of Prison Life we are speaking & therefore the Cause of our Continued imprisonment is not I Beleive out of Place Here. Now I Have given the Cause & The Effect of that Long in prisonment you may yet see any day you meet a man that suffered in them Southern Pens or Prisons. Yes, I can Safely say that any man who lived three months or over in any Southern Prison & is yet living Bears on His Body or in His System the Effe[c]ts of that Imprisonment & will to His Grave & How many Brave Gallant Northern Hearts Lie Buried in & around those Prisons.

I cannot Remember the Exact Number but to the Best of my Memory, it is about 80, Eighty Thousand, the Rebel Records show to Have died in their Hands but the Records of our Enlistment Rolls call For Between 40 and 50 Thousand more who Had Fallen into the Rebel Hands as Prisoners but were never accounted For & are not to day. They are Still marked missing & not accounted For on our Rolls & fill unKnows Holes, not graves in Southern soil & to Prove to you that this was Possible & there Fore liable to be so, While I was in Andersonvill[e] & Before I Had been there three months, I Heard there that the Rolls of the First Five Thousand men who died there were Lost & therefore those men were never accounted for to our Government. The Rule the Rebs Had Was Every three months or there about to send to our Government a list of all Prisoners, who Had died in their Hands since their last Report with their names, Co. & Regiment. Now if the Neglect or Carelessness of other Southern Prison were the same as those at Andersonville, it would be very Easy to Lose 40 or 50 Thousand names of men who died in their Hand so that we may Consider that about one Hundred & twenty Thousand died in Rebel Prisons & those who Lived to came out are yet Living, a Living Death. That is the Effects & now my Friends, I Have given you the Cause & also tried to give or show you the Effects of Prison Life & will again resume it.

The Rumours of Exchange still Continued & about the 12th or 13th of March after being about 4½ months in Danville & 6 months a Prisoner, we were moved out of Prison & Placed in Box Cars, Freight Cars, about 50 or 55 of us in Each Car. The Doors of the Cars were Kept Closed

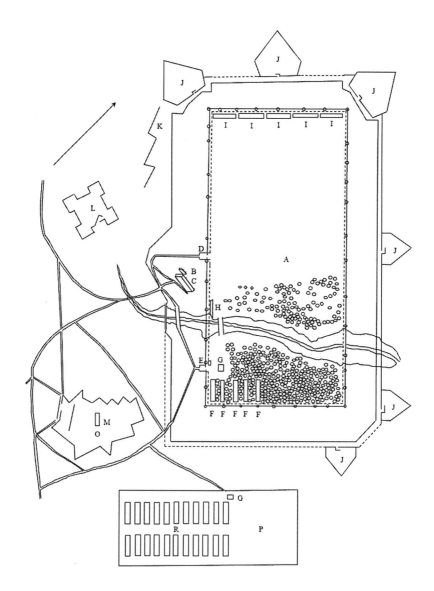

Except a bout 18 inches of space Just Enough For a man to stand in & Breathe the Pure air of Heaven. All the air we got had to come through that small place, you may Imagine the Foul impure air we were Compelled to Breath in that small space & the Consequences to our weak & Emaciated Frames after six months of such Fare and treatment as I have tried to describe in these my Reminiscence of Prison Life.

There was but one Rebel Guard Kept inside by the open door at a time & was often releived from the roof of the Car where the rebels Guarding the train were Kept. In this Close Filthy space, we were Compelled to stay for 5 or 6 Days & Night Without being allowed to get off during that time to allow some other train to Pass. I Can not remember any thing Particular that occured during this time on the train.

At the End of the 5 or 6 days the train stopped we were told to get off & were only too glad of the opportunity. When I reached the ground, Looking around me, I saw we were in Heavy timber with spaces of Clearing here & there, the station we stopped at, was Andersonville then unknown to us and Comprised the Depot —& one Frame House. We were marched about a Half Mile East from the station & Halted before a Large double Plank Gate where we were Halted, Examined & Searched again to See if we Still Had any Valuables. The officials were Finally Satisfied with our Pockets if they were not with our appearance & we were turned over by the Guards, who Had brought us from Danville to the Authorities there. The Gate was opened & we were driven in to What that Hell Hole of the

Opposite: Rebel prison at Andersonville and surrounding fortifications, based on Walker T. Woolley's 1867 map, Library of Congress. The interior dimensions of the prison were 812 feet wide by 1712 feet long. The palisades stood 15 feet high, made by sinking pine trees on end side by side in the ground. There was a swamp on each side of a running stream.
A. Interior of prison or stockade
B. Bakers quarters
C. Prison bakery
D. & E. Entrance to interior stockade
F. Sheds for prisoners
G. Rebel commissary sheds for daily issue of rations to prisoners
H. Water trough for drinking purposes
I. Sheds for cooking purposes
J. Earthworks on line of outer stockade (22 guns in total)
K. Rifle pits
L. Earthworks mounting 4 guns
M. Earthworks mounting 11 guns
O. House inside of main Earth Work
P. Hospital Stockade
R. Hospital sheds for prisoners, open sides and ends, 17 having no floors
-----Death Line inside stockade, 6 paces from Palisades (18 feet)
ooooo Burrows underground, made by Union Soldiers for shelter
-o-o-o-o-o- Stockade with sentry boxes.

Two

March to October 1864

Never while our Mercifull Creator Lets me Live & retain my Sences, Can I forget that date, the 20th of March 1864. No, if I wanted to, I Could not Forget it For I am Reminded of it Every time I See my Features & Hair in a Glass. Yes, Everytime I receive a twinge of Pain & think to myself where did thats Come From, the answer is Andersonville. Everytime I Have to Sit down from Weakness while walking for Exercise & I wonder to my self what makes me So weak & again I Answer Andersonville & now that I am there allow me to try & describe it as it was on that 20th of March 1864 we were driven in & I was with others, Amongst whom was Bill & Henry Lavelle Put in Detachment no. Fourteen.

A detachment was Formed of 270 men. They were devided into messes of 90s & then the 90s were again devided in 30s. Those thirties were again Devided into 10s. They were devided up so in Orders to make it Conveient to Issue Rations too. The Rations were drawn & Issued on the Same Principal as Richmond & Danville. I Had again a mess of 10 to draw Rations For & Issue to them & in my Mess was Bill & Henry. Brett I lost track of when we moved from Danville & never Saw Him again but was told in about 6 weeks after that He died.

We Fastened our Blanket & Pup Tent together & Erected it as a tent. By scratching around, we got little sticks & Pinned the Blanket & Tent & we then Had a place to Crawl into from the Sun. So now that I am out of the sun, I will look around me & describe the best I Can What I See before I Begin to Wrastle with death for the next Eight months but Understand, My Friends, my Description of Andersonvill[e] & my Life in it is given from memory alone as was that given in the other Prisons so I will begin with the outside view as I see it from my tent.

Looking west I Can see the Rail Road Depot a little Aimly Amongst the trees. I see also a Dwelling House looking a Kind of white & near the Depot on the outside of the Stockade & to the left as I look West is some Buildings Built for the accomadation of the Rebel officers in charge of us & between us & them & nearer the Stockade is a Rebel Battery of I think 4 or 6 Guns with a Few Tents near them for the Artillery men. Just beyond them & nearer to the Branch, is the Rebel Camp or a camp of two Rebel Regiments. Those are all on the south side of the slope of Ground & also on the South Side of the Little stream that Supplied us inside with water.

Across the stream & on the north side opposite the Infantry Camp is another Camp of two Rebel Regiments & between them & us is another Battery. Those Cannon were Loaded & always Kept Loaded with Grape & Canister. The object of them Batterys was that in Case of any Disturbance Amongst us or any attempt to Break out, the Battery on the South Side was Situated so as to Fire or Rake the North inside of the Prison, this is the Side I am on & the Battery on the North Side would Rake the South inside of the Prison with two Regiments of infantry to Support Each Battery. So, we are well Protected from the outside with a Brigade of Infantry & two Batterys of Artillery.

Now for our interior, the stockade was Built of the timber, Cut of the Ground We occupied & was made by Cutting the trees about 20 Feet Long & Heaving them square like the Logs For a log House. The[y] set them in the ground about Six Feet Leaving about Fourteen Feet over Ground & Placing them as tight or Close together as the[y] Could, the whole Forming A Stockade or Fence 14 Feet High & Enclosing about Fifteen acres, a little Longer North & South than East & West. The Formation of the Ground on the inside was slanting or sloping with a Free Slope from the north & South Ends of the Stockade & terminating in a narrow swamp in the Center through which this narrow stream ran that came in from the outside & west Side after draining the Rebel Camp through which it Ran for the Formation of the Ground. The Rebels were Camped was of the same Formation as ours inside. That narrow Shallow Stream Caught all the Refuse of Rebel Camp Before it Entered the Stockade for our use. It Came in from the West Side, ran Clear through the Pen & went out again through the East Side of the Stockade. In width, it was about 4 or 5 Feet Wide & about 5 or 6 inches of Water in it. On Each Side of this stream was the Swamp & I think it took up about 2½ or three acres of the Fifteen Enclosed leaving us about Twelve acres for our use of Sleeping or Exercise & I may as well now & Here State

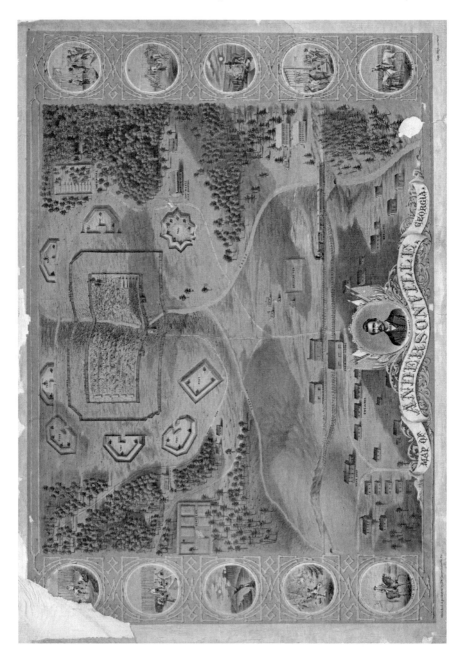

South-West View of Andersonville Prison showing the dead-line, photographed by A. J. Riddle, 17 August 1864 (courtesy Library of Congress).

that to that Swamp we Had to go for all Nessesitys of nature. It is really nessesary for me to state so that you may Later on from some Idea of the Place we Had to Eat & Sleep in.

When the Hot months come, the water of that Stream was all the Water we Had to drink if we wanted any. The soil was a Sandy Soil very loose & the timber taken of it was yellow Pine. The Water out of that Stream, we could not drink so when we wanted water, we Had to go to the dead line & try to get it there Fresh after it Passing through the Rebel Camp & Bringing with it the Refuse & Filth from them. Such was the Water we Had to use or go without.

The Dead Line was about 14 or 16 feet on the inside of the Stockade & Made by Setting a Post about Every 12 or 14 feet apart & about three feet High & on the top of those Post was Nailed or Fastened a 2 × 4 scantling that Composed the dead Line & Extended Clear around the inside of the Stockade & a dead Line, Death Trap, rather it Proved to

Opposite: Map of Andersonville, Georgia, sketched and published by J. W. Cooper, Latrobe, Pa., n.d. (courtesy Library of Congress).

many — many of my Fellow Prisoners but I will do those Rebels now Guarding Justice by saying that they did not Generally treat us Harshly or Cruel with very Few Exceptions. They were as good to us as they could be under the Circumstances but amongst So many, there were of Course Some naturally inhuman & those took Every advantage of their Position as Guards & our unfortunate Position as Prisoners by Firing on us, at the Least Provocation or otherwise abusing us but the Majority of those now Guarding us was Kind.

They were old Confederates & Had Fought us but the time Came soon when it was Death to Place a Finger on that dead Line, Death to touch it in any manner Even to be Pushed against it by another or Even to touch it Ignorant of Knowing what it was or what it was placed there for. Yes, Death to be near it Even for it was not always the man who touched it or that the Rebel Guard Fired at that got Hit. No, some times a man 30 or 40 feet away would get Hit, the Guard being so much Higher would overshoot & Hit some other than the one He Fired at.

The Rebel Guard or sentry was stationed about Every 5 or 6 Rods apart & in this way about that distance apart on the outside of the stockade, there was a ladder or steps Erected & on top of those Steps was a small Plat Form & on that Platform Stood the Rebel Sentry. As He stood,

South-East View of Andersonville Prison, photographed by A. J. Riddle, 17 August 1864 (courtesy Library of Congress).

the top of the Stockade Came about to His Breast so that He could over look the whole Stockade & there fore Immediat[e]ly over the Dead Line only 14 feet from Him so that a Guard Firing down from that Height was Just as apt to miss His man as Hit Him but if He Missed the Object fired at He was certain to Hit another. He might Shut His Eyes & Shoot & He would be Sure to Hit a man So that we Knew when Ever a shot was Fired, some Poor fellow got Hit. I may as well Here say that during my stay there I never Remember but one day to pass without one or more shots Fired.

On our First day as I said we got our tent up & got a short peice of a stick to place at our Feet. The first Prisoners who were sent to Andersonville arrived there on the 26th of Febuary & therefore got there about three weeks before us. They were from Richmond and all old Prisoners or men who Had been Prisoners about as long as I was. When they Came, there was chips & Light Limbs & Brush with the stumps of the trees but now all is gone, not a green thing inside the Stockade, not a Blade of grass. No, if there was, I Pledge you my word I would Have Eaten it & be Glad to get it but no there is none there, nothing but a few stumps left & we Have no ax, no spade, no nothing to dig or chop them.

Those men we find already there look about as we do ourself, Ragged, Dirty & Starved & from the Smoke made from the Pitch Pine, they are Smoked as nice as any Ham, only a great deal more so For to go down to the Stream to wash our Face & Hands without Soap would only make the dirt Stick the Faster. So we abstained from Washing, For fear the dirt might Come of[f] & we might Catch cold or we might not Know ourselves or our Friends might not Recognise us but From Whatever Cause, I do not Remember Washing or trying to Wash My Face & Hands but once or twice there during my 8 months in it.

My Friends, it seems to me if not to you that I am Rambling around from the Point. What you wish to Hear & I do write of namely my Prison Expeirence but to tell you the truth, out of the mass of Sights, Scenes & incidends that comes up before my minds Eye. I Really do not Know How or where to begin but as I Hope to come to the End Some time, I must make a Beginning.

My tent, it sounds grand to Say I had a tent in Andersonville dont it but it Really was worthless for any Purpose only to give us shade from the Sun. The Blanket & Pup tent was Badly worn but answered very well as a Sun Shade & we were glad to Have it as there was only the three of us, Bill, Henry & Myself. There was Still Room for two more to sleep under it For we Had no other Covering but Slept on the Earth without a Rag under or over us but our tent. We could Just Sit up under it. I took George Stewart, the one I Bought the Coffee Essence From at Danville & A Friend of His named King.[1]

Stewart & King were Neighbour Boys before Enlisting but King I think Belonged to the 25th Ills while Stewart as you Know belonged to the 21st Ills. Stewart & King were Americans & you Know the Nationality of us other Three. King Belonged to my mess but Stewart did not. Those Detachments of 270 men were Supposed to remain near Together & Form a Kind of a Company as it were & there was supposed to be a space between Each Detachment of 8 or 10 Feet left as a walk or narrow Road.

There was two main & only Entrances to the Prison Called the north & South Gates, on account of them being on the north & South Sides of the little Branch or Stream. The two Sides of the Pen were always Called the north & south Sides, both by Prisoners & Prison officials. There was one Main road or street running East & west opposite Each of those Gates Just wide Enough to allow a Wagon to drive in to Issue Rations to us so that there was but one Public Street or Road on Each Side of the Prison Sufficiently wide Enough to allow us to walk around Freely. Those narrow spaces between Each Detachment were too narrow for any Purposes only to allow us to go in & out to our Sleeping Places, For you will Please Remember all through this narrative that For the one man Who Had any Shelter or Protection from the Weather, there was a Hundred who Had nothing whatever but Had to Lay on the Bare Ground & sleep in the Same Clothing He Had on all day. They Had no other.

Those Gates or Entrances were made of Heavy Lumber, well nailed or Bolted about 10 or 12 feet High opened in two Halves or Folding & when Closed, they made that place as strong as any other Part of the Stockade. There was a door or wicket in the Gate so that when they Could Come in or out without opening the Gate. As I Have Said My Place of Rest or unrest was on the north side about one Third of the distance from the north Gate to the East Line of the Stockade & Close to the Street or Road & on the north or Left Hand Side going E[a]st from the Gate.

I make Enquiries from some of the old Stockade Prisoners at what time we get rations & am answered at about 3 or 4 Oclock. It is near that time at Least I Gauge so from the Feelings of My Bread Barometer & yes, there Comes the Ration Wagon in our Gate. I go down to see what they are doing. I See a Four Mule Wagon Come in & on the Wagon is three men, one of them driving the team & two others standing up in the wagon. The two men Standing up are our own men, Prisoners on Parole & so also is I think the driver.

The Team is Halted & the man in the Hind End of the Wagon takes out a slip of Paper & Calls out Detachment No. one. The Sergeant of that Detachment Quickly Steps up with His men, some of them Has an old Blanket or Peice of Pup tent or a Blouse with the Lower Ends of the Sleeves Tied up & the Front of it Fastened tight so as to Form a Kind of a sack. As soon as the man Calls No. one, He Quickly Pulls up the End Board of the Wagon & Grabs a Hold of a Scoop Shovel & Commences to Shovel out the meal, the men with Blankets or What Ever they Have Hold it so as to Catch the meal or Else it, a Blanket or tent they Lay them on the Ground & let the Meal Fall on it as it is Shovelled out.

It is all done as Quick as Possible & as soon as the rations for that Detachment is all out of the wagon, the wagon is drove on a short distance & Number two is Called, a Partition Board across the Bed of the Wagon is Pulled up & the man goes to shovelling out the Meal. The Sergeant of that Detachment is a little slow in Coming or His men are too weak to be Lively or Quick Enough to get there in time & He only Catches a Part of His meal in His Blanket. The Rest of His Detachments Meal is Shoveled on the Ground & they Gather it up the Best they can, dirt & all. A little sand & dirt Eaten with the Meal dont Hurt much. Oh no, it Just Helps to fill up & Really those men are too slow, they Have no Business to be so weak & will Know Better the next time.

So on goes the Wagon a sho[r]t distance & Detachment No. three, He again Pulls up another Partition Board & goes to Shovelling — & soon the Rations For no. three are Issued on the Ground. The wagon is turned around & Drove out for more Rations. The men standing around & there is alway a crowd of men Standing When the Rations are Issued & those men now Pitches in to that Pile of meal on the ground. The Serg[ean]t of the Detachment Hurries up & the men Quits taking the Rations & He takes whats Left & Devides it amongst His 270 men.

This is the way the Rations were Issued to us if the Sergeants of the numbers Called were Promptly on Hand all Right, if not, then their Rations were Dumped out as I Have shown & if once shovelled on the Ground, He was Luckey if He got a Particle of it, for the Crowd was always so Great Around the Wagon. It was Impossible almost to get the men away from there as long as a grain of that meal or anything Else Eatable was on the ground & Mercy to See those Hungry Starved Creatures Scrambling & Scratching Amongst that Filthy Sand & dirt after a Particle of Meal. The Sight was Sickening & Enough to Make a Man looking on Curse the Cause that made them do so or Curse the man or men that oblidged them to Fight & Scramble for a morsel of food as a Hungry Animal would & this too by men, Smart, Intilligent & Well Educated men, who Had Followed all Walks, all Professions of Life before Enlisting men From their Comfortable Homes, Farmers, Mechanics, Clerks & Store Keepers, Merchant, Doctors & Law[y]ers & as I said from all Walks of Life Here Huddled in a Pen Like Hogs & Like Hogs driven By Hunger to act, I Have Shown.

Yes, I will also say that I Have only given The mild side of the Picture, the actual Scene Itself would be an utter Impossibility to give with Either Pen or Brush. That wagon always Brought in the Food For three Detachments, 810 Men. Imagine if you Can the Amount of Food Brought in that wagon for that number of men, it was an Ordinary 4 Mile Government Wagon & the Bed Containing this Food — Food — No — it was not Food — for that name applied to Food Intended For Human Beings means Something Clean Healthy & Nutritious — but this Feed — yes, that is a more Proper name For it, is only Fit For Hogs — & as to Hogs, it is given to us & as Hogs, we were Compelled through nesesity to use it. But that Wagon Bed was not Half <u>Full</u> when it Came in for 810 men. No, it was not Even that so you may Imagine the Amount in it but by this time, They are ready for our Detachment & we are ready for them. Our Rations are drawn & devided Just as they were in the other Prisons as I described while in Richmond & I Have got my first Ration in Andersonville & will describe it to you.

A Pint Cup would Hold my dry Meal — Meal — Please Excuse me for misnaming that stuff — Ground Feed would Be a more Proper name for it. Yes, Ground Hog Feed, Feed is still Better for that is what it Actually was & I will Prove it to you that it was nothing Else. For the Corn was Ground Whole Hulls & all with a Very Fair Portion of Corn Husks, Corn Stalks & Corn Cobs through it. I Hardly Ever Remember while there to Receive a Ration of that Feed without getting some if not Peices of all the above in it & they never once issued to us Boiled Meal. Now as none of us Five Had been raised on Hog or Cattle Feed, we Concluded to Sift all Foreign Substance out of it & I obtained a Nail Some Way & Punched Holes through My Half Canteen & Sifted that Substance through it & From My Ration or Pint, I obtained about one Third of a Pint of Coarse Corn Meal. This is a Positive truth & with that one third of a Pint of meal, I Had also about from 1½ to 2 ounces of Bacon.

Bacon, well yes, it was originaly intinded as Bacon but now it is nearly Half Rotten & well Supplied with Skippers or small White Maggots & all smeared with ashes & with very rare Exceptions, our Bacon was always in that Condition & never at any time Exceeded two ounces in weight but oftener neare one ounce, the Siftings from my Ration of Feed after I Picked out the Corn, Cobs Husks or Stalks, I Burnt on My Half Canteen or Sifter, as it now is & made Coffee from it in my Quart Cup.

I Have truthfully given to you the Quality & Quantity of my Rations that Had to do me 24 Hours for we drew only Daily about 3 or 4 Oclock & about 2 or three times Each Week they would Issue to us Extra about a Tablespoonfull of Feild Beans or Rice. The Bean was a Small Black or dark Brown & are called the Southern Feild Bean. You now Have the amount of my daily Food & the Quality or Quantity never Exceed that given for Fuel. We Scratched around & with our Knife or Spoon of if Fortunate Enough to go a Piece of a chip, dug up Roots of the stumps or roots in the Swamp but that was a Rather Dangerous Place to go to & stand still for any Len[g]th of time for if so we would sink into it as it was more Like Quick sand than anything Else & we were all so weak that very Few men there if they sunk once to their Knees in it, Could Pull them selves out without Help & many Lives was Lost By it & From that Cause alone, I Persuaded the other Boys Sleeping with me to do their Cooking in the same manner I did Claiming & with truth that if it was Less in Quantity than to cook it as it was Issued to us.

It was Certainly Healthier for us, For God never intended Corn Stalks, Corn Cobs & Corn Husks For Human Food. I Persuaded them to do so & I Beleive it was that Course that saved us Five so long without Sickness. While one was cooking, the others would sit around & wait for only one could Cook at a time as we Had only the one Cup & by putting Plenty of water with our little meal, we could make a Pretty Good Drink of Corn Meal Broth or soup & if we were Fortunate Enough to get a Rib in our Meat Ration, we Put the Bone in with the Meal to Flavor it. No, we Had no Salt & never Had.

It was a slow Process of Cooking & Sometimes the last man would Have to Cook His Food in the dark for we took it in turns. The first man to day would be the last man tomorrow & we considered ourself very Fortunate in Having our own Conveinence for Cooking For I Can Safely say that the Majority of the men there Had not a Single Article of any Kind to Cook their meal or Feed in & if they Could Beg or Borrow anything of the Kind, the[y] Had to wait untill those owning it were through when they would then Cook it as they drew it because it was more in Quantity & would Satisfy them Better & the time Few of such men Ever lived to come out for the Food Killed them. Others again Could not Borrow any Article to Cook their Feed or were too Ankious to swallow as soon as they received it that they Eat their Feed Raw, to Eat that stuff as it was Issued. I Cannot Call it Food that would be a Libel on Human Food So I must Call it by what it was Feed. Those men who Eat it Raw Soon Felt the Effects of _it_ & Died in Suffering & agony.

On the north south & East Sides & outside the Stockade, there is Very Heavy Pine Timber with a Space of 60 Feet between the Stockade & Timber all Cleared of[f] so that if a Prisoner gets away, they Have to Pass this Cleared space in full view of the Guards before the[y] Enter the timber but why, with the timber all around us, did they not Leave some at Least of the trees Standing in the Stockade for a shelter for us from the sun but no not even a Schrub is Left, all gone & we Have to take that Hot Georgia sun. A good Portion of us Even now in March Half Naked & a good Many Bare Headed & more than a good Many Barefooted & nearly all Bare Legged & amongst the latter, your Humble Servant.

Now we have put in our First day & seen about all there is to be seen of our surroundings & Had our Supper & alway after supper Comes Bed time. So I Lay down on the Soft sand but before I go to Sleep, I Hear the usual Camp Guard Call of No. one Nine OClock & all is Immediately taken up By No. 2 & Repeated, so on — Each Sentry untill the last I Believe was about 60. That call was made Every Hour always started by No. 1 & the object of it was to See that Each Sentry was awake & Every

94

thing in His Vicinity all right. For instance, if one Sentry Failed to Call His number, they would Know at the Guard House as well as Every Sentry on Guard at the time that that sentry Failing to answer was Either asleep or some thing Happened to Him & immediately on Him Failing to Answer, there was a File of men & an officer sent to that Post to see what the matter was.

That was the Same Rule with us in our Army when troops were in Garrison or in Camp when Far away from the Enemy so that the Sound Seemed Natural to me. But the Fact to myself was Far, very Far, from me being alls well & with those thoughts, I went to Sleep. When I woke in the Morning & after the Rebel sergeant Had Came in & Counted us or called the Roll, Knowing I Had several Hours untill Ration time, I took a strolle around to Kill time & will Endeavor to give you what I saw.

In the next Detachment to me was a Body of Sailors, Captured in a night attack on Fort Sumpter in an Effort that was made to Retake it from the Rebels but it Failed & those men Captured there was about 150 or 200 of them. A Fine Splendid Lot of men who stood By Each other Like Brothers, these Sailors were in the Detachment East of me with only this narrow Passage way between us & from there East to the Stockade, it was Thinley settled by Squads but I go west towards the gate by which I Entered as thick & close together as the Ground allows them.

There is Plenty of Room to Walk in the street so on I go & Pass by where there is some men, a little Blacker than the others. I look Closer & See their Hair is Short & Kinky. Thunder, them fellows looks Like Darkeys & I ask a White man or a man that would be White if He was Scalded Good so as to take the Black off Him. What is them fellows? Why, He sais, them Niggers Massachusetts Darkeys.[2] They were Free before the war & the Rebels turned them in <u>Here</u>. There is about 17 of them there, the other or slave darkeys were all Put back in <u>slavery</u>.

I Pass on & get to the Gate, it is open with two Guards standing in it & a Rebel Lieut[enant]. There is also a Bunch of about 15 or 20 other Jonnies standing around Looking in at us & above on the top of the Stockade is a Rebel Sentry, one on Each Side of the gate that was about the Position of things there daily. This is the north Gate.

I now start south Keeping a Respectfully distance from The Dead

Line & go down about Four or Five Rod when I Come to a Crowd of Maybe 5 or 6 Hundred men Jostling & Crowding Each other & all Faced to the dead Line. All seemed Ankious to get there, the Rebel Guard right over them stands with His Rifle all Ready, His Finger on the trigger Guard, His Left Hand Grasping the Barrell, intently watching one spot in the dead Line & that spot is the Water Coming through the Stockade after Passing through the Rebel Camp outside. Those men are then waiting untill their turn will Come or untill they Can Work themselves up to that spot & get a drink of that water before it Enters our Pen to Pass through the Sink of a swamp as I have described. Yes, there is men there waiting & Has been waiting for an Hour & may be will be another Hour before they Can squeese themselves up & through that Struggling mass to get a drink & if very Weak may never get there or if the[y] do maybe as the[y] stoop to get their drink with the Pressure from Behind, they may be forced against the Dead Line to shot or some other Poor fellow or Fellows in that crowd get shot by mistake, for a Ball Fired into that Mass of men is Bound to Kill or Cripple more than one man.

The place where that water Enters is narrow & shallow with a slight Fall as it leaves the dead Line & right under the dead Line So that a man Even reaching His Hand under the dead Line for water would be shot Just as Quick as if He tried to Climb over the Dead Line. So that when a man got to it in getting the water, He Had to be Cautious & Carefull to not go too Far. It was a death Trap & Proved so For Even if a man was wounded, it Ended in His death by Gangrene.

I Passed along but Hello, what the deuce is those Holes in the sides of the Bank? They look like Dog Houses or Dug outs. Yes, there comes a man or what out to be a man & Actually the only way you Can tell it is one is that as soon as He crawls out, He Strai[gh]tens up & walks, yes, the Poor Fellow Had no Blanket, nothing to make any Protection from the sun so He dugs Hole in the Side Hill & Crawled in to [and] out & its only from the Hole, He goes in & out at that you Can tell it is occupied for a man walking down was Liable to step on it for Solid Earth & go through it & disturb the occupant inside the Hole. If made for me of Course Could not accomadate two & the man Breaking in through the top or Roof of Course would Create a disturbance inside & you Could then Hear a Circus going on Untill the intruder got out.

That mans Habitation was Ruined on account of the man above Coming down on Him so he would move & dig another or Else take the open air as the Balance did & Maybe the Poor Fellow Had not stren[g]th Enough to dig Him another Hole & there were scores, Hundreds of those Dug outs but when a Heavy Rain Came, those all disap[p]eared. The Entrance to those Holes all Faced to the Swamp on Both sides as the ground Descended that way.

I Pass on & cross the little Branch & am now on the South Side. This Side is Every way Laid out as the north side is, this South gate is the same as the North one & Here on account of it being nearer the officers Quarters, there is Generally more Rebel officers Standing around, yes & there stands the Infamous Wirtz,[3] a small Pinched Dried up Peice of Rebel Poison, a Swiss by Birth & looks about 55 or 60 years of age — A Cruel Sinister Look on His Face & the Reputed Cause of thousands of My Gallant Comrades Death as well as the Cause of the Living Death of the Thousands of others, who lived to get out. It will be nessesary to speak of that imp of Hell occasionally as I go along.

Outside of this South Gate is the dead House So called, I give the description of it from Comrades, who Had Seen it & gave it to me there at the time. In going out the gate & Close to it on the right & therefore the north side of the Gate was a spot set apart for the dead. Along the Stockade there they were Laid on the Ground without any attention being given untill next Morning when the accumilation of Dead for the Past 24 Hours were taken away to be Buried in this way. A Four Mule Wagon & I May Here say that this same Four Mule Wagon that delivered our Rations to us as I Have described is the same wagon.

I now mention this Four Mules & Wagon Would be driven to the dead <u>Pile</u> & there Loaded with dead Bodies, Loaded as you would cord wood, Clear up to the Bows of it. This I Have seen the two men Handling the dead, one of them would take the Body By the shoulders & the other by the Feet & Swing the Body in the Wagon Pitching it in from the Ground & Piling them up Heads & Feet so they would Pack Closer & when the[y] got them up to the Bows of the wagon, I Have seen them chug, Chug the Bodys in Between Each other to tighten them as a man would chug in a stick of Cord wood on the Top of His load to tighten the others from Falling of[f]. Yes, I Have seen them when the[y] Thought they Could get one more Body on chug & Push & Twist it in to fill up tight.

This wagon was used from Early morning untill they got the dead all Hauled away then taken & Loaded with our dry meal or rations as described & Hauled in to & Issued to. As My Friends, Can you Beleive this, I State is as a Fact & the Truth if you Can not Beleive it, it is useless for me to say anything more of Andersonville For that Fact is not a Circumstance to what I may State & also with Truth before I finish my Prison Life, Let us follow this load of my Poor de[a]d Comrades & see the Burial them once Gallant Boys Receive. The[y] are Hauled about a mile & a Half, the Wagon is stopped Backed Around to what to a Long trench & there they are Pushed, slid out of the wagon & in to this Trench untill they are all out when Back goes the Wagon. You may Imagine How Busy that wagon & those men were in Hauling of the dead. When I say there was often from one to two Hundred Dead to be Hauled of[f] in one morning, I Have Known of a Hundred & twenty Dead men to be taken out of the Stockade in one morning & all those were men who Had Died during the night. Now add to that 120 all who Had Died during the day & the dead From the Hospital & you may Have some Idea of what I am trying to describe.

At Sick Call in the Morning, all who required Medical attendance went to this South Gate & were allowed to go outside to the doctors. The place of Receiving them was in the open air & right Beside the Rows of their dead Comrades Laying there to be Hauled away. If a man inside was unable from sickness to walk there some Comrades would Help Him out to the doctors. If the man Could not Come or be Brought to them, He might stay inside & die, for a doctor never set His Foot inside of that Pen while I was there. It was Come to me or die, for I will not go to you For that seemed to be their Motto.

I will walk away from that Gate East & down their street about 30 feet wide. Now, Here on this South Side, the Prisoners seem to be Thicker, more of them. The street is pretty well Crowded & I Have to dodge sometimes in order to Pass without Jostling against some Poor Fellow. It looks More like a Crowd at a Circus. Yes, I guess there must be a Circus or something going on for see there is a Crowd Gathering & they ar[e] yelling. I Squeese in & See what this is all about & I see what, Why two men Fighting, yes two Skinney, Boney, starved & Ragged Creatures Fighting, yes & viciously too from their actions there. One man Has made a Blow at the other & missed Him & with the Exertion of tryeing to Hit the Other Fellow & missing Him, he is so Weak that He loses his Balance & Falls down.

Three or Four Comrades, after Some Exertion, get that man on His Feet & Holds Him up a little while to steady Him when some Fellow Calls out time. The two Boxers make a few Passes at Each other & down Tumbles Both of them Both falls From Weakness but both are again Picked up & the seconds of Each of those Pugilists get down on one Knee. The Crowd places a Champion on His Knee, another Fellow commences to Rub the Muscles of His Arm or Rather to Rub the Place on His arm where the Muscle ought to be & when they are Rested, the[y] are put standing up steadied a while on their Feet & then told go in & win, whip that other Fellow.

The same thing is again Repeated for three or Four Rounds when the two Poor Fellows get so Weak, the[y] Cannot Stand alone & the Crowd Calls out Let them go. They are Both Game & Neither Whipped. I Look at those two men, they woul[d] Probably be 24 or 26 years of age & weigh if in Health & with Proper Food from 160 to 180 Pounds & now after Fighting 5 or 6 Rounds, there was not stren[g]th Enough in their arms to draw Blows from Each other. No, there is not a scratch on Either of them on such as made by their Falling down, they are both unable to walk & stagger a Few steps then drop down on the ground to Rest where I leave them & go on a short distance but Look, see those two men there Just in Front of me.

One of them in tryeng to Pass another Has Jostled against Him & the Fellow sais what did you do that For & before the man Can Make His Excuse, the other Boy strikes at Him & misses Him & Falls down. The Crowd Hollows a Fight. A Fight, Make a Ring, Fair Play. Give them Room & soon there is a Ring Formed & a Repitition of the other Battle Follows. Oh yes, there was no Trouble there about getting up a First Fight if a Fellow Felt like Having a Fight. All He Had to do was to go out on the street, step on some Fellows Bare feet intentionally or otherwise or Rub against Him. Yes, Even look cross at some of them in [—] give them any Excuse whatever & you Had to fight Him.

You could not get away for as soon as one man used An Angry word at another, the Crowd was always so thick that they Immediately Closed around you & before you Knew it, there was a Ring Formed & you Had to Fight & when you Found you Had to [go] at it, you went with a Will with usually the Results I Have described & Generally a man was always Ready for a Fight for there was but very little diffirence in any of us.

We were then all old Prisoners All Hungry at all times & there for all Cross at all times now in this Prison Life, I wish to avoid a Repetition of the same scene as much as Possible. For I Expect I Have Enough to write of without Repeating the same incident wise so you may Imagine that For the next 7 or 8 Months, those Fighting scenes & their Causes are a daily & Hourly occurrence. In Fact, they were almost a Pastime for they Helped To Break the Monotony of our Forced imprisonment & in all of them that I Saw or Heard of, I never Knew or Heard of any ill consequences to any of them Fighting Parties For the men were all too weak to draw Blood from Each other & I Beleive the most of us Had no Blood at all to Loose so that the only Consequences arising from them was an additional weakness to them from their Extra Exertion & I will now close that Part of Prison incidents & go to some others.

We will Pass about three weeks time & that will Bring us to about the Middle of April for the last Few day, new Prisoners were coming in. Fresh Fish, we called them in order to Designate them From the old Prisoners. For all the old Prisoners Had a Fellow Feeling For Each other. Not that we Had any the less Feeling For those unfortunate new ones but we well [k]new that those new Prisoners if they Lived Had to Endure for about 6 Weeks or two months, all the Agonies of Hunger & Starvation. But my Friends, you may say are not you & the other old Prisoners Suffering so & I answer, no, although our food & Treatment is as I Have described & there is not a Particle of diffirence between the Food & treatment of those new men, Fresh Fish & ours.

Still we do not suffer the Pangs as they will for the time I have stated & For this Reason, we are so long used to it that to tell the truth I Belive our stomachs are contracted & I will speak for myself supposing the others the same way. I do not Feel Hungry in the sence of the word, no, but I am so weak at all times that it Requires Considerable ambition & Exertion for me to move around & the only time in the 24 Hours that I Have a Hungry Feeling is for about one Hour after I Eating my Rations then I do suffer the Pangs of Hunger but after that time, I loose [lose] that Feeling & become weak Listless & in a cross or Fighting Humour.

But those Poor Fresh Fish just Caught, Just in From our own Lines where the[y] Had Plenty to Eat, their First Question would [be] Boys when will we draw Rations & when the[y] got them, they would Eat more Ravenously then Even us. The next day or two, they would be wild crazy with Hunger, restless & could not sit or stand still but all the time moving, walking, thinking of Food & they could not [—] thing for them selves than to move around but the Poor Fellows Could not Help it. Oh, but I Know How their Feelings were, yes, I had been all through that <u>mill</u> — then they would offer their Blouse, Boots or Shoes, yes, or their Pants, a <u>Fact</u>, For Some thing to Eat. Any thing they Had Could be got from them For <u>Food</u>, Feed — but they Had to live through it & none but the Mercifull God & themselves Knew or Can Know what they suffered untill time Blunted the Edge of their appetite & they got to Feel, I, we Felt, yes.

I Could walk through that Prison & tell from a mans Actions about How Long He Had been in Prison. If He was in only two or three weeks, he would be walking around with a Hunger Longing Look on His Features & if in from one to two months, He was Wild, Crazy with a starved Expression on His face & in His actions but if He Had reached the Limit & Began to get Reconciled to His Lot Feeling Something like what we Felt then He would go around Careless, ready to Right with a dont Tread on the Tail of my Coat[4] Expression on His Face & when you saw Him that way without you Felt as He did, you stepped out of His way, gave Him a Wide Berth & let Him go on His way Rejoicing with the Consolation of that He would not go far untill He met some Fellow like Him Self & Just in the same Humour when Crash, Greek Has Met Greek or Bones met Bones & then For the Tug of War but an unbloody war, you Have been there & Know what it is.

From now on there is almost a daily arrival of new Prisoners Coming in. The Campaign Has opened East & West & they Come in by Squad of 60 or 70 & some times three or Four Hundred or more so that the[y] cease to be any change to us Except for the news the[y] Bring in of the movements of the Diffirent Armys, Their Positions & Prospects of them coming to take to Recapture us & take us out & often in those new Batches coming in, an old Prisoner would Find a Brother, Cousin or some Neighbour or Company or regimental Comrade & you may Imagine their Meeting. The one Just Come in Clean with a good Uniform Fat & Healthy Looking, the other Skin & Bone, Dirty & in Rags. Yes, we could then see the contrast between a Northern Cracker Fed & a Souther[n] Corn Feds, yes, Truly & Truthfully Corn Feds as we were.

The Pen now was Getting Filled up pretty Fast & there was not any vacant space & we thought Pretty full but we yet did not Know How a Rebels Conscience Can Expand as well as they Can Squeese in Yankees into a small Pen. As I have before said on account of the Swamp in it, there was only about 12 Acres of dry Ground that we Could occupy to Either sleep on or walk on & I suppose now about the Latter Part of April, there was about 20 or 22 Thousand men on that 12 acres or about 2 thousand to an acre. Oh yes, our Neighbours were very Close if not very near.

It was now so crowded that it was impossible for them to Issue Raw Rations to all of us on account of Wood. They Had not yet Issued any Wood to us but left us to do the Best we could, Either Dig Roots to Cook it or Eat it Raw & the Coarse Feed was telling Heavily on the men with scurvey & other Diseases, Arising from the unhealthy Feed & impure air Arising from the Swamp. So they Built a Cook House Just outside the Stockade on the Edge of the Branch & near the north Gate & Issued Cooked Rations to us Every other day.

I will leave you to Imagine what Kind of Corn Bread, as they Called it, or what Kind of Mush, that mixed Corn Feed, would make For there was no change in the Quality of it after Cooking but if any thing worse for us for Just think of that stuff Baked in loaves & when Issued a Half Loaf of it given to Each man, the outside of it sometimes a little Browned, More often Just crust Enough to Hold it from going to Peices while Handling then on Breaking it up, next the crust would be Just wet & inside of it Entirely Raw or wet. Then Pick out of it, corn cobs Husks Stalks or anything Else you Found & did not want to Eat the mush for we got it in mush — oftener than in loaves. But it was Usually a little Better when the[y] would Pour Hot water on it, it was not so Bad but if they which they very often did, Pour Luke warm water on it by mistake then it was not So good but such as it was, we Had no other & Had to use it. This all was shovelled out of the Dead Wagon as I described in our First days Issue for be assured if there is a change of any thing for the Better, I shall mention it.

This Cooking is done by our own Men out on Parole of Honor & any man could get out that way, For they were at all times ankious to get men out on Parole to do the work outside as it saved them being oblidged to Have their own Men do it for Every man of us that went out to Cook, dig Graves or Pits for the Dead or chop Wood or Clerk for them or for my other purpose left them one more man to Guard us & the[y] found men willing to do that for the Previledge of being outside & get an Extra Ration. We thought very little of those men at the time & I think very little of them yet their appetite was stronger than their Patriotism so the[y] satisfied their appetite & Left Patriotism to Rot in the Pen.

The Rebels now allowed three men to Go out side with a Rebel Guard to Gather up wood & Bring in to cook our Feed. They did not detail their men for that Purpose but left it optional with their Guards whether to go or not but if He went, He could only take three Yanks with Him & then He was Held Responsible for their Return & the only way our Fellows could get to go out was to Bribe or Buy a Jonnie to take them. It was very little any of us Had to use Either to Bribe or Buy so we Put our Heads together & mustered amongst us Four, Bill, Henry, King & myself, 4 Buttons of our Blouses. It looked rather a small Bribe, a Button a Peice for three of us & one Extra for Luck but we determined to try & get out on them so Bill told me to take them & Bill, Henry & Self Went to the North Gate Early in the morning.

The Weather was Fine & there was a good many Rebs standing around the Gate. I watched for some Reb that I thought might be Kind Hearted Enough to take Pity on us for I Knew my Temptation was not very large 4 Buttons. Although our Buttons or as some of them Jonnies called them, Buttons With Chickens on 'em. Our Buttons were Brass with a Spread Eagle on them but some of them not Knowing an Eagle from a chicken Called Them Chickens. A Fact so after us waiting some time, I saw a man with a Phiziognomy Like an Irishman & I Beckoned to Him to Come in to me. He came & asked if I wanted to go out. I told yes, so He said, Bring your Partners & the three of us followed Him.

I thought His actions a little Strange for all the other Rebels I Had seen taking out our Poor Fellows would First ask what they Had to give for taking them out & I have seem them stand & Bicker for more than the Poor Fellow Had as though it was a Fortune they were trading for but this man asks no Question & we follow Him. He gets His Gun & as soon as we are Clear of the Gate, I offer Him My Four Buttons but He Refuses to take them with the Remark to Keep them & give them to some other Fellow to get out again as He did not want them & that He Had been watching me for some time & Knew I wanted to get out so to come along & get a Breath of fresh air & that He would Keep us out as long as He could Stay.

We all went out about a Half mile from the Stockade in the Timber. Oh, What a change from the Crowded Sickening Pen. Here in Gods Pure Air with Every thing Green & Clean around us. Bill said for me to stay & sit with the Guard & Henry & Him would Gather up the wood & Bring it to where we were. There was plenty of light Limbs Lyeng around, the Guard offered no objections but told them to not go Far & Him & I Sat down & talked about the War, Politics & any thing we could think of. He did not seem to be any way uneasy about the other two Escaping from Him & I asked Him why He was giving us Such Previledges. He Said He Knew we would take no advantage of Him & try to Escape for that He Had thought of that before He came with us. The Boys Had soon Gathered Enough & then we Had a pretty good time for a couple of Hours when He said we would no[t] have to go back as it was near time for His Guard duty so we Picked up all we Could Carry & I assure you it was not much but such as it was it was valuable in there.

We got to the Gate & our Guard in Bidding us good By said when Ever you want to Come out, Come Here & I will take you. We thanked Him & went & before we got to our tent, we could Have sold what wood we Had Scores of times for wood was very High, there a Stick 18 inches Long & 2 inches thick was worth 50 Cents in our money. But we did not sell a stick of it for it was Just as valuable to us as we still Continued in our mode of Cooking as Described. No matter Whither Bread or Mush, we Picked it over & cooked it so that what Ever little the Quantity, we Eat it was at least as clean as we Could under the Circumstances make it & it was also Cooked & now to speak of the Kindness of that Reb Guard & the Confidence He Reposed in us & the Risk He Him self ran in taking us so Far from the Prison & allowing Bill & Henry to Roam around. They did not go Far Certainly but at any time, they were Far Enough for Escaping if We Had Come out with that intention. The Guard & I sat on a Log shoulder to shoulder & I could at any time almost Have snatched His Gun when He would Have been at my Mercy but He Had Confidence in us & I say God Bless Him for showing that Confidence & His Kindness to us.

I never saw Him again although often went to the Gate to try to see Him & go out now. It often Happened that three men when the[y] got their Guard sufficiently Far from the pen that they would watch their opportunity & Jump on Their Guard, disarm Him & Kill Him & then Escape but those men were always with very Rare Exceptions Caught with the Hounds & Brought Back & Punished by Flogging or 36 Hours in the Stocks or sometimes Both. In one case, the three men Captured & Compelled their Guard to go with them for several days & those men I think got through so you see our Guard Knew all this as well as we & therefore you see the Risks He Ran for if He allowed any of us three to get away from Him, He would have been Severely Punished or Shot.

All Prisoners Brought in were searched & all taken from them that the Rebels wanted, Even their Blouses, Boots or any Part of their Clothing. This was done by their Guard while Bringing them to Prison but my [—] always searched at the Gate Before Admitted inside & then all money or other valuables if they were not well Hidden were taken from them. There was only one Exception to this Rule & that was a Brigade Captured at Plymouth, North Carolina.⁵ They were all Captured in one Body & they Surrendered on Conditions that nothing on their Persons should be taken From them & for once, those men were allowed to come in without being searched.

Just before they were Captured, the[y] Had Reinlisted as veterans & Had Received their veteran Bounty & all Back Pay so this money with all their other Personal Property, they Brought in with them & some who Had Revolvers Brought them in with them & one man, a Regimental Color Bearer, Had tore His Flag from the staff when He Found they were going to be Captured, Wrapped it around His Body under His Clothing & Brought it in with Him but that was not Generally Known but to a few untill the morning of the Fourth of July. We Called This Brigade, the Plymouth men & there was a lot of them near where I slept.

Those Plymouth men Having plenty of money would Buy our or any Part of our Rations Paying any Price almost for them, our one or two ounce Ration of Meat was worth 50 or 75 Cents Greenbacks & you I Hope understand by this time that it was no trouble for us old Prisoners to abstain from Meat so they got Plenty to Sell to them at that Price but only the old ones sold their Meat. You Could not buy from the new Prisoners their meat for any Price & from now on Greenbacks was Plentifull at least with some the Rebels.

I Heard it was [—] Adjutant Built a small Board Shanty inside & near the North Gate & made arrangements with one or two of our men to sell Provisions to us. I will now give you the Price & Class of those Provisions you could Buy, a small spring Chicken For 5 dollars, A Quart of Flour 2 dollars & 50 Cts, Irish Potatoes about Four dollars Per Pound, Sweet Potatoes about two dollars Per Pound, Eggs 50 Cts a Peice, Coffee 25 Cts A Table Spoonfull in the Grain & Browned or Roasted, Salt 25 Cts a Table Spoonfull, this is all in Greenbacks.

There is very little Southern Money Amongst us & the Rebels dont want it. They want our Money & the diffirence in value now of a Gre[e]nback & Confederate money is 60 or 65 for one of Greenback. Business now got lively & the Yanks showed their inginuity in trading & manufacturing Articles required For Business or Trade. A good Many Coffee Pots & other articles for Cooking was brought in by those Plymouth men & they when they first Came in seeing no use for them Easily traded them of[f] for Food & the old Prisoners for them & now made good use of them.

Others would make small Buckets or Pails out of Pitch Pine & again others who Had good Boot Legs Would Cut of[f] the Legs of the Boots & Plug up the Bottom of the Boot leg with a Block of Pitch Pine. Patience, Friends & you will soon see to what use they Put them there was vessells of all & any Description that could be made to Hold Water. Others again Had Erected on the main street little stands Made from sticks or Rough Slabs For Retailing out the Products of the Southern Soil.

Oh yes, things are now lively Business, Brick [—] trade [—] & the market well stocked. The Business Portion was all between my Residence & the Gate & suppose we take a walk down that way & see the trading. No, I Have no money & therefore Cannot Patronize those Merchants who are doing a Wholesale & Retail Business. It would take an Astor or Vanderbilt or Jay Gould[6] to live Here & Keep up with the Present times Here in this Hotell of 15 of Hells Acres & now let us take a walk towards the Gate. So come along there, listen to them merchants Calling Customers. Heres your nice Fresh Soup only 10 Cents a Cup —& another Heres your nice Ham sands witch or Dam[n] sand Which, I dont Quite understand what that Fellow says, but no matter, he only asks 50 Cents a Peice for them and another Heres your nice Fried Potatoes 50 Cents a dish but let us go on now.

We come to a stand, on it is Fried Potatoes, Biscuits, those San[d]wiches. How do you Sell those Buiscuits? They [a com?] sised Soda Buiscuit & He answers 50 Cents & those nice san[d]wiches are 50 Cents, a small Peice of light Bread about the Sise of your Open Hand, Cut thin & a Peice of very thin Ham about one third the Sise of the Bread Composes that San[d]wich. The whole Could be Placed in the Mouth twice & only 50 Cents. He Has Boiled Eggs also 50 Cents. This is a Retailer & there ar 2 or three Dozen of those fellows along the street.

We Pass on & meet a Fellow Hardly able to walk from starvation Him self & in Rags, Filthy but he also is in Business. He Has one of those Boot legs & as He Comes near, He Calls out Nice Fresh Bean Soup only 10 Cents a Cup. I call Him to me & ask Him to let me see His Soup. He dips His tin Cup, an Ordinary Pint, one into His Boot Leg & Brings it out full of what — oh of Bean Soup. There is maybe a dozen Beans in that Cup, the Rest is all Water & Floating on the top of the Water is a Dozen or two of those Bob Tailed Grey Backs. Some of them let alive for the Soup is not Hot.

The Poor Fellow Cannot Help that & nobody Regects [rejects] His soup on account of them. If He wants to Buy the soup, A Man Buys it & if He dont like to drink them, He will Pick them out with His own dirty Fingers befor[e] He Drinks it or Else Shut His Eyes So He wont see them. He Knows they are there in it some where for they are in & on Every thing. Id ask the Soup Merchant How much He Sells Each day & He sais oh, Maybe 10 or 12 Boot Legs Full but I ask How do you Boil it? You Surely do not Boil it in the Boot Leg. Oh <u>no</u>, He answers there is a Fellow in my Detachment Has one of those Coffee Pots He got from the Plymouth Fellows & I Pay Him for the use of it to Boil my Beans in. I ask what do you Pay Him for the use of it?

He answers I give Him two Cups full of soup but the <u>Cuss</u> Generally fishes out all the Beans & Just leaves My Soup as you see but the Boys Like it & it is Healthy So I am making money & intend to start a Bank when I get <u>Home</u>. Home, Poor, Poor Comrade, your Home is Here Close only a Mile & a Half or two miles from you & the chances are one to a Thousand but you will [—] Dead inside of a week or maybe inside of the next 24 Hours but that Poor Fellow, Wild Eyed, Hungry, Himself starved & Ragged still thinks of Home & the Loved ones Waiting, Watching & Prayeng for His safe Return. Yes, He is in Business & there is no limit to His Ambition & may be at the very time I am speaking to Him, He is Thinking of His Wife or Loved Children & thinking of How much money, he Can Save & take Home to them & God alone Knows How much they might need it & Him there Facing Death Each Hour of the day & Breathing it Each Hour of the night from that Cess Pool of a swamp.

This, my Friends, is only a description of one man but it applies to thousands of us there & is Light description too & there is Dozens of men Making Soup as He is Some in Boot Legs & some in Rough Coars[e] Wooden Buckets or Vessells they Have made but it is all about the same Quality Rice or Bean about a spoon full of Either to a Quart of water & is Readily sold to those Having the money. So we go along, there is a place under that Rotten Blanket Tent you can get your Watch Repaired & there a little Further on, you can get a suit of Clothing made. Yes, thats a Tailor Shop under that Rotten dog tent. Why, yes, you see he has a suit allready for Sale Coat, Pants & vest. {You ask what are they made of?} Why, an old Government Blanket Furnished the Cloth for that Suit & He will sell them too.

There just beyond that tailor Establishment is a Musical Instrument Factory. Yes, dont you Hear the Fidde Playeng. Oh yes, He made that Fiddle Himself, it is made out of a Gouard He got from the Guards. Sweet Music aint it? Yes, He makes them & the Prices Range according to the sise of the Gouard from two to ten dollars & see that Excited crowd there let us see what they are doing. Oh, its a Chuckerlook Bank.[7] Yes, that man is doing a Banking Business & His Business is lively. See there is 4 or 5 Playeng or Depositing their money in that Bank for it usually turns out that way. It does not Require much Capital to start a Bank of that Kind. No, A Box with three Dice & a Board with the Figures from one to Six is all Required & if you Have a few dollars, you can Put your dice Box in your Pocket & your Board under your arm & go along untill you see a place Suitable for Business, sit down, Place the Board across your Knees, take out your dice Box, shake or Rattle the dice Thoroughly then turn the Box Bottom up Covering the dice then Hollow out with a Voice of thunder, Bank is open! Come up Boys & try your Fortune, no Limit to this Bank, all sure to win!

No Limit in Playeng chuckerlook means that a man Can Bet Any thing from one cent or dollar to a Thousand or more dollars & Can Double His Bet as often as He Pleases, where if there is a limit to it, the Banker sets the Limit by sayeng from one to Five then a man Betting could only Double His Bets Five times. Say the first Bet was one dollar then the second would be two, third, 4 — Fourth Bet — 8 & fifth Bet Sixteen dollars He then would Have to go Back & commence at one again but if His first Bet was 5 Cents or 5 dollars, He Could double on that amount the same as He did on the dollar.

Now the Bank is started so that Poor Ragged Fellow Walk up & Put a dollar down on the Figure 3. The Banker Raises the dice Box so all Can See the dice but there is no three turned up & the man loses. He bets again on the Same Figure & this time, there is two of the dice with three on them turned up. The man wins two dollars or an amount Equal to the amount He Bets for Every time the Figure turns up that he has bet on & there is a good many of those Banks going.

This is our Business street, our Broadway, our Exchange & a lively Business is carried on in Business Hours & Business Hours are from day Light untill dark & those Having money Spend it [Fast]. The South Side is the same but after the Prison got so Crowded, I was with the warm weather getting weaker so that I did not go over on that side but once or twice. It took too Much Exertion & I Confined My Self to My own the north side.

The descriptions I Have given or will give you must take as the description of all. Now for some little time, I Had been selling my Meat Ration to one of those Plymouth Men to try & get a little money to start something that would give us a little more of anything to Eat besides what we were drawing For myself & Poor Comrades, Bill, Henry & King, were getting Pretty Low & delapidated looking. I do not include Stewart for He always went away in the morning & came back to sleep & He seemed to be doing very well. He looked Fat & Felt so & I supposed he was getting [—] more to Eat that the Prison Rations. But us, Four Skinney, Boney, Ragged, dirty Creatures, were Just able to Crawl or sneak around but yet we were in Health, thanks to God & our way of using our Feed, We Had Escaped from those Diseases that Had already Carried of[f] Thousands of Brave men & was yet doing so, I Had those true & Kind Comrades, true to their manhood & true to Each other. For never did I Hear from any of them during our Captiveety or while we were together, any word or act but such a true man & comrade should Be Kind & Considerate to Each other then for those three & myself.

I Had sold seven meal Rations & Had now three dollars & 50 Cents in Consulting the Best use we could make of it. Henry, He would get a chucker look outfit & we could run a Bank as there was Millions in it & we would all soon be Rich. He got the Box & Boa[r]d & Him & I went down to the corner of our little alley, where it Joined the Main Street & opened our Bank with our three dollars & 50 Cents. I will leave you to Imagine our Feelings with our all invested in the Banking Business & while we were waiting for customers to Come & make their Deposits For we had to be Carefull to not let them know that our Capital was so small, it was yet Early in the Morning but you Know the Early Bird.[8]

We soon Had the Bank a Running with the usual Luck in Such Business Sometimes winning & some times losing but gradually Increasing our own Capital untill at one time about 10 OClock, we Had about 22 dollars. I wish, My Friends, I Could describe to you the Picture we Made, Henry & I, while Running that Bank & Particularly Henry as He yet looks to me after 27 years. Yes, I Still see the Poor little Ragged Dirty Boy, naturally a little dark skinned & slim but no, Black, smoked Black from the smoke of the Pitch Pine & slim. Well, no, My Friends, not slim now but a living Skeleton, Skin & Bones with God Breath still in Him. Yes, Literally a Living Breathing Skeleton. Yes, I still See Him as we would win a dollar Greedily reach out them Bony Skeleton Fingers & Clutch that dollar Bill, draw it to Him & Put it amongst our other money & place one Hand on it to Keep it in place & also Keep any one from taking, stealing it for it was not an unusual thing for a Bank to be Robbed then as now. Only the way of doing it was diffirent there at them times, the way a Bank was Robbed was in this Way.

There was some men there who lived by Plundering & of Course, those men usually were a great deal stronger & Quicker than a Poor old Prisoner, who Had been Living for months on Prison Fare. Those men were always Prowling around & when the[y] saw anything to Steal, Especially from a man that looked sick or weak, they took it often Knocking Him down if He objected, which a man naturally would no matter How Sick & Weak He was of this class of theives. They wore the Blue but I Cannot Call them Comrades of them. I will speak later on when the time

Comes & it was for this Class of Rascalls that Henry was watching with a club by His side & His other Hand on the money, for one of those men to Come along & see a Pile, Big or little, Layeng on a Board & the man running the Bank if he was weak or Sickly & the Fellow though in a Fight or Tussle He could get away with Him, He would grab the money & Skip out. That was their mode of Robbing a Bank in those days.

I had noticed Henry for some time being uneasy & as Business Had sla[c]kened up a little, I asked Him what was the matter? He said he was getting afraid some Fellow would clean us out & we ought to Quit. We had 22 dollars but as usual, I Had a little Capital & Began to feel Like a man of Business & a Bloated Bond Holder so I told Henry, it was too Early & our Luck Had been good. So we would continue & if our luck changed, I would stop so we Could get Some thing to Eat out of it anyway. So we Kept on Playeng & our luck did turn for at noon, I Had only Eleven dollars & a Half we went up to Bill & King, Left the Box & Board with them & Henry & I went down to the market to Buy something For dinner For I was Bound to have some thing to Eat. A Banker & His Family, Certainly we will Have dinner.

I do not Remember Just what we Bought & the Prices you Know but I used 10 dollars on what we Bought for dinner. We took it to our tent & all Eat of it untill all was gone. For myself, I Can say that I felt like there Had been some Kind of a change Made inside of me but to save me, I Could not say from My actual Feelings whether I Had really Eaten anything or not. Of the two, I would rather say I Had not Eaten anything for I felt Hungrier after than before & that was about the way the other Boys Felt. For see Henry is looking around in the sand to see if by any Possible Care lessness, a crumb dropped but no, He looks disap[p]ointed at not Finding any.

I asked Bill How He Liked His dinner. Dinner? He said was it dinner, I Had? Well I Knew I Had Something Strange from the way I Feel but I did not Know it was Dinner For it did not last Long Enough for me to give it a name & Henry Said Confound it, I wish we Had our ten dollars Back. We could go into Business again. I told Him to be Patient that it was Customary for Business men & Bankers Especially to take an Hours Rest after dinner & for them to Lay around on a sofa or Lounge Until Business Hours. Sofa, He Said, where will I find a sofa to Lounge on? There, I said, Pointing outside to the Hot sand & oh the De[vi]l —

<u>Dickens</u>, he said, yes, that would be a nice place to Lay down. I would soon be Rolled down Hill into the swamp so that sand is alive see it role around like there was Life in it.

Yes, My Friends, Henry is Right. It is literally alive but alive with what? With Grey Backs, they increase & multiply in that Hot Sand So that when the Sun Shines on it, you Can see it Heave, role & Glisten in the sun & it is & Has been so & Continues so while there is a Human Being left there for them to Feed upon & Suck their Life Blood & now Can you wonder at our Uncleanly Condition of Body & Rags, Can you wonder at them Eating, yes, Literally Eating men up alive. You may not, My Dear Kind Friends, Beleive this, it Looks so u[n]reasonable to think that a man with Life in Him Could or would allow Himself to be so Killed by such vermin but Remember they will not stay on a Dead Body & I again Pledge you my word, I am stating nothing but actual Facts & will Prove it to you by actual observation a little Later. For you Remember while in Danville what I Said about the scratch of a Pin or the scratch of the Finger Nail or any thing that would draw Blood, there we were Comparatively strong to what we are now & there also we were Layeng on a Board Floor but Here we are in the open air Exposed to the weather as the Lord is pleased to Send it weakened Physically & Mentaly From Long Confinement Starvation & Exposure & you cannot wonder that men in that Condition with a Feeling that they are Neglected by their Government & Forgotten by their Friends should get Careless of life & give up at the least sign of Physical weakness & let them once give up & lay down for 4 or 5 days & during that time Neglect to Skirmish & I may Safely say that Nothing or Nobody on Earth Can save them, no, not Even if they were Perfectly sound & well in Health when they Laid down. For in that time with the Condition of His Flesh when He Laid down, there would then be sores on Him from one Cause or an other Either from Him scratching Himself or sores Caused by Layen on the Bare Ground with the Bare Flesh next to it.

Amongst the[m] Most of the men & Especially the men longest in Prison, there was Hardly Rags Enough on us to Keep our Bare Bodys from Mother Earth when we Layed down. Oh yes, we were Just Right For that warm Climate, Very Cooley, Very Airily but also Very, yes, Very Muchly, very Thinley Clad. {You may ask my Friend why, oh, why did you let those Poor Comrades die such a Horrible inhuman Filthy Death, that is if it is true what you say?} I will answer it for it is but a Human & a Natural Thought & I will Speak for Myself although I may use the word we as I Have been doing I mean myself. First then it was a life or Death Struggle at all times & we were so long used to seeing such sights that we Really thought nothing of it & would Say Poor Fellow He will be soon gone or if he was Dead Poor Fellow, His misery is over. Second, we Had all we Possibly could do to try & Keep those death Dealing Vermin of[f] ourselves for it look Considerable ambition & Exertion as well as a Pretty Strong Stomack to strip of[f] the few Rags we Had two, three or Four times a day & try to rid ourselves of them & third, we Had lost very near all Fellow Feeling for our Fellow man in our struggle for Life & it was indeed a Friend & Dear Friend that a man there would go to any Extra Exertion or trouble for. For the Lower or selfish Side of Humanity was the side that was uppermost, there it was mostly & with Rare Exceptions Every man for Him self & you need not be surprised at it for none but those who were there can Imagine what men Can Endure & Live.

& I may Here say while I think of it that during My Prison Life & Parties Early in Andersonville, I noticed that men from the Western States or from any Rural district took their Imprisonment better than the men who Enlisted from the Cityes & amongst the diffirent Nationalities, the Irish & Dutch or Germans stood it the Best. That was my observation of the Endurance of the men from the diffirent Parts of the Union & from diffirent Countries & now as our noon Hour is up & I see Henry from His Actions is Ankious to see what we are going to do now as our Bank is near Bankrupt. I tell Him get His Board & Box & we will try our Luck with our dollar & a Half.

So down we go to our old stand of the morning & I spread out our one dollar William that looks better than to say one dollar Bill & our 50 Cent Shin Plaster & after waiting a short time, a Fellow Came along with a Bundle of Green Backs in His Hands. He stopped looked at my Pile then at me & Said, Hello, Runnin a Bank, are you? I Politely told Him, yes, to Pitch in & try His Luck. He asked what my limit was I said from Five to twenty five.

Now according to the Rule of the Game, if it was dollars, I meant He could not Bet Less Loan 5 dollars at a time nor more than 25 but Really when I spoke I meant Cents & not dollars but He thought it was

Dollars So Planked down a ten dollar William & I Hesitated about Raising the Box for if He won, I only Had a dollar & a Half to Pay Him & He might win three times & then thunder, where would I get 30 dollars to Pay Him. I Kept on Calling for more to Come & make their fortune in Order to get a little time to make my Mind up For the Fellow looked Stout & Strong & I was afraid if I lost, there would be a tussle for He looked like a chap that would stand no Foolishness but that ten Dollar Bill settled it, I could not Resist the temptation & my chance to win was 5 to one against Him.

Henry is looking like we are in a Bad Box so Here goes & up Comes the Box Exposing the three dice & Confound them, one of them Has the number that Fellow bet on & He Has Won. I Hand over to Him the dollar & a Half & tell Him that is all I Have & that we Have Just started. He Sais Bank Busted — Eh — I tell Him, yes, the Bank is Bursted & we are strapped. He looks at the dollar & a Half & then at me & I think He is going to give it Back to me but no, He puts it in with the other He Has & Walks of[f] & I suppose goes to Bragging amongst His Friends that He Busted a Bank. I tell Henry to take Back our Bank Furniture that we Have no more use for it. The Bank is Busted, Payment is suspended — & we closed our doors, Forgetting to Hang out our Shingle with inscription, Bank Closed.

That was my First, Last & only attempt to Better our Fortune by any Trading, a Speculation Whatever, while a Prisoner of War & it was a Failure altogether for we Had a Ten dollar dinner out of the Proceeds & Part of our System felt for a short time at Least little old times but will their old times Ever come, I Begin to think never. How Can I live where so many, many men stronger & Healthier than I dies under the same treatment but my Motto was & is always do the Best you Can under whatever Circumstances you are Placed & Never say die untill you Have to.

No Jonnies, I will try & Live as long as I can & Eat all you give me. I Know you are short of Bread stuff & Provisions Generally so that the longer I Live the more Ill Eat & Every Mouth Full I get from you is so much taken of your Substance & therefore Weakens the Rebellion so that if I Cannot Fight you in the Feild I Can Stay Here & Eat or Help to Eat you up. These, my Friends, were my Thoughts & Feelings as well as the thoughts & Feelings of my three Comrades in misery & also the thoughts & Feeling of others as well as us & that may Partly account for our Stubborness in not Dieng under the Many ways the Rebel authorities Had Prepared for us but Thousands were Succumbing to it. But there was some tough ones that still Defied their Inhuman Cruelty to us.

You must Consider during all this time Camp, no, not Camp life but Sink Life, is going on the usual Fighting & Stealing amongst ourselves With a Shot occasionally from the Rebel Guard to Remind us of who & what we are & Here before I forget it, that Rebel Guard who took us out for wood told me at that time that they, the Guard, got the same amount of Food that we did but the Quality was Better & their meal was Bolled so there was then Considerable diffirence in the Quantity for they got there a Full Pint of Pure Meal, where if the stuff we got was sifted as fine as Bolled meal would be there would not be one Fifth of ours as fine as theirs. This I forgot to mention at the time as I Expect there will as I Know there will be Plenty of little incidents Forgotten.

King now Has a touch of the scurvey in His mouth. It is the first Symptom of it any of us Has Had for up to now we Had been very Fortunate & I Knew our danger & told Bill befor[e] long we would all Have it for we Had but the one spoon to Eat with & I Knew if we used that spoon & allowed King to use it, we were Certain to get it from Him in that way for in no other way is there danger of Catching it but by using the same Spoon or Article used for Eating but there was no Help for it. We Had to take our chances as King was one of ourselves but I lost Bill by it afterwards.

Stewart, I did not Know much about what He was doing & I asked King what He was doing & if He would not get Him something to Stop the Scurvey on Him as if not, we would all Catch it from Him. King told me Stewart was Running a Chuckluck Bank with some Friends of His on the South Side & Had plenty to Eat & Plenty of money. I asked Him if He never Helped Him or gave Him money & that as they were Neighbour Boys at Home, it was His duty to Help Him. I told King to ask Stewart when He Came Home that Evening and also to tell Him that we Bill, Henry & Self were strangers to Him & did not Expect anything from Him & that what Ever He would give Him should be used for Him Self to Stop the Scurvey so the rest of us would not take it from Him. King told me it was no use for Him to ask Stewart for any thing as He was & always Had been Selfish & that He Had already asked Him for some to Help us all as we were Kind Enough to give them Both shelter with us when we all Come in first & that He, Stewart, yet Came there & used our shelter to sleep in but no, He would not give Him a cent.

I told King all right I would ask Him so when Stewart Came that Evening. I told Him How King was & our danger but He Refused to do anything for King. He did not deny but He Had plenty of money & was Living well but said He wanted for Himself all He Had. I then told Him He would Either Cure King of the scurvey or He Could not sleep there anymore. He said He would not give Him a Cent & Sleep there too. I told Him I guessed not & if He did not Skip Lively out of there then as Quick as He Could, I Had an Idea He would not Enjoy His High Living any more or at least for some time to Come & that His Banking Business was over. I Jumped on my Feet & He Jumped out & Skipped away. I never saw Him any more but Heard when inside our own lines that He died on His way Home.

King got worse & Bill was the next, Henry, then took it & I felt my Gums getting sore. What the dickens Could I do? I took a walk out on the main street & Ran across one of My Regiment, one of Co. D men from Momence KanKaKee County.[9] It was the first time I saw so I asked Him what detachment he was in & I found He was in the second detachment from me. He said He saw me several times but did not Speak to me. He seemed to me to look Pretty well for being So long in Prison. His Clothing looke Pretty good at least they were Whole while mine was—well never mind mine now & He also looked like He was not depending on Just what was Issued to Him.

I asked Him where He got His Clothing & How He managed to look so well. He said He Had traded with some new Prisoners for the Clothes & was in a little speculation so was going very well. I then asked Him if He Had any money. He said a little but I asked Him How much He then Had & He Said about 9 dollars was all He Had. I asked Him to lend me some telling Him I would Pay Him when we got out & also the way myself & Comrades were with the scurvey but no, He said He could not share any as He needed it all in His Business. I then told Him to give me three dollars that was one Third of what He Had or Else I would take the whole nine dollars from Him. He was a little Taller & a good deal stouter than I was but I guess He thought that as I said I would take it all that I would have done so. I Beleive He was Just about Right For I Happened Just then to be in that Kind of Humour thinking of How we

116

were Fixed in my tent So He gave me three dollars but with a very Bad Grace.

I went on down the street & Bought a Quart of Irish Potatoes for two dollars & a Half & Paid 50 Cents for a cucumber about three inches long and as thick as my thumbs. I walked Proudly Home — Home — well yes, it was the only spot of Earth I could then Call by the Dear Name of Home & there was my Poor Sick Comrades but I Soon Cheered them by Relating my Success at Highway Robbery, For I Beli[e]ve it was Really nothing Else. I Cut the Cucumber in Four Parts & told the Boys to not swallow any of it but Just Hold a small Peice in their mouth & suck it untill the[y] got all the substance out of it & then spit it out as the scurvey was yet only in our gums & if we Co[u]ld Keep it out of our Stomachs, there was little danger of Fatal Consequences from it but if it Ever got inside of us then Good By, John, for it would not be Long.

I then Counted the Potatoes & there was twenty two in it so I told them Each one of us use two Potatoes Each day as long as the[y] Lasted but to not Chew them, only Scrape them very Fine & first suck some of it to Cleanse the Gums then retain the rest in the mouth as long as they could & we all done so, swallowing but very little of them. They did not Cure us but they Checked it for the time being & gave us a chance if we could Have got about twice as much more, it would then have Entirely Cured us but none of us Knew where or How to obtain Either money or Potatoes so we Had to do the Best we could, thankfull for what we Had got.

The main or Principal thing was to Keep our spirits up & not despond. King was very quiet & not talkative & Bill was a good deal the some way but Henry was Restless & wished to move around as much as he Could So that Him & I often would take A Stroll together & we now go for a walk & short though it is, we will see Enough of Human Misery. This time I go towards the swamp for it is Here the outcasts of our Ragged Starved Society Congregates. They are men who Have no Hopes of living & Have no Friends there to take any intirest in them, are Sick almost unto death Generally from scurvey which is working in their systems & they want to be near the swamp for Conveinence Sake.

For Certainly no Human Being in His Right mind would go near that Disease Breeding swamp only from Nesssity & Conveinence & I well Know when I see any man go there to Remain near it that He Himself

Has given up all Hopes & that it is only a Question of a Few Hours or at Furthest a day or two untill he is Carried out, a Corpse For the Healthiest man that Ever Breathed the Breath of Live Could not Breathe that Pestelential air For 48 Hours without Creating the Germ of Disease in His System & now let us take a look at it under this Hot Burning Sun.

My Friends, you may think those descriptions unnessesary for me to give or are over drawn. No, I Pledge you my word there is not a Description of a mans appearance of any Scene that I give you but what is Realy under the Reality of the actual scene it self For Beleive me, Pen Could not describe nor Language Express the Real Truthfull appearance of the Prisoners & their surroundings. How much less then Can I? No, I Can only give what I saw & choose such words as may give you, my Friends, some little Idea of us in that Hell Hole & our Surroundings in it, our Personal Feelings of Hunger Misery & our Longing <u>desire</u> for Home, Friends, Food & Home Comforts & Friendship, with our thoughts of what we Had been & what we then were as also for our Natural Sympathy For all Human Suffering & again I say what man or what Pen Could give you all this in writing so that you would Have all those feelings, I Have mentioned as we Had them there in Andersonville & other Prisons. No, my Friends, it would an Impossility for me or any other man who was there to overdraw the Picture of our Misery Either with Pen or Brush & that swamp you must see so as to Form some Idea of it & the Kind of Air Exhaling From which we Had to Breathe night & day & Beleive Me, I am choosing a time too to show it to you when it is Comparatively speaking innocent of all Disease Breeding Compared to what it will be in the nex[t] months of June, July & August.

I do not mention that sweet month of Flowers May. It will speak for itself when we get into it for at Present, we are in the Last of April. So that I think you will be thankfull as you have to see that swamp sometime. That you see it now Even in the Present Filthy Condition that to see it Later, For after this I shall give no Description of it, Leaving it to your own Imagination if you should give it a Thought & so to Continue. From where I slept to the swamp was about 12 Rods so I did not Have far to go & as I Came near it, I Could see men Layeng around in the Hot Boiling Sun in all Positions on their Backs with the sun Beating on their Faces, on their Sides or Layeng Face down, all in diffirent Positions, a Languid & Listless and all Hastening to death by Disease & Vermin.

I go up to one & move Him, shake Him. He Finaly with out moving His Body sayes weakly, what do you want? Leave me alone & let me Die. I ask Him, whats the matter with Him? What ails Him & He answers scurvey. If this Face is turned up to me & mouth open, I see His Gums all inflamed & Rotten, the Flesh of the Gums Eaten away in Patches or He Has Pulled out His Gums in Peices with His Fingers & not a tooth in His Head, he has also Pulled them out with His Fingers. The Flesh is too Rotten to Hold them in & if He did not Pull them out Himself, they would Have dropped out & he might Have Swallowed them in taking a drink of water or s[w]allowing a mouthfull of Food & it is not the Condition of His mouth that is Killing Him. No, but He Has of Course in Eating & drinking taken some of that Putrid Flesh or Matter into His Stomach & that is what is Killing Him.

Poor Fellow, who in your Northern Home is waiting, watching, Hoping they may yet see you & Embrace you in Loving Arms. Who, if they Could See you in your Rags, Filthy in your Present Condition with Death standing by you, waiting, see you in your Misery & Loneliness Without a Friend near to ask you if you wanted a drink or speak a Kind word of sympathy to you or one to whom you Could send a message of Love to those at Home. No, you are alone, alone amongst Thousands & not one of these to take interest Enough in you to stand beside you & Even See you Die. Again I say, who of the Northern Friends of this man Lyeng Here if the[y] saw Him as I saw Him Could Ever Forget the Cause that Placed Him there & its Effects on Him & thousands of others.

There is Hundreds like Him along the Edge of the swamp so I move away from Him & Here is another one this man is dieng From a Fever. The Doctors Could not Come to See Him & He, Poor Fellow, Could not go to them so He Crawled down amongst the others to die. This seemed to be the General understanding that if a man Had no Friends, no one to Care from Him & no Protection but the open air, when Ever He Knew that he was sure of dieng, He Either crawled there or Had some of the men Help Him get there & once near that swamp, He did not Linger long in this world.

I again move on & see that man or what was once a man but now a mass of living Corruption. His Body & Limbs are Covered with Scurvey Sores & around these sores are, I might say, Hundreds of thousands of those Vermin Eating Him up. I pass from that sight, it is Sickening &

would be a Mercy to Knock Him in the Head & End His Misery. I move on & See a Few Rags Covering Some Human Bones, go up to it, it is very still & does not move. I touch it, it is cold & Stiff <u>Dead</u>. I ask a man How long He, that mass of Bones, is dead. He says about an Hour — yes & He may be there for 2, 3 or 4 Hours Longer or may be there untill Morning For the Rebels never Came inside to Carry out a dead man. Oh No, that Place was too Filthy for them & we might all Die & Rot there for all they Cared & if the Yanks wont tote their own dead out, they can Keep them there. No, we Had it Carry out our own Dead & it took Four of our Fellows to Carry one of those Skeletons & as a Temptation for the Dead to be Carried out, they Four Men Carrying out a Dead man were allowed to Carry Back with them all the wood the[y] Could Carry So that Carrieng out the Dead was a Business speculation & a Payeng Business too.

As wood was so valuable, one of Four Men able Carry out a dead man Would be able to Carry back with Him wood Enough to Sell for 5 or 10 dollars so that this Dead man Remains there Amongst the dieng untill Four of those men Finds Him & Car[r]ies Him out & now let us remain by this Poor Corpes for a little while & see what will Happen before He is placed in the Dead Pile outside.

See that man come & look at Him to be Sure that He is dead then Hurries away as well as His Stren[g]th will Permit. Yes, He is gone to tell His Comrades He Knows where there is a Dead man & see He Brings three more with Him back. They are Four old Prisoners & look Hardly able to Carry their own Bones but they Each take Hold of a Leg or an Arm & Slowly Lift the dead Body up untill they get it on their Shoulders. It was a Pretty good lift for them & they stagger on towards the North Gate.

They do not go very Far with the Body untill they Meet Four More Men, who Considers themselves Stronger & Better able to Carry that Body than they are & one of this last Four Sais drop that Body, we want to Carry it out ourselves but the Four in Possesion will not give it up & tries to Pass on With it. The Four last Comers then Pitch into them. They drop the Body & then there is a Free Fight over the Remains of that Poor Soul Body.

The Four new ones Conquers & Pick up the Body & move on but do not go Far untill they in turn meet Four more & then another Fight Ensues & while they are Fighting, Four others snatch the Body up & off with them with it to the north gate then turn down along the dead line across the Swamp & on to the South Gate & out with the <u>Body</u>, when they are allowed to get the wood For that is the object, they were all after. It was not Love for the Poor fellow that those men wanted to Carry Him out For but for the Profit to be made by Carrying Him out. Sometimes a Body would change Hands oftener than that & Sometimes the First Four getting Him woul[d] carry the Body out but that would be only when any other Four in that Line of Business would be afraid to molest them.

My Friend, I often Have to Break in on my Narrative & give you scenes or Descriptions of things as the[y] occur to my Memory or Else I may Forget them Entirely. For my object is to give at least if I Can one of the different Scenes or incidents as the[y] occured in Prison so that you may Form from the Whole, some Idea of our Life there. So to Return to the Swamp I have not yet described it.

Look the whole Len[g]th of it from East to West & you see a string of men Barelegged, Bare Headed & I might Say Bare Backed too. They are in the Little Branch of Water, Some tryeng to wash their Face & Hands, some throwing water over them to Cook themselves & Some of them Lyeng down Flat. It feels good to them, there is no Clothing to be injured by it. There is only 5 or 6 inches of water running & it may drown or wash of[f] them those Thousands of Vermin Sticking on their Poor Flesh & Picking their Bare Bones & swarmed on their Rags.

That is a sight you may see at any Hour of the day then look along on Both sides of the Bank & See those dug out from Here. We Have a good view of them, see the Poor delapedated Human Creatures Crawling in & out of them like Animals. The South Side of the Branch you see has got very little of the swampy ground. It is nearly all on our Side & the dry ground Comes down Close to the Branch but see the whole space in the Swamp Covered with men. No, Skeletons wading, waddling, struggling around in it, now driving their arms down Even to the Shoulder, feeling around for what, for a Root of any Kind of a Plant which they dry & Cook their Feed with it. Yes & some of those Roots they Pull up are no Thicker than Stocking yarn.

That is what those Poor Fellows are doing & in wha[t] a Mass they are struggling, Feeling in. Look, the day is Hot, the sun almost Boiling Hot & that Mass those men are in looks like it too is Boiling. Yes, it is actually moving & a Kind of Bubling up like yeast from the Heat of the Sun, that

Mass of Quick Sand Maggots & Filth. That is the only Description I Can give but it is Far, yes, Very Far From being what it actually was & Expecialy Latter in the Hot Burning months.

I will Close the Month of April with the Filthy swamp scene & Enter the sweet Month of May, the Month of Flowers, the Bea[u]tifull month of Nature but Here, where is Natures Beauty — gone, all gone, taken, Spoiled by the Hand of Man. Of this month of May 1864, I have very little to tell For the Reason that there is very little that I Remember of it only that in this month, the Mercifull God in His Goodness showed by His Mighty Hand that He Had so not Forgotten us if our Government Had or Seemed to us to Have. Yes, He showed to us His mercy by sending us 21 or 22 days almost insesant [incessant] Rain day & night. It Created a good deal of inconvenience to us for we were wet Continualy & Had to Lay on Wet sand. It also Entirely Demolished those Dug outs but with all the inconnvenince, we appreciated it as a Blessing. It drowned out & washed away Millions of those Pests of Vermin & thoroughly Cleansed & Purified that Swamp.

It Commenced on the First & Continued almost Continualy untill about the 22 or 23rd. The swamp was full from Bank to Bank & Ran like a mill. It washed out & carried away the width of itself on the East Side of the Stockade, about 12 or 15 Rods of it, Leaving a gap there for several days & the Rebels Kept a Heavy Face of infantry there to Guard it For Fear we would take advantage of it & Break out. They also Kept all their men under arms Night & day & Had Both Battery trained on that Gap with Gunners standing by Ready to fire at any moment night or day.

At night, they Kept 2 Large Fires Built so the[y] could see any movement Made by us almost as well as in the day but in spite of all their Precautions & danger, some Few got away by swimming, at least they Left us that way but whether they were drowned in the attempt or Escaped I never Knew. The Rest of us watched Close for a Chance to make a General Break but no, if we Had only a Clear Feild, the Armed Rebs, we would have taken our Chances with but the water, we could not overcome & it was between us & them & instant Death to all Entering it but a First Class & Strong Swimmer & in our Weakened Condition, it would be suicide to attempt it so, we Could take no advantage of that wide gap & when or as the water Receded, they Had timbers & men Ready to put them in so by the time the water Had all gone, the Stockade was again as it was before but we could Feel & Breathe the Pure air. That was now there instead of that Foul & impure air we Had been Breathing.

So much Constant & Heavy Rain Had made the Mortality greater than it Had been Before. For the men, who were allready down Sick from any Cause, when the Rain commed, Died & those, who were Weakly or Sickly, got worse but those of us, who did stand it, Felt the Refreshing Effects of the Comparatively Invigorating air & I now Felt but Little Danger of what I Had most Found, yellow Fever.[10]

Yes, I often thought during the month of April that when the Hot months Came & with the Crowded Filthy Disease Breeding Condition of Andersonville that it Certainly would be Impossible to Escape Either that Epedemic or some other Fatal & Contagious Disease. Yes, often have I thought of that as I would Look around me in the daytime & see the Condition we were in & our Surroundings & think of the Harvest any such a Disease Could Reap from the yet remaining struggling Thousands of Brave men.

For a man Could in there Show His Bravery & Loyalty to His Country & Fellow man as well as on the Battle Feild & we were Bravely, Nobly Struggling For life with the Chances of 100 to one against us. Still we would not give up untill it was Gods Will For while there is Life, there is all ways Hope & we still continue the Battle & if we are not destroying our Enemys, we are destroying their substance in the shape of cracked or Crushed Feed & as little as [—] of us get of it, it takes a Considerable [amount] of it to give that little to 25 or 30 Thousand men.

For during this time & you may Consider that from now Untill about the 8th or 10th of September, that Prisoners are Coming in almost daily in squads more or Less in numbers. We are as you Know in the last of May so we will take a Skip into the Month of June 1864. This month Comes in dry & Hot & now the men are again beginning to suffer. Most of the new Prisoners, Fresh Fish, are from Grants Command in Virginia & they are coming in By the Hundred. Men, some of them, not two week From their Families & Firesides, men from the Merchants Desk from the Wholesale & Retail Counters, Men Fresh From College, men yet showing in their appearance & Actions, the Refinements of the Society from which they so lately Had been in & what a Contrast two or three Short weeks Has Made not they in the Society of still their Fellow Beings but of what appearance. You, My Friends, Know but by their actions or rather the actions of some those strangers might think the[y] Had got into a tight den of wolves & there were Human wolves Amongst us.

Up to this time, I Have Hesitated to mention them but now I must show you to what Degredation & Crime, Even Hunger & Misery will drive a man or some men to For some time past, there Had been an occasional Rumour that a man Had been Murdered for what little He Had, May He Carelessly showed a Little money on Buyeng something to Eat or He might Have neglected to Hide His watch while inside & the[y] saw it. No matter what, a man was Killed So Rumour said & Rumour is very often Right but we Know that men were Robbed & in daylight, in Presence of Hundreds Standing By & of thousands within sound of the Voice. Yes, Forcibly Robbed on the main street & in this way, those marauders, Murderers, usually went in squads.

Nobody Knew them from the Rest of us & of Course, their mode of Plundering gave them the means of Living Pretty well so that they were strong Compared to others & when a new Batch of Prisoners would be coming in, they were usually there watching & when they saw a man come in that they Judged from His appearance Had money or valuables, the[y] well Knew His First thought after Entering For they new men always Came in Hungry would be to get something to Eat from one of those many little stalls on the street & if He Had money & the means of Buyeng He would walk up to one of those Stands, Buy. Some of these Human wolves Had followed Him & if the[y] saw a good looking Pocket Book, one of them would Grab it from Him & Walk away. If the man Made any trouble, another one or two of them would Knock him down & Escape in the Crowd & by the time the man was up, His Pocket Book was gone.

This mode was very Common — & no one Except the Man Himself Cared much but if the man showed Fight & Beat them of[f] without them obtaining what the[y] wanted, some of them would Follow Him all day & watch where He slept & then Either Rob Him or sometimes murder Him. Then it was an Easy Matter to dispose of the Body, the swamp was near or if it Happened near where the[y] themselves slept, they would Bury the Body amongst them selves.

They were an Organized Gang of Eastern Roughs & all occupied the south East Corner of the Stockade. Their depredations were Committed Generaly Amongst the new Prisoners for the old ones Had but little if any thing to lose & they would Fight to the Death for what little they Had I think Considering the diffirence in numbers between the old Prisoners, I mean by this men who Had been in Prison 6 Months & over & the new Prisoners that in this month June & the two Suceeding Months that there was the Greatest Mortality amongst this new one For this Reason, the weak ones, ones of the old Prisoners, Had all or nearly all died of[f] & those Living of them were Tough Hardy Men or they also would Have gone under while the new Prisoners Mostly new Levies & men but a short time in the service & there for neither toughened or Hardened by the Hardships of war or manner of Former Life soon succumbed to the Prison Life & its Hardship & I will give you a few Illusterations.

In walking around, I would often meet Such those men as I now describe. I see one of these new men, His Clothing & appearance Show Him to be not Long in Prison & that His Former life Had not been one of Labor. I see Him sitting down on the Side Hill facing the swamp & near it with His two Hands under His Cheeks, Elbows Resting on His Knees & a Desponding, Longing Look on His Features. Oh God, How well I Know that look & its Fore runner, Death. The man looks Strong & Healthy, I Know it is not Sickness. Yes, My Dear Kind Friends, I Know that mans thoughts for well I Know what is Killing Him. Many — many — many such unfortunate Creatures Have I watched & many I Hope I Have Saved too from that death, the Hardest I Beleive of all Deaths, the death of a strong Healthy man without Disease, without Sickness & without any apparent Cause, the Death of a Broken Heart.

Yes, I Know His thoughts & will give them to you. Look at Him in the Position and appearance I Have Stated, He is Thinking but a few days ago, I was at Home in my Comfortable Home in the North with my Loving Wife & Children. I was doing a Good Prosperous Business with Kind Loving Friends around me. I Had all the Comforts & Pleasure of Life & now in those few days or weeks, What a change. Mercifull Father in Heaven, what a change. Here I am alone — alone amongst Thousands — alone without one Friend on Gods Earth, Wife, children, Friends, where are you all gone & I Here alone & Left to what, to a life of Misery, Filth & Starvation as those Poor Human Skeletons around me show. No, it is not life but a living Death, a lingering Death after Sufferings daily, Hourly, for maybe a few weeks or months but Death Certain in the End & I may as well sit Here & die at once or soon than wait &

Linger along as those Poor Creatures are doing whom I see around me. What Have I to live for I shall never, never get out of this Filthy Hole & See Wife or children again.

Those My Friends are that mans thoughts for many times Have I felt or He now Feels but never Sat down & Nursed From Fed on them sweet thoughts though they were & although I Had no wife, no children, I too Had a Home & Loved ones. I often thought of, Dreamt of & wished For with all the wistfull Longing of the Human Heart but never allowed my thoughts to Long dwell on that Subject.

No, my thoughts, I Kept Steadily on the Present & How I might Live to again see them nor neither did I allow any mans thoughts to Dwell on Home, that I Could Prevent for well I Knew the Consequences. Yes & well I Knew the Consequences to that man Sitting there so I walk up to Him, touch Him on the shoulder & say Hello, what are you doing there Breathing this impure air? You ought to be Knocking around taking Exercise as I am. What Part of the North are you From? What Regiment did you Belong to & How long are you in the service? Have you a Wife & Family & How did you Leave them? These & other Questions I Put to Him in Order to draw His mind from what was Killing Him.

He would answer Careless & listless untill I would mention His Wife & Family then I Could See His Eyes Glisten & Tears Gather. Ha, you Love them then I Know He is a Married man for he Has not answered that Question in words but His action shows He is for He Cannot Speak. I Have Found His Weak spot, Love of Wife & Family & work on it Rousing His manhood to bear up for their sakes be a man & live to go Home & Make them Happy. I tell Him to look at me, a Skinney Bunch of Bones with a few Rags thrown over them. How long I have been in Prison & that I intend to Live & go Home no matter How Long the[y] Keep me or How Bad the[y] treat me. They will Have to shoot me to Kill me & that there is Thousands of us there Feeling just that way & none but a coward would sit down & die Like a Dog without making an Effort to Live at Least if not for Himself, For those Loved ones waiting, watching, Hoping for His Return to them.

With these & such arguments, I thank God, I was often successfull in waking them up from those Death Thoughts they were indulging in — - but with others, I Had to use diffirent Arguments & Some take an Entirely diffirent Course with some after tryeng as above & it Failed, I would Give Him a Box in the Ear, A Kick Him with my Bare Feet or Hammer away on Him untill He got mad & then He would Jump up & start for me when I would tell Him to stop. Hold on. I Had accomplised all I wanted in getting Him Roused up & He would get ashamed of Himself & walk away. Others again I woul[d] Kick & tell them get out & the[y] Generally did, Supposing they were Sitting in my Place or spot of Sleeping Ground & that I was only Claiming My own.

This, my Friends, was one mode of Amusement or Pastime for me all through or while I was able to walk around there. I was often Successfull & also often Failed For these would all be new men. The old ones never gave up untill they Had to & then they Soon were Carried out. I one day Met one of these men who told me He was Captured in Front of Grants army on the Picket Line & He was not yet two weeks since He Eat His Dinner in His own Home. As soon as He Enlisted, He was Rushed to the front Placed on Post of one of the most important duties a soldier Has to do a Picket Post, Captured & Rushed into Prison & such a Prison — & all this is done almost before the Last meal that man Eat with His Family Has thoroughly digested in His Stomach. So you can Hardly wonder & the Thoughts or Feelings of that man if He allowed His thoughts to work in that way.

At another time, I met a Stout Healthy Red faced Smart intilligent young Irishman with a Sergeants Stripes or Schevrons on His arm. He looke like he was Just from My Mother Country & I Stopped & asked Him How long He was in the Country. He said it was Just three weeks since He landed, so in three weeks He Had Enlisted, was Promoted to Sergeant, Captured & a Prisoner. I give you those as samples & you may Imagine there was Hundreds of Just such in that Prison Pen.

Another time & during this month in going around, I Saw what I Promised sometime Back to Prove to you a man Eaten alive by Vermin. I will not ask you, my Friend, to see the sight but Beleive me, I saw it, a Large Hole Between that Poor Creatures Shoulders & Just Below the Shoulder Blades where the Back Bone Joines them a Hole almost as Large as a saucer, His Shoulder Blades & Back Bone in Plain View &---& I again saw a man — Excuse me I must say it — I met Him down on the Edge of the Swamp Naked. Yes & sane in His Right mind for I asked Him why He Had Sold His clothes all & He said to get Food that He was starving. He was the only one that I saw Entirely that way but there was Thousands of us might as well Have been so, for all the comfort we got from our Rags, yes & Really Better for us if we were so Except For decency Sake for then the vermin would Have no Home, no place to Play Hide & Seek on our Poor Bones but that Poor Fellow mentioned died in a few days, Baked to death by the Hot Sun. He Had no Shelter from it & no Protection from it.

You, my Friends, may take those I Have given a samples of Thousands of others with that one single Exception & you may also Consider that our Prison Life daily & Hourly Has been & will Continue to be as I have tried to describe it by scenes or incidents only as the time Passes picture to yourself the daily increasing of the Suffering & misery of the Living & also can increase of Deaths the increase of the Suns Heat & Increasing with it of the Filthy Unhealthy Condition of the Prison Pen.

I Say this now, as I am about to go I might almost insensible state for the next three month & during that time I shall be unable to give but very Little from Personal observation as I Have Here to fore done & during this time whatever I can Remember to Have Heard that I think is truthfull & will intirest you, I will give it or any thing that may give you a Better Idea of our Prison Life than what I Have or Can Hereafter Relate. The most that I can now Remember during this time that I am Lingering Between Life & Death will be in regard to my self & Even a Part of this time Passed to me in Such a manner that I do not Remember Even myself for my Memory is Clouded but I Know I was there & that is all.

So now to begin this Period of From about the first of July to the First of october or there abouts. For Some time Back, we all Four Had Been Suffering From the Scurvey & it was Naturally increasing on us as we Had not anything whatever to use to check it since we Had that Quart of Potatoes & our Present Condition about the First of July was very Bad. We all Had the Scurvey in our Gums & any of us Could at any time have Pulled Every tooth in our Head out with our own Fingers without a Particle of Pain & we Had to be Carefull in swallowing our Feed that we did not also swallow our teeth & it was not a very unusual thing for us when in tryeng to Pick out of our Gums, the chaff or coarse Hulls of the Corn to also Pick out with our Fingers a tooth which we Quickly Pushed Back again in its place. This I Have often done & so also did I see others do. You, my Friends, may not like to beleive this but you may charge it to Prison Facts for it is the truth.

King & Henry were very Sick but Bill managed to Keep on His Feet

& draw our Rations & done the Best He Poor Fellow Could to prepare them for us. I suppose before I go I Had Better give you Some Little Description of myself while I am able. This we be the only one I shall give, I Have before told you My Friends that my Pants were worn of[f] about up to the Knees & the Bottoms of them Pretty well Frayed that my Blouse, the only upper Garment I Had, was worn of[f] up to the Elbows & Ends Pretty well in Ribbons. Well Just Imagine My Blouse Entirely Sleeve less & the Body of it almost Bodyless with what Remained of it — well More Hole & than your Humble servant & what the dickens, How shall I describe my other & only Peice of Dry Goods. Ill be — Blamed if I Know — only to say that they were — well — Leg less <u>also</u> & that I Had to watch them Pretty Close or the[y] would leave me alltogether & if that Happened I would be Legless <u>sure</u>.

My Personal Appearance in Features I Cannot Give you for the simple Reason that I Had not seen myself since I was a Baby, at least it seemed that Long to me. If you can Imagine a Human Being from the description I give of myself then also add to it months without washing Face or Hand with the Smoke From Pitch Pine Glued on to all Exposed Surface & a [—] of Hair on the Head & Face of ten months & you may Have some Idea of me on the First of July 1864 & that Same Picture will answer for about 15 thousand Men there & I may say that they would not all of them Come Quite up to that, no, a good many would Fall short of making s[o] good a Picture & others who saw me then might say I Had Favored my self in My Drawing. One of Bills Legs now Commenced to draw up, a contraction of the Cord from scurvey. So also did one of mine the Left or wounded one & I was now Confined to my tent unable to leave it & Blind at night. They Call it moon Blind[11] as soon as it got dusk, I was Blind From. Now this time I loose all track of King — & also Henry. I only Remember William Best. King, I do not even remember seeing after I was Confined to my Shelter & Henry, I saw once after which I will mention when that time comes but How or when He got where I saw Him, I do not Know.

Time now Seems more like a Dream than a Reality & very little I remember distinctly. I am not Sick in a strict sense of the word. No, it is scurvey, scurvey in my Mouth, Scurvey in my System, Scurvey all through me. It is nothing but scurvey. Bill, Poor Bill, still Hob[b]ling around me when I am Wakefull or sensible Enough to ask Him if there is anything to Eat. He always Has a Mouthfull of thin Corn Gruel for me For after our Mouth got Bad that was the way we took it in a Kind of a Drink & the meat, we swallowed the Best we could for we dare not try to chew it or anything & for some time, they Had issued Beef or what once Had been Beef.

I Hear they Had Captured 600 Head of Beeves from Sherman & Ran them down to us & it was that they were giving to us. The amount was about the same as the Bacon Ration & the Quality also. For those Beeves were Killed along in the Latter Part of the night or very early morning then stood in the Hot sun until the[y] got through Hauling of the Dead & when we got it, it would be covered with Fly Blows—thick & this was our Beef Ration.

The next I remember Bill told me He would Help me crawl out if I wanted to see those men Hung. They were going to Hang 6 of those Raiders For Plundering & Murdering our men.[12] I Have Heard the[y] well disposed of the Prisoners Had Organized themselves in Companys & Captured a lot of these theives & murderers & Had tried them outside the South Gate by a Judge & Jury of our own Men Prisoners. Wirz Furnishing the Guards to Guard them after our men inside Captured them & Brought them to Him. They Had been about 2 Weeks doing it & were now Ready to Hang 6 of them Just inside the South Gate. The Rebels Furnishing the Lumber For the Scaffold.

Those six I think were

Father William J. Hamilton (courtesy Diocesan Archives, Catholic Diocese of Savannah).

all Eastern men & Found Guilty of Murder. For our Fellow Found Body Buried in the ground over which some of them slept. Some of them Confessed to the Murders, the[y] were to die for & some denied them but acknowledged others they Had Committed. They were attended to the scaffold by a Catholic Priest, Father Hamilton[13] & the only Minister of any Religious Beleif that I Ever Knew or Heard of visiting the Prisoners in Andersonville.

Tell this I Heard & now while speaking of Father Hamilton, I will say that I saw Him several times myself & He once attended Bill & myself & I think Henry & I Had a talk with Him & if I remember Right, He told me His mission during the war was to visit the Diffirent Prisons in the South & attend the Northern Prisoners in them.

He remained in my shelter for some time was Pleasant & Sociable. I Had often Heard other Prisoners speak of Him & His Kindness & also say of Him that He would talk to them up on any Subject but War that is that He would not or could not from some cause or motive, {& Here let me say that a few years ago, I was speaking to a Personal Friend of Father Hamilton but did not Know it at the time & He told Me the Cause of Father Hamiltons Silence to us of War Matters} speak to them of the Positions of our armies or the Rebels. On that Subject, He was silent but on all others, He would Freely talk to them.

This is the first time I spoke to Him & as He appeared So Kind, I determined to try & obtain From Him some information of matter outside for Rumours were wild in Regard to the movements of our troops under Billy Sherman, But we could not rely on any thing we Heard So I asked Father Hamilton several Questions, some He would not answer & all I Could obtain was that Sherman Had Cut Loose from all Communication & was on His march to the sea in what direction, He could not tell me & also that our troop Cavalry Had made an attempt to Reach us but Failed. I also Learned the Cause of our non Exchange. Now I will return to where I left of[f].

Bill Helped me out so I could Sit & Look across towards the south Gate & I See a Solid mas[s] of Human creatures Crowded, Jammed together near the Gate & Looming up over or above their Heads, I see timbers, one long Beam Extending East & West & Hanging from that Beam 6 Ropes with a noose on Each one & under these Six Ropes, a Frame with what lookes Like a single Plank running the same Len[g]th of the Beam above. I soon see a Commotion amongst the Crowd & between the scaffold & Gate, the crowd opens & I then see ascending the Scaffold from the West End of it, the End next the Gate, those Six men, one after another. The[y] Range along Each one of them standing directly under a Rope & amongst them six appears to be one young Boy Beardless & Looks out of Place there Amongst those murderers. They seem to take things very Easy & do not appear at all uneasy as though it was Fun or that the men was not going to Execute them only doing it to scare them. That is the way the[y] appear to me.

They are on High Ground & so am I with the Swamp between us & about 15 Rods distant soon a man goes along Pulling a white Sack over their Heads. It looks like a Pillow Case or Small Flour Sack then the Noose is adjusted around their necks. The Plank they are standing on is Pushed from under their Feet & the Six men drop Kicking, Strug[g]ling but look, look, the one, a Heavy man[14] on the East End of that Gallows, see His Rope Has Broke & He falls to the Ground but is Quickly on His feet Looks Wildly around Him as though He does not understands where He is & How He came there. He looks Bewildered, scared at the crowd then Looks up & sees His Companions Hanging, Kicking & He springs wildly away from them with a Peice of the Broken Rope yet around His neck.

He throws out His Arms & Brushes the Crowd out of His way, making a lane For Himself through that Human mass as Easily apparently as a Machine would mow down Grass. For the Poor weak fellows Falls on Either Side of Him & Rushes in my direction. The Rope Broke & the man away before an man seemed to Realise what Happened but now Hear the Roar that goes up as the[y] Realise it & then after Him comes the men, who Had charge of Hanging them. They are the same or a Part of the same Body of men, who Had Tried & Condemned them & they were the men, who Captured them & Broke up the Gang of theives & we were then organized as a Body of Police to Protect us from our own men, Keepe order in the Stockade & Punish offenders.

Those men are now after the Run away & let us follow Him with our Eye. See Him dash through those Poor Skeletons of men, Brushing them away from Him right & Left as some of the Poor Creatures Forgetting their Physical Weakness attempt with their Child Stren[g]th & Long Boney Skinney Arms to stop that mad man in His Wild race. Ha,

He is down, gone, Disap[p]eared. Yes, He Has stepped on one of those dug outs & gone through it but He is out & makes a few Wild Jump. He is now Just across the swamp from me & Close to the Edge of it but down He goes again through a Dug out & as He crawls out from it, a Dozen men Jump on Him & Leads Him back.

He is Begging to be Let go & when He got to the scaffold, He sees His now Dead Companions in Crime Hanging there, Knows then it was no Fun done to scare them but a Dead Reality & Knows now what His own Fate is by seeing theirs & He again makes an attempt to Escape but He is now amongst Men, who He cannot Brush aside & they Quickly satisfy Him of it by Forcibly taking Him to His own End of the Gallows & Hanging Him, this time sure Enough. I take one look at the Six Bodys & tell Bill to Help me Back.

Poor Bill it is all you can do to Help yourself with what little stren[g]th you Have but Like a true comrade, you are willing to try & Help those who are unable to Help them selves & I got back to my shelter. I did not Know the day of the month then but a comrade who was there & in the Party who Hung them tells me it was the 11th of July & now I must go Back as we are at the 11th of July.

We must go Back to the morning of the Fourth. At Sunrise that Morning I Heard a Great cheering amongst the men. Bill was up & I asked Him what was up. He Hurried in Back & told me Hurry out & see the sight. He Helped me get out as Quick as I could & He Pointed down towards the swamp in a south east direction & said right there where those men are, a man Raised the stars & stripes Just as the sun got up[15] & that is what made the men cheer. I could not see the Glorious old Flag for the man Hid it as soon as He waved it & I Looked towards the Rebel Batteries & saw the troops all under arms with the Rebel Gunners standing Ready. The crowds, the cheering Had Brought out, Quickly dispersed for we Knew at any moment they were Liable to fire.

That day we got no Rations. Wirtz said He would not Issue any feed to us untill that man & Flag was Given up to Him. The next day, no Rations & He got no Flag. The next day, no Rations nor He a Flag. The mortality in those three days was so great on account of our Fo[r]ced Fast & the men seemed Determined to die sooner than give up or tell of the man who Had the Flag that Wirtz on the Fourth day Had Rations Issued to us. This is the Flag I mentioned that I Heard a Plymouth man

Brought in with Him & if I think of it, I will once again Have to mention it & now we will again Resume from the 11th.

Time Passed with me in this Kind of a Half Dream, Half wakefull Condition. Time passed I Know not How but I suppose things were going on in the stockade as usual. You may Remember some time Back I intimated that when my thought would Revert to Home & I Knowing the Effects those Thought would Have on me, if I Indulged in Them, I said I would get up & walk around & Find something to distract my Mind From Thoughts of Home & if I Found nothing more Amusing, I would Kick some of those Fellows I Found Sitting down Indulging In those sweet Thoughts of Home & which I wished to Banish from my mind. If I could not Banish those Thoughts from My Mind by Banishing those Poor Fellows From their sitting Positions, I would then walk around & soon Find some other Poor Fellow that From His appearance I Thought I Could Lick & Raise a Row with Him & Generally one or two of those Rows were sufficient to drive Thoughts of Home from My Mind.

Now Raising a Row For the Fun of the thing did not Pay always & was a Luxury I could not often Indulge in & only did when Nesesity compelled me but you of Course always understand those rows of mine for that Purpose were allway Raised with some fellow Weaker or looked weaker than I was & I will say Confidentially that I some times I got Fooled in the appearance of them but no matter, it Had the Effect I desired & that Satisfied me.

But now as I Lay there unable to get up & with nothing to distract my Mind from any thoughts I want to give way to but those Back Biting & Bosom Friends, I want to think of Home but Cannot make up my Mind if I Ever Had a Home. I will give you my thoughts as I Laid there. Have I Ever Had a Home or any other Home than this? Have I allways Lived Here, Raised Here & in this way, yes, I think I must Have been there always For I cannot Remember any other Home distinctly Enough to be Certain of it so it must be so. But what is that I Imagine I see or Imagine I see, it must Have been ages & ages ago since I Cannot Remember distinctly what Happened then. It seems as though I am looking through a Mist or Fog, I can see nothing Plain. Can Remember nothing distin[c]tly of it but like a Dream to me, I Imagine that Long — Long ages ago, I Had some other Home but where it was or who were in it. I cannot Remember I Cannot place them, not a single Person of my Family not a single Individual or incident of my Former Life Can I Remember or Place So I must Have always lived Here Raised Here but if so when I Came or How long since I have no Memory of. Nothing is distinct but the Present & that only at times & then I only Remember William <u>Best</u>, May He Rest in Peace.

My Friends, these are my thoughts as I Laid there during the month of July 1864 & a Part of the two following months, August & September. I say they are my Thoughts but Can you Imagine My Mind & Feeling during this time or what my actual Condition of mind was. No, you Cannot for I do not Know Myself but let me Bring a Part of my Mind Home to yourself Individually & you may then more Readily Comprehend my state of mind if not my Physical Condition. Dreams or the Mind when the Body is Resting in Sleep Imagines a great many thing absurd or otherwise and all Human beings are subject to those Flights of Imagination while asleep & are Called Dreams. Now suppose, you Had Dreamt of something Pleasant & woke up. Every thing, the Slightest incident of that dreams, on you waking is as Plain to your mind as if you were actually Looking at or going through it. Yes, it is Plain & Pleasant but you again go to sleep with those Pleasant thought & wake up, your Dream was so good that you Desire to tell your Friends of what a good dream you Had but in Trying to Recol[l]ect it, you cannot Remember the First thing of it the first incident of it. You Know you Had that Pleasant dream & that it is Floating as it were in your memory. You can yet see with your minds Eye those things as though through a mist or Fog but you Cannot Place them, Cannot Remember them distinct Enough to give them a name or Describe them. Such my Friends was the Condition of my mind when I would try to think of Home, I would Imagine that at some time or other I used to Live diffirent, have diffirent Food & my surrounding were diffirent but where, oh, where, I could not Remember.

I Have Lain Hours & days thinking such thoughts but could never During this Period solve that Problem. Was I or was I not Born & Raised in Andersonville, Georgia? No, I Could not Solve it So Concluded I was a Child of that Place. The next I Remember I was Sitting up & two young men we[re] standing by me, one of them said is that you, <u>Ed</u> & looking up I saw Harry P. Weir,[16] now living at Weir City, Cherokee County,

Kansas—& Harry introduced [his] young Friend, Richard Thacher,[17] now living in Neodasha, Wilson Co., Kansas.

I asked Harry when He was Captured & when He Came in to the Prison. He said He was Captured on the 22nd of July, the day Genl McPherson[18] was Killed near Atlanta. He Had been about 3 or 4 days on the Road Coming So it was now the last of July. I asked Harry if He Came from our old Regiment For He had Belonged to Co. B of the 42nd. He said He was Captured from the 111th Ills Infantry,[19] that He Had been Transfered from our Regiment to it & that His Friend, Dick, was Captured the same time. He was & Belonged to the same Regiment with Him. So Harry Brought me no news of my Gallant old 42nd Harry, at that time, was about 19 or 20 years old & Dick was a year or two younger & I Had never seen Dick untill that day & they Had got in to the Stockade the day before.

Richard Thatcher's Civil War enlistment portrait at the age of 15, 1861 (courtesy University of Central Oklahoma Archives/Special Collections).

Harry was pleased to see me as He found Some one in that Hole, who He Knew, but was sorry for My Condition. They asked for information about our Feed & Treatment & I gave them all the information I Could & after talking some time, Harry asked me if I would not like some Yankee Coffee. I told Him, yes, but did not Know How to get it. He said He Had a little. They took my Cup & soon Returned with some Coffee to me & it did taste good indeed & For about two weeks, Either one or Both of them would come daily to me with a warm drink of Coffee & often through Each day would Come & Rouse me out of my Half Dead & alive Condition & talk to me For after I was Helped to a sitting Position I would be sensitive Enough but as soon as I Laid down, all was Blank Except those Dream thoughts. I Remember nothing only when Sitting up.

One day Dick Came alone as He sometimes did with my Coffee & I Remember Noticing some thing the Matter with Him like those new desponding Prisoners I mentioned before so I asked Him & Found it was so. He was getting to give up. The sight of so Much Human Misery Was too much for His young Mind & He was giving way to it. I gave Him the old Recipe, told Him to Knock around & Not to let His mind dwell on Home & when He Felt that way to go & steal something so as to get Punished as A Theif. The Punishment was Flogging by our Prison <u>Police</u>, if a man was caught stealing or For Him to Knock some Fellow down to do anything so as to get His mind of[f] Home thoughts for they would Kill Him Quicker than the Prison treatment would & that if He loved Life sufficient to Ever Hope to get Home to take my advice. You Have Seen the Fruits in Prison of desponding men Death. Now let me show you the Fruits of taking my advice there & I will give it from the mans own Lips.

On the 22nd of April 1889, the day Oklahoma was opened,[20] Harry P. Weir & I was at Richard Thacher's Home in Neodasha.[21] I was there to get His affidavit & Harry Came with me, & during our Conversation, Dick made the Remark that to the advice He got From some one in Andersonville, He might Thank for His Living to Come out of it. Mrs. Thacher, Dicks wife, was Present & She said, yes, Dick often spoke of that man & the advice He gave Dick but Could never Remember the man or the Circumstances under which He received it. I asked if He Remember the advice & He repeated it & said at the time it sounded strange advice but He Followed it. [Th]at it Came From an old Prisoner & He Had at the time Confidence in the man giving it but to save His Life.

He could not Remember who or what the man was & often wished He Could as He thought that man by that advice Had saved His Life. I will Remembered the Circumstance For to that & others like it, I owed my Life. So I asked Dick to let all thoughts out of His mind of His Present surroundings & in Imagination return to Andersonville & Remember the first day He Had Entered the Prison. He thought for a short time & I asked Him if He could place Himself where He used to sleep.

He said yes. I then asked Him if He Remembered the next morning after He arrived of Him & Harry Meeting or seeing an old Comrade of Harry's & Making Coffee & Bringing it to Him Some times bothe of them & Some times Himself alone, speaking of Some Circumstances that He Remembered & so let Him to the Morning I gave Him that advice & it all Came to His mind for the time Being as plain as the time it occurred & the tears Came to His Eyes as the Picture of that morning in August 1864 Came to His mind but Enough that He as Fully appreaciated it as I did His Kindness & the Kindness of Harry to me when I needed it & never — never shall I or Can I forget them, but to Return the Kindness of those two were making me feel much stronger & I asked Harry one morning where they got their Supply of Coffee For they were now about two or three weeks & Still Coffee every day.

Harry said when they were Captured, Dick Had about a Handfull of Coffee unground in His Haversack & that they Had seen me before they Had used it so that in Order to make me a drink, they Cracked 2 or 3 grains Each day to make Coffee for me but that now it was nearly all gone. 2 or three grains I said of Yankee Coffee would not make all the Coffee the[y] B[r]ought to me. The[y] said no that one of them I do not Remember which Had traded Either a Gold <u>Pen</u> or Knife for some molasses & the[y] Brownd or Burnt some of their meal, adding a little molasses to the Burnt meal & making Coffee of that, added the two grains to it to Flavor it for me & after the Coffee was all gone, they still continued Making Meal Coffee for me while they Remained in Prison.

This incident, My Friends, I am Proud to Have & give it in my Prison Experience as it will show you the Better side of Humanity in that Hell Hole, which drew out all the Baser & very Few of the Better Sides of Human Nature. Those two Friends still Continued to wait on and assist me all the[y] Could. They were more Like Brothers to me than strangers. Brothers, I may safely say, very Few Brothers would in that place Had done For Each other as Both of those Noble Boys done for me & Entire stranger to one of them — & the other only, a Regimental Comrade. When Every grain of that Coffee was worth its weight in Gold, yes, I Have no doubt there was men there who would give any price for a Single Grain of that Coffee to Have it to think that Before they died, they Had once again tasted Coffee from Gods Country & those Boys denied themselves Even the taste of it, drinking the Corn Feed Coffee & giving the other to me.

The next, I Remember, it is after dark & sometime in the night, I am woke up & Harry & Dick are standing over me telling me to Rouse up & come with them. I ask where to & they say to our lines that all of

Shermans men are going out. There is a Special Exchange for them & For me to Brace up & go with them. Shermans men, as we called them, Had only been in Prison about two months or over & were supposed to be fit to go along without Help to walk Straight & were not supposes to be all Doubled up Like a Jack Knife with scurvey & scurvey sores all over their Body as I was but my Friends, you do not Know of Course the Improvement time Has Made on me since my last Description of myself so I will now tell you what my Condition was on that night that Harry & Dick Came to me.

Both my legs were drawn up very near in the Position a mans Legs would be when sitting on a chair but my Left Leg was the worst. On Each Hip was a Calloust Patch nearly the Sise of my open Hand & on the outside of My Knees where that part of me touched the Ground was a Calloust Patch, my legs were Both Covered with Scurvey Sores & I Had one on the Back of my neck But my Body so far as I Can Remember was free from that Disease that is the outside on account of the Position of my legs & Bodily weakness, I could not Stand up without a man under Each arm & then Could not walk, so I told Harry & Dick that as I was in that Condition, it was impossible for me to go with them much as I wished to but they said the[y] would Each take an arm & carry me.

I told them if they were caught taking me out, they would be Kept Back & not get out at all, besides being Punished but they said they would take their chances that they wanted to take me with them & did not want to go without me. I Refused to go on account of the Risk they would Run in assisting me but Had I been able to stand alone & walk from the Dead Line to the Gate, a distance of 14 or 16 Feet, I would Have Risked it for then if Caught, I alone would Have to bear the consequences of Flanking out, as we Called it. But to Have them two Boys take the Risk of assisting me in the Condition I was in. No, A Thousand times rather death For Even if I got out, the chances as I then thought Even if I did get out would be death in a short time any way & I might as well die there than Have them Loose their chance of Liberty, For as yet they were Both all right & able to get along so. They Reluctantly bid me good by & that was the last I saw of them untill as I Have said in April 1889.

Now to give you an Idea of Flanking out, Shermans men being So short a time in Prison were all supp[o]sed to be yet able to walk & if I Had taken advantage of their Kindness & gone to the Gate with them &

waited there untill some mans name was Called & the man Failing to answer, I would answer for Him as though I was the man when I would be supposed to step Quickly Forward when I answered Here—& walk out. If I could Have done that the chances would be about Equal that I would Pass the inspection of the officers in Charge & get through.

But Supposing I am there, Harry & Dick Holding me up & I Answer Some other mans name & Harry & Dick starts Forward with me, the very first step they make the Guard stops them telling them go Back, their names were not called. They would be oblidged to Leave me when down I would Have to drop unable to Help Myself & More than Probable the Real owner of the Name I answered for would step up sayeng that was my name when I would be caught as well as Harry & Dick or again Suppose that Either or Both their names was called before I got a chance. They would then be Compelled to Leave me or loose their chance For when a mans name was called He Had to answer Here Quick & move out or some other Fellow would answer for Him & go out & His chance would be gone with Him. If their names were called, you see they Had to go or lose their chance & if they remained with me, they would not be allowed out with, so that there was no Possible chance for me in my Present Condition & if they were Caught, they at least Had a Certainty of Entirely losing their opportunity of getting Home with a good Prospect of 36 Hours in the stocks as Punishment, where all the[y] could do to me was to Put me in the stocks.

I Knew all this but they did not Realise it or if they did in their zeal to take me with them, overlooked it. In all this time, I Have not mentioned Bill. His Condition was growing worse but still able occasionally to get up & go around a little. There was only one of His Legs dowlled up & He managed to get a Hold of a Couple of Sticks, which He used as Crutches. The next I Remember about dusk or Early in the Evening, a man Came to me. I did not Know the man but that He was a Country man & Belonged to a New York Regiment but I Knew where He slept about two Detachments north of me, but He Came & asked me if He Could not Come with His Friends in the Morning & Carry me out. I told him, yes, if He got there before any other Fellows got me. He said He would be on Hand Early & I told Him all right.

Now this is about the first time I Remember giving a thought about Dieng & that is How I was Reminded of my <u>Neglect</u> So I Laid there &

the last thought I Had before I went to Sleep was that I Had to die that night as the men were Coming Early in the Morning to Carry me out, So therefore I must be dead when the[y] Came. I woke up Some time during the night & my first thought was that I was Dead & after waiting & listening to Hear of some thing new so I would be Sure. No, Everything was dark & I felt around & Hello, that Bill. Is He dead too? I next Felt of the Ground & was satisfied I was not yet Dead For I Remembered where I was. I did not wake Bill but I thought of 9 Rations of Beef that was there under my Head for safe Keeping.

My Mouth Had been too Bad or I Had been too Sick to Eat or swallow the Beef so Bill, I Remembered, Had dried or Jerked it & put it under my [head] for me & I now Remembered it & that as I Had to Die that night, I might as well take that Nine Rations of Beef with me, as leave it for some other Fellow for I Knew Bills mouth & System was worse than mine. His trouble was all interiorly but How was I to get out side of that Hard Dried Skipping Beef. No, it was not Slippery. If it was, I would have Had no trouble whatever but no matter How Hard it was, it Had to go with me in to the next world & I would Have the Satisfaction of at least Having one good Feast of Beef Before I died.

In the dark, I Pulled that Beef out from under my Head Regardless of How it look. Looked, I Could not see it if I did look but might well Imagine & so may you its Condition Coming from where it did. I Can Remember tryeng to Hold it in my mouth to soften it so I Could swallow it but I was always good on the Hang on & I Hung on to them Nine Peices of Beef, Soaking them in my mouth & then letting them get inside the Best or Easiest way the[y] could untill all were gone & I felt Better Satisfied now that I was taking that Beef with me but How I swallowed it or it got inside of me is more than I Could or Can tell for I went to Sleep & my last thoughts were those fellows would Have to carry that Beef out with me in the Morning but Just about Break of Day, I woke up & Hello, I am not Dead yet is my First thought & my next is about that Beef, wondering it Had not Killed me any How but no, I feel Better & stronger & I Know for several days I Have Lain Unable to move but now I Can move my Body around & I try to Sit up.

Yes, Hurrah, I am able to again sit up myself Without Help & as there is no limit to some mens Ambition, I try to straighten up but Hello, My Legs is not Built that way. If they were I think I could stand up. Well,

I Reach over & take Bills sticks or crutches & Placing them, I wiggled, mind out, Giggled up as near Straight as I could Get & I Suppose as I stood there Drawn up to my Full Height that I Stood the Lofty Magnificent Height of Full Three Feet.

But Remember, this is the first time in nearly three months that I Have been up & during this time, I Have been down Pretty Low so that I think three feet, the first Raise is pretty good & now I feel Better, Stronger than I Have for some time but where are those fellows that were coming to carry me out. I am all Ready & if the[y] come now while I am up, I Can Help them so that I will not be a Dead Weight altogether to them but Here whats the matter with me going down to them as they wont Come for me. It is not very far & if I do Fall, it wont be long untill some of the Fellows will find me or untill Bill misses me so Here goes & I trudge along some How & get down to where those Four men are sleeping. They also are under a covering & their Feet is towards me so I Pick the Fellow out that Had asked for the Honor of Carrying me out & Hit Him on the Feet to wake Him.

It was not yet clear daylight & the Fellow sleeping Half opened His Eyes Sayeng get out, what do you want? I said I came down to be Carried out as He agreed to Carry me out that morning & as He Had not Come for me, I Came to Him. When I Commenced Speaking, He Commenced opening His Eyes & when I got through, He Fully Recognized me & His Promise but instead of Him Fulfilling His Promise, He Jumped up on His Feet & Roared out, Hes, Come, Hes, Come. That woke His three Comrades & when they saw me standing there, they all yelled out & all Four of them Skipped, Leaving me to Explain to the Crowd which there yelling Had awakened.

What the matter was I Humped Back & Bill was not yet awake but I Woke Him & when He saw me, He said Hello, Ed. Not Dead yet? I told Him no that I Had Just Returned from a Walk & told Him where I Had been & its consequences. I told Him what I Had Eaten & He said it was a wonder it did not Kill me but He said you will Pull through & get Home & Poor Bill, always stuck to it that I would get out alive.

In a short time, my Friends, the Carriers Came down & seeing me Sitting up asked if I was not Dead. I told them I thought not & they said it was a Blamed Shame to Fool them that way. That they Had Contracted for wood the day before depending on me to Help them out & now I might go to the [hell] & they walked away mad. I did not see what they got mad at Except it was that I woke them up before their usual time.

I now Had spells of Feeling Pretty well. Bill gave me His crutches so I Could Hump around when I was able or wanted to & He got a Stick somewhere that He managed to get around with. He Had now got acquainted with the men or one of the men, who Issued Rations or Shovelled them from the wagon & would some times got a Half or whole Loaf of Corn Bread from them & with that addition, we Managed to Hold our own Pretty well. Some times we would both be unable to move & then some one would draw our Rations & Fix them for us. How I do not Know For I Have no memory of my surroundings from the time I was taken down.

I now Hear that they are moving the Prisoners out to other Prisons & that there was a special Exchange for the Fort Sumpter Sailors. They are now gone but I Heard that when the[y] got Orders to go, they Refused to [allow] a man to move a foot towards our Lines untill Every man then Living should be taken along. The Cause of that was that there was some of their Comrades Sick in the Hospital & the Rebels did not want to Bother with them but the sailors Refused to go without them & said they would Carry them all the way sooner than leave a man of theirs Behind them or they would stay & Die with them, Brave Gallant Tars.[22] Glory in your Manhood, you won the day & got your Comrades out of their Hands & I Hope you all got safe through.

The Rebs were moving the Prisoners almost daily to some other Places of Safety as the Rumour was Sherman was on His way towards or in our direction So the Rebs were thinning out as Fast as they Could find Rail Road transportation for them, Running some to Charleston, South Carolina & some to Salisbury, North Carolina & some to other Prisons Further south. Now my Friends, I Stated that I Had no dates only such as My Memory Furnished & also that in this, my Experience of Prison Life, I should State Facts but that they would be given regardless to the time of their occurrence.

So Speaking of Rumour Reminds me of two or three weeks of Exciting Sleepless days & nights we Put in there in Andersonville on that Same old Dame Rumours account. I think it was in June or the Fore Part of July we were then Certain that Sherman Had Started on His Famous March to the sea but we Heard that He Had Detached a Large Body of troops to

Come & Liberate us & about that time the Brigade of old Rebel troops, who Had been Guarding us, were taken away & I Heard sent to Atlanta & in their Place as our Guards, we got a lot of old Grey Headed men, that was too old for active service in the Front & young Beardless Boys. Children would be a more Proper name for them for in years the[y] Ranged from 12 to 15 years old while the old mens age Ranged from 65 up & you may Imagine what the chorus would be when they would Call the Hour at night, the old mans Quivering voice & the Boyish Piping voice in answer.

About this time also, that is when those old & young Guards were Placed over us, Wirtz Issued His Infamous Order of thirty day a <u>Furlough</u> to Every Guard to go Home & see their Friends For Every Yankee Prisoner they shot & now indeed it was not safe for one of us at any time to be near the dead line For those Grey Headed Hell Hounds & the little Imps, their Companions, would Shoot at the Least Provocation & some times without any Provocation what Ever for the sake of the 30 day Furlough & to go Home & see their Friends & tell them of the Hated Yank they Had Killed or Maimed in Order to Have the Pleasure of Coming Home to see them.

Yes, I have stood & watched them when they wanted to shoot, draw their Guns to their shoulders, Fire & then Quickly dodge down Behind the three or Four Feet of Stockade they were resting against & soon the Releif would Come & place another man or Boy in His place & take Him away & that Fiend, young or old, would get His thirty day Furlough & away that was His Reward of Merit For His Inhuman act & at this time, June or July, there was Fully Thirty Five Thousand men in the Stockade, three Thousand men to the acre to Eat, Sleep & Exercise on. Every available Foot of ground was taken up.

The little alleys or walks between the Detachments were occupied day & night & a Person Could walk Blind folded over Every Spot that A man Could Lay on at night & never touch the ground with their foot & I will Prove it For before I got So Blind at night, I Had occasion to go & see a Friend I was in some little of a Hurry & now let me show you my Progress.

The first step out from my shelter, my Foot Encontered a Body of a man & He grunted or said something, its all the same. No matter, I Knew He was not Dead So I Stooped & Felt along past His Body untill my Hand touched another Body I felt Between them lifted my foot Carefully & Pressed it down sidways between them untill it rested on the Ground. If the men were awake, I told them to Lie still but if the[y] were asleep, I was Carefull no[t] to wake them for I was not sure of any mans temper, stepping on Him when asleep. They were Short Enough in temper when awake in that way & Back I Had to Pick my way & when I started, I was in a Hurry too to see my Friend, a Kind of a Sick Call you Know, but that settled my night walking. I give this incident that you may Have a Better Idea of our Crowded Condition.

3 thousand men to the acre in them Hot months that does not of Course include the swamp, although the[y] Had to Sleep there as close to it as a man Could get & Keep out of it. Imagine if you Can, the Sanitary Condition of that Hole at that time & during this time, there was a notice. Bill saw it & told me that at the South Gate, there was a notice that any man who wanted to Could Enlist in the Confederate Service. Sell our Country & Become a Rebel. Well, He got a few but very Few & such men as He got were Better from amongst us, they could not stand the Pressure & gave up their manhood their Principal, if they Ever Had any, their Country & Perjured themselves. For what? For a Peice of Corn Bread & Bacon, for that was all they could get as a Rebel Soldier.

I must now also speak of Tunnelling. I Have not mentioned any incident of it & Andersonville would not be Complete without it for at one time, we Had Great Hope we Could Liberate ourselves by its means. After the Prison Became a little crowded, the Rebels Furnished a very few Long Handled [—] Shovels for us to dig wells & the wells the[y] dug were intentionally Generally dug near the Dead Line. There was Quite a number of them dug when the[y] commenced using them as a starting Point for a tunnel, the object being the nearer the Dead line the shorter the distance to tunnell. The[y] would aim to tunnell Below the timbers or about Eight Feet Beneath the surface & Continue on outside the Stockade 50 or 60 Feet. That would about clear the open clearing outside & Bring them up in or about the Edge of the timber.

The usual sides taken for tunnelling were the North, South & East Sides. The west Side is towards the Rail Road Station & Rebel Camp. Very few of those smaller tunnells were Continued to a Finish for some Traitor would Report them for the Reward of a loaf of Bread & Parole & it was Customary for Wirtz to come in & go around the dead Line with a lot of Darkeys with long Iron Rods & go about where he Expected to find the Tunnell & then Have the men drive those Rods Here & there in the soft sand untill they Found the tunnell then the[y] would dig down & Cave it in. He was usually Accompanyed by some Guard but all ways Remained inside the dead Line & with I Beleive two Exceptions, I never Saw Him amongst us otherwise than in the dead Line but what I more Particularly wish to state is the Preperations that was made for a General Breakout of the whole Prison.

I do not Remember the Exact time but it was before I got Entirely down in my Half Sleepy Condition & during the time of the two or three weeks of our Excitement but I will give it as I Heard it for at the time, I was unable to go around. I Heard that all the men in Andersonville, who were able to make a dash & on a way out for themselves & those unable to do so, Had Formed themselves in to Companys & Battallions all under the Command of one Major, who was in Prison with us & Several Captains & Lieut[enant]s. Those officers, when Captured, Had Removed from their Persons all the Insignia of their Rank as Commissioned officers & allowed themselves to be Captured as Enlisted men, thinking to be Paroled or Exchanged Sooner as Such than they would be as officers so that they were Known to but very Few in their true Rank.

The Rebel Authorities Knew they were there & Had made several attempts to find them out & Remove them for they, the officers, were more valuable to them than Enlisted men. A Major in Exchange Value was Equevalent to about 18 or 20 men & the other officers in Less Proportion,[23] so you can see the motive the Rebs Had to find them out & Remove them. Well, I Heard the men were organized under those officers & Each Company or Batalion Had its alotted duty to Perform but first to Prepare the way.

They Had Dug Four Large Tunnells on the Four diffirent sides of the stockade then tunnelled along the stockade for some distance & the day came that they w[e]re to make the attempt. That same night, it was Generally Known & all was Excitement that before a nother morning, we might be Roaming freely through the woods trying to Reach our own Lines then about 150 miles from us but we also Knew if the attempt was successfull, Lots would lost their Lives in the attempt For the Rebel Brigade Had to be charged & their arms taken From them. The two Rebel Batterys Had to be charged, captured & spiked. Without all this First being done by the First Rush out of those organized companys, it would be a useless risk of Life for those Poor Fellows Coming Slowley alon[g] after them unable from Hunger starvation & sickness to take Part in the First Rush & the object was to Leave a Free Passage for some Hours, at

Least for all those able to walk or untill the Rebs could get Fresh Troops from some other Point there to Follow & Recapture us & during this time, I Knew thousands of those men would go through safe while other Thousands would die in the woods From starvation & over Exertion.

Oh, to see the nervous Excitement of Little groups who were unable to be in the First Rush, Gathering together Planning How they would stick together & if the[y] could only get a Rebel musket & some Amunition, they would be all right & go through or die together. Others again would be planning the Route the[y] would take & How they would surprise their Friends North when they walked into them all in Rags as they then were & their Friends would not Know them. What a surprise it would be. Oh My Friends, the Hopes & asperations that agitated those Living Skeletons that Forenoon & How few today Living of them & now for the plan of Escape from some Paroled Prisoner.

Our men Knew that at 10 oclock that night, there was Expected to be a Heavy Freight train due at the station a Half a Mile away & the object was to capture that train when it came in, Load it with all the men the[y] could get on it & that were not able to Hurry through the Country, run that train as near as the[y] Could to our Lines then destroy it & take chances through the Country. But to Capture that train, the[y] Had to be out of the Stockade at a Preconcerted signal to be made after dark giving time to accomplish their object of Escape & get to the station before that train was due at the Signal.

The Rush was to be made at the Parts of the stockade undermined. Push strongly against those timbers, which with the Earth weakened around them & the Pressure of the men against them, the timbers were to be thrown down & Four outlets made to Freedom & Gods Country then as the Gaps were made away was to dash the Companys to their assigned Duties, some to attack the Infantry on Each side the Branch, others attack the artillery & others dash for the station & be ready to Capture the train & again others dash for the officers Quarters. The main thing was the Infantry & artillery & to get arms in our Possession as soon as Possible for we Knew that during all this, the men would be Continually under the Rebel Fire & Hundreds lose their Life in the First Rush but we Had Thousands to lose if it was nessesary For the Liberation of the others.

You may Imagine the state of Agitation & Excitement we were in

147

when in the afternoon, Wirtz came with a lot of His Tunnell Finders & went to Each of the Exact Places, which Had been Tunnelled & caved them in. Some weak minded Traitor Had told Him & if He been Known, it would have been Death to Him from the Hands of His Comrades.

[As] I Have mentioned some of those Plymouth men even Brought in Revolvers. Well six of those men, who Had Revolvers agreed by Solemn Promises to dig a tunnell & if the[y] got out to Fight to the death Before they would be Recaptured. The night their Tunnell was Completed & Just before they were to Enter it to Escape, some one, I am not sure who but think it was Either Bill or <u>King</u>, told me of it & the certainty of Either Freedom or Death if we Could get out with them. I Hurried with the one who told me to the Little tent or Covering where the Entrance to the tunnell was. It was about 5 feet from the Dead Line at the East side of the stockade & when I got there, some of them were all Ready in the Tunnell working their way through. One of those Remaining told me to Follow Him as He was the last of the 6 to go & when I got out on the other side to go to a large Pine tree, which He showed me & there I would Find them Waiting. The understanding was that when a man Entered the tunnell the next man Following should give Him time to about get at the other End before He Entered.

The outlet opened about 60 feet outside the stockade & the tunnell inside was Just large Enough for a man to crawl on His Hands & Knees so that a man Entering it could not turn around but would Have to Back out if He could not go ahead & now it Came my turn, I was Halfway down Head First when I Heard Bang from the Rebel Guard nearest the Hole at the outlet & I Knew the men Escaping were discovered & waited. Soon the last man in the tunnell returned & said the Hole was Guarded that the Alarm Had been given & it was no use to attempt it.

The next morning Early I saw the three Rebel Horsemen in charge of the Pack of Hounds, Blood Hounds & one Bull dog Composed the Pack, Bring the dogs to the Hole. They soon took the scent & away East the[y] went Howling. Through the timber through the day I Heard that the last man out of the Hole in His Hurry to reach the tree appointed as a meeting place, He stepped in to a Pile of Dry Brush & the cracking of the Brush alarmed the Guard, who Fired His gun [at] the Prisoners.

When the Alarm was given Skipped out & Had about 8 or 9 Hours start of the Hounds. They could not Put the Hounds on their tracks at night For the Horsemen could not Follow them. The third day after the Escape one Horseman & three Hounds I Heard Came Back. The men were as good as their word & did Fight for Liberty, Killing or Crippling two men & 9 Hounds & the[y] Escaped or at Least I never Heard of them Being Retaken & Know they were not at that time.

I think it was in the latter part of July that there was an addition made to the Stockade on the north side of I Beleive Eight acres or making in all Including the swamp about twenty Four Acres this time that the new Part was opened. I was down but Remember Hearing the Boys Speak of it. I do not Remember Ever Seeing the new Part but once I think I saw it once from a distance & if I Remember right in one Corner of it or near the North West Corner was some Rough Looking sheds that was intended For Hospital Purposes but never use for that Purpose to my Knowledge.

I Remember Hearing of what they call the Providence spring[24] but never saw it For at the time it Broke out, I was unable to go around. Now, My Friends, I Cannot Say that I Have given one Hundreth Part of my Experience of Prison Life in the Stockade of Andersonville but I Have tried to Remember Sufficient of Each of the different scenes & incidents were an Hourly occurrence & I must only Leave it to your own Imagination what Kind of a Picture the Whole would Form & I will now Return to Bill & My Covering.

I Have mentioned that the Prisoners were shipped or Run out almost Daily to other Prisons & when I was able to get out from my Shelter & take a look around, I Could see that they were thinning out Fast & that now if I was able to walk or move around, I could do so without-[−] against another fellow. Yes, there [−] a plenty of Room but Bill & I could not make use of it. No, we were Both now all to Remain stationary or almost so for neither of us Could stand up. Bill more from Physical weakness Caused by Scurvey in His System & I, on account of the Doubled up Condition of my Legs more than weakness although I Believe I was a Kind of weak too or inclined that way. How we got our Rations of feed? I do not Remember or whether we got any at all. I only Remember Bill & I sitting there & Looking around the almost deserted Prison. It must be now near the first of October or there about when some men came in. Who they were I do not Know but think they were nurses from the Hospital & carried Bill & I out the South Gate and on to the Hospital & Being Placed under covering.[25]

THREE

October to June 1865

I do not Remember very distinct coming Here nor for Several Days after, only that it seemed to me some men Had Died near me or by my side. The next I Plainly Remember is that the nurse or some man told me My Partner wanted to see me. It appear Bill Had Retained His senses & Knew where I was For he Had sent for me. I then Found that I was Placed at one End of a Row of Raised Bunks Make of Rough Boards or Chunks all under a Fly or Canvas spread above but no Ends to it, both Ends were always open.

I was Laying at the South End of this Line of Bunks which Contained seven men & Bill was Laying at the North End so I got up & crept along to Him. I found Him Partly Raised or Sitting up. When He saw me Crawling along to him the Poor Fellows Eyes glistened & when I Came near Him, He asked me if I was able to sit by Him, as He wanted to talk to me. I told Him I was & I sat on the Edge of His Bunk. He seemed to look Pretty well & was Perfectly Rational.

Now Bill often talked with me of His Wife & two children & also of a Brother in Law of His Named John Gallagher, who was a Boss stevedore[1] in Chicago. He Had so often Described Gallagher that I could well Imagine Him, & also His Kind Wife & Loving children, one Boy & one Girl. Thought of His Wife & children Had often troubled Him & I Know He, Poor Fellow, Had often — Often thought of them, yes, much & many times oftener than He spoke of them [to] me. For He Knew what I thought of the Injurious Effects to us of often Thinking of Home & the loved ones there but He well Knew that He Had my Sympathy when He Spoke of them in a Rational manner — & a Friends Sympathy is sweet & consoling to a man in Distress. Distress, My God, were we ever out of it. While there, they address of Bills Family I never Knew or if I did & I

Expect He often told me, I forgot it. But my Friends, let me tell you How He Came to be in the Service & I think you will Feel for Him the same Sympathy that I did in this His Last Mortal Agony, For Bill is Dying.

Bill, before Joining the 88th, Held I Beleive some Position in His Brother in Laws Packing House, Parker's—& one Evening Him & some Friends were taking a social Glass after work & By some means, Bill always thought they fixed His drink For He never was a drinking man. While in that Condition, His Friends took Him to a Recruiting Rendezous. Bill Enlisted in the 88th Ills or Chicago Board of Trade Regiment. The next morning when He woke, He found Himself in Co. Quarters & asking How He Came there. He was told He Had Enlisted the night before & He told them if He Had Enlisted He would stick to it but He was not Prepared to leave His Family —& I Beleive that was what worried Him in Prison. His Family was not Provided For as He would wish them & He Had to Leave them that way.

I never Heard Him Regret Enlisting only that His Family was not Provided for. I will again speak of Bills Family after I get out of Prison & will now Return to Him. He again Mentioned them & when you get Back to Chicago, go & See My Wife & Little ones & give them these, they are all I Have to send them & He took of[f] His neck His scapulars & gave them to me to give His Wife with other Verbal Messages to Her & the children.

Andersonville Tombstone of William Best (photograph by Kevin Frye).

I told Him I would take His Scalpular & Messages to His Family if I lived to get out but that I Had no Hopes of Ever getting out. He said yes, you will get out & go Home. I saw Him droop & I placed my arms around Him, sat to His Back. He settled Heavily against me & Bill, my true Brave Friend & Comrade, Breathed His last Good By. My True, true Comrade, yes, Free in Every Sense of the word For He Had been Tried in the Deathly Furnace of Hunger Starvation & Misery & Disease & I Ever, Ever Found you, My true Friend, true Comrade, yes & more than true Brother, again Farewell & may you Rest in Peace From My Heart & Soul. I wish it to you & all True Comrades who Died there or Els[e]where For Love of Country & Love of Principle & Honor, Farewell.

Bills Death seemed to Have aroused me out of my Half Dead & alive Condition that I Had been so longin[g] & in mind at least, I again began to feel like my old self. Bill Died about the 10th of October, I tried to impress that day on My Memory & I now Had an object to Live For, yes, I was charged with a Message from the Dead to the living & in order to deliver it, I must live myself & with Bills Last Breath, He said I will Live to deliver it. From now on, My Mind is more clear & active But my Bodily infirmitys Keep me Pretty well confined to my Bunk & I felt if I Could get my Legs Straightened, I would be all Right & many, many Hours Have I Lain there stretching & straining my Legs to Force the cords to give way & let my Legs out to their Natural Len[g]th. Yes, it was on usual Pastime for Hour, days & weeks to Lay there on my Back & Stretch, Strain untill I thought I would Pull myself in two but after a Couple of weeks, my Right Leg began to give way to my Presevering & got a little Longer.

Oh, How ankiously Have I watched Each days or weeks improvement in it For I Began to think the[y] were so long in that Condition that they would get Set & Remain so & if I lived, I should Have to go through Life in that Deformed shape. So I would stretch & strain untill my Stren[g]th would Fail or I could endure the Pain no Longer & then wait, Rest & go at it again. So you may consider that my Pastime in the Rebel Hospital daily with a Gradual imperceptable Len[g]thening of my right Leg. But the Left one always Remained the same while there & I will now Return to my Surroundings For Realy it is not untill now that I am sensible of where I am.

So I ask the men around me How long I Have been there & some of them tells me about 10 or 12 days & that I seem to Have Brought Death with me for that since I Came, there Has several men Died from my side & from under the same Blanket or covering over me. Well that I cannot Help & I do not think that I Killed them so now to Resume our Bunk for it Extended the whole Len[g]th of the Covering of Canvass was Capable of Seven men sleeping on it & it was Raised about 2 1/2 feet above the Ground made of Rough Material & on it to sleep on & cover us was old Blankets & Peices of Blankets.

The whole Hospital covered Quite a space & a Portion of it such as I Can now see are Just the same as the tent I was in & in this part of the Hospital were the most Cases or Cases that never supposed to be Dangerous or Critical. The other men in My tent were all Confined to their Beds for the want of a Better name, I will call them Beds. It was the usual Prison Complaint with all or most of them scurvey & soon our Doctor Came alon[g] on His visit & when He saw me Sitting up, He Kindly asked How I Felt. I told Him I felt Pretty well or would, if I Could, get my legs straitened & told Him what I was doing to Stretch them. He said if I Could stand the Punishment, that it would in time Help me. I liked the looks of Him & His Kind way of speaking & spoke Freely to Him & told Him I wanted if Possible to get able to Knock around. He said He would do all He could to Help me then Looked at my neck, made out His Prescription & Passed on to the others.

After a while, we got our Rations & I got about a Half or three Quarters of a Pound of Corn Bread. It was well Baked & Eatable. The meal was not Bolted [boiled] but it Had none of the other Material such as we Had in our Bread Ration in Andersonville. It was Coarse Corn Meal Bread & we could Eat it, that is those men who were not too sick. I do not Remember for certain whether I got any Meat of any Kind while in Hospital or not but Rather think not For I beleive if I did I should Remember it that Ration of Bread Had to do me 24 Hours for Food was only Issued once a day.

Pretty soon the nurse came with my Medicine & for the first time in Prison, I am to taste the Southern Remidy For scurvey & almost all other Diseases our men Had. It was a Kind of a cure all & I Beleive it was the only Medicine they Had, for it was the only Medicine I Received while there & the only Medicine I saw any one Else Receive but then almost all the men Had the same Disease — scurvey. {But you ask what

was this Great Medicine, this Great Cure all? Tell us so we can use it if
we want it for it must be valuable.} Well you wont Have far to go for it
for Look at the medicine Here in my Hand with directions of How to
use it from the nurse. Put a few grains of it in your mouth then suck
them untill you get all the substance out of them but spit out, dont swallow any of it & Repeat the dose as often as you want to but that Medicine
Has to do you untill tomorrow.

Those are the directions the nurse gives me as He places in my Hand
this Splendid Scurvey Specific, this Great Cure all & look at it. You Know
it, it is almost at your very door Look & see there nice ~~shoe Mak~~ Sumac
Berrys[2]. Yes, thats the cure all, thats the Remedy For scurvey & all other
Diseases a Northern Prisoner Has Fallen Heir to, in those strong smelling
if not sweet scented Southern Hell Holes & By the By, let me now while
I think of it tell you what I Have often Heard the Boys in the stockade
say lots of times. That is that there was only a Paper Wall between Andersonville & Hell & I guess for Yankees the[y] came Pretty near it.

Well, I used my Medicine as Prescribed & some of the men near me
did not get any of it. They Either Had not Enough to go around or Else
those Poor fellows were too far gone to be Benefitted by that specific &
so Passed my first day. I Call it such as it is the first I Remember. The next
morning the Doctor came again & I asked Him if there was no other
Medicine than ~~Shoemake~~ Sumac & He said no, they Had no other & some
times Could not get Even that, so that they Considered themselves very
Fortunate when they Had it but said He would try & Keep me Supplied
if He could but was allowed only to give so much Each day to Each man
as it was often scarce. For my neck, He could do nothing, the[y] Had no
salve & my only chance was to get the scurvey out of my system. When
my neck would Heal, the other sores on me did not amount to much.

For this day we got a Biscuit, Flour Biscuit of Ordenary Sise instead
of Corn Bread. The doctor seemed very Pleasant & For a Rebel Army
Surgeon, was Quite Sociable with me & would often all through the time
I was there, treated me Kinder than I Could Expect & would often Bring
me in when He Could a Biscuit in His Pocket. Although He said it was
strictly against Orders to give the Prisoners anything but the Prescribed
Food & Medicine. Still He would also Bring me in a Handfull of Shoe-
make [Sumac] Berry & Beleive me, my Friends, I Fully & thankfully
appreciated His Kindness & good will to me.

We will now Have to Pass two or three weeks as I Have stated for untill this time is Passed I Have been Confined to my Bed or tent but now with the aid of my short crutches, I will Endeavor to move out so I place them under my arms & swing both Legs out in front of me. I Suppose I swung to[o] far for when I went to stand alone & draw the crutches up for another swing Forward, I fell Back Flat & I thought my Legs would snap in two. Gee Whiz, I Thought sure I was going to be tied in a Knot. I Laid still, I Had to untill the Pain was gone then I raised myself slowley & took shorter swings. It was still Painfull but it was neck or nothing & I moved along but soon Had to stop.

Still the next day I tried again & so Each day untill the cords were more Limber & did not Pain so much & I will now describe what is in My immediate Neighbourhood. All around on the side of the Hospital Grounds near me are Rows of tents or Flys Just the same as the one I am in with a good Wide space or street Between Eac[h] Row & all occupied Full of our Poor Fellows. I did not go far for I could not but a little East of me is the Rebel Guard so we must be near the East side of the Hospital & near me to the South is a little Brook. There I now go often 2 or 3 times a day to Bathe my neck & other sores. It Cooles them & I feel Better for it.

About this time My Bed Fellow (I do not Remember who He was) died & I Kept His Pants & Jacket. It was a cavalry Jacket, a trifle to[o] Large for me but then I might grow [in] to it. There was lots of Room in me For improvements & I wished to Provide winter clothing. I slipped them of[f] Him before the nurse came for we were not allowed to take any thing whatever from a Dead Comrade. What Ever He Had was the Perquesite of the Nurse. Those nurses were all our own men & Except when the[y] came with our Medicine or Rations or to Remove a dead man, I never Remember seeing ours in the tent at any other time but those mentioned. He was a New York man.

In my next Bed Fellow, I Had a Pen[n]sylvania man, I think His name was John Anderson[3] & Belonged to Either the 79th or 97th Pen[n]sylvania Infantry. I Remember His name for Reasons you will see a little Later. This man was very near Dead when the[y] Brought Him in From the Stockade which was close to us & north of us & yet Contained a Number of Prisoners men, who were unable to walk that Half mile to the Rail Road Station & to move them, they would all Require to be carried or Hauled so the Rebels Left them to feed the Hospital, from & according as the men died in the Hospital the[y] went or sent to the Stockade & Brought out the worst to take the Places of the Dead men Removed as the Capacity of the Hospital was Lim[i]ted & would Hold only about 15 Hundred.

The Mortality there must Have been Large & I Hear it was Anderson was unable to Eat His Ration when He would get it but would Sometimes a dozen times a day ask for some thing to Eat. If it was Corn Bread day, He would not touch it. His Disease was the same as <u>Bills</u> Had been but if it was Biscuit day, He would take a little nibb[l]e of it & that was all. If He could get that little Bit when He called for it, He was Satisfied but always it Had to be given to Him for He was unable to Lift or Help Him Self & I done what I could to Help Him.

I still Had my Quart Cup & wood was Here plentifull. There was no stockade, no fence but Just a close chain of Guards around us & the[y] never Hindered me from picking up what little Brush I wanted & could carry So I woul[d] make a fire, Burn some Corn crust, make Anderson Coffee. I always managed that when He wanted a drink to Have some of this Coffee for Him or if He wanted to Eat to Have a Peice of Biscuit for Him by me, saving my own Biscuit for Him & I would take His Corn Bread.

I do not Just Remember How long He Lived but think about 8 or 10 days any How I Know some times I used to Have a Terrible Longing for a Biscuit & was often tempted to Eat my own when I got it & Let Him go to the Dickens but when I would look at that Poor man La[y]ing there Helpless Expecting when He wanted a drink or a Nib[b]le of Bread, that I would Have it for Him. I could not Eat it & would think He cannot last much Longer & then you can Eat it so I would Put it away for Him & He never to My Knowledge asked for a drink or Crumb of Flour Breaded Biscuit but what I Had it for Him.

One day He asked me if I would Read some for Him out of His Prayer Book & I told Him, yes. He said to take it out of His Haversack under His Head. I done so & Read for Him Such Prayers as He wished untill He told me to stop. I asked if I might Keep the Prayer Book so as to Read again anytime He wanted & He said yes, Keep it. He Had not that day asked for Food & only very seldom for a drink & I thought He would soon go but at dark, He was yet Living & I did not think He would Live untill morning. The Biscuit was in His Haversack under His Head

& I wanted to Eat it but then He might come to Enough to ask for Something to Eat before morning & if I Eat it & He should ask for some, I would feel Bad so no, I would not touch it. I went to sleep & woke up my first thought is He Dead yet? I Reached my Hand under the Blanket. No, He is yet Living. I again went to sleep & again woke Felt of Him. He was yet alive. I think the Fourth time I woke, I put my Hand on His Breast. It felt Cold but I wanted to be sure so I Slipped my Hand under His Clothing & Placed it over His Heart. It was Still & cold & He was Dead Sure this time so I sat up, raised His Head & Pulled out His Haversack took out that Biscuit & Eat it. I also Found a small ink Bottle with a tight top to it. Such as we Had in the army, we could Carry them in our Pocket. I put the Bottle in my Pocket & went to sleep.

I Slept Late the next morning & was awake La[y]ing there with my dead Comrade when the nurse Came along Just before it was time for the doctor to Come. He asked me what time Anderson died? I told Him I thought about 11 Oclock. He then Reached under His Head & Pulled out the Haversack, put His Hand in & asked me where the Prayer Book & inkstand was. I told Him I Had the Prayer Book. Anderson gave it to me & the inkstand I took after He died. He said I must give them to Him or He would Report me. I told Him, no. He might Report me but I would Reep what I Had. He then Said He would take them from me but I told Him He Could not & if He attempted to that, I would Brain Him & I grasped my Crutch & Raised it. He Knew my Condition on account of my Legs but He also Knew that while I Had the use of my arm, it was not safe with that crutch in it so He took the Body about 9 or 10 Oclock & I Kept what I Had, the Prayer Book I Brought Home & gave it to my Sister Mary & that same day, I traded the ink Bottle to a Rebel Guard For some sweet Potatoes & they Helpe to check the scurvey on me.

That nurse was not a warm Friend of mine after that but I Considered that I was Better Entitled to them articles than He was For from the time Anderson was Brought in untill He Came to Carry Him away, He never Came near Him to see Him or give Him a drink but He must Have Known what He Had. No matter, He did not get them. Those sweet Potatoes Helped me greatly with my scurvey so that I was able to go Humpily, <u>Hump</u> along, pretty good. I thank you & I Began to Feel like they the Rebs were not treating Just Quit Right in not giving me more to Eat as I was getting Very Ambitious that way.

I Had Heard that it was very Hard for them to get any one to wash the Bandages for the Gangrene or wounded ward. The Reason was of the danger from taking the Gangrene for if the skin was Broke on the Hands, a Person would be taken with the Gangrene & that in our Condition was almost Certain & Lingering Death. The man who washed them, on account of this danger, the Rebels gave a Double Ration to & the next time the little doctor as I Called Him Came, I told Him I would wash the Bandages. He advised me to let that Job alone on account of the Risk but I told him I would take the Risk & was not afraid of taking the Gangrene. So He said He would get the Job for me & Have one of the nurses Bring them to me Each Morning & Come for them in the afternoons as I was not well able to walk.

The next Morning a Roll of those Bandages Came & I took them to the little stream I mentioned, unrol[l]ed them & Gee Whiz, what a sight. What a sweet Job to wash them Bandages in Cold water & without soap. I looked at my Hands to see if there was the least scratch on them. No, I could not see any but then there might be under the Coat of Solid Blanket that Covered them. But I thought if there was a scratch under neath it, I Could not see it & the Gangrene would Have Close work to find it so I Hunted up a Chip & scraped of[f] the Bandages the Best I could then Rinsed them out in the stream, Rung them out & the[y] were washed. I Brought them to my Tent & dried them & when dry, it would be very Hard to tell What was the original or Present Color of the cloth, but the doctor was Satisfied & said it was an Artistic Peice of Laundry work & I was Satisfied when I got my Extra Ration.

My Biscuit was now stopped as I was not a critical case although I might Personally Be a Hard <u>Case</u> & I Know Myself I was Hard Looking but with a very slim Case but my object now was to Enlarge that case of mine by stretching or Expanding it & the only way to do that was by Putting Plenty or all I Could get into my case & let it Expand, Grow, stretch & get Fat. My Friends, dried Apples would Have been Splendid for that Purpose but you Know the apple crop was not in yet so I used what was in Corn Meal.

The man that was given me to sleep with in Place of Anderson was a great Long Hoosier. His surname was Carter[4] & He Belonged to some Indiana Regt. I never Knew His Given name, nor His Company & number of His Regiment. He was naturally a Tall man & His present appearance as a Living Skeleton made Him look to me from my Low statue of three feet about 10 feet tall. He actually looked to me then as a ten foot Rail would now dressed up as He was but I found Him a good Comrade & as an Introduction to Him on His first Coming to share My Blankets, I asked Him How long He intended to live? He said that was a H[el]l of a Question to ask a fellow & asked what I wanted to Know For? I told Him I Just wanted to Know because if He Died any way soon, His Clothes would not Fit me. They were a little too Long in the Legs yet but if He intended to Live a short time untill I straightened out then His Pants. What are you driving at? I dont intend to Die Here & why do you ask? I told Him I was very glad to Hear Him talk that way but that if He was going to sleep with me, His chances were good to die soon as He would make the 7th or 8th one, who Had Died from under my Blankets. Oh, get out, He Said, I aint Dead yet although I am Blamed near it & He Looked like He was very near it sure, but He showed good grit & I liked the way He talked.

He was not Confined to the Bunk. His Legs, though Long, were sound & I made use of them by making arrangements with Him for Him to get wood, make the fire & Cook the Coffee & I was to Furnish the Provisions. He willingly agreed & I found Him true & cheerfull & He never left me untill we Parted in the North. Such was my daily Life.

The little Doctor was still as Kind to me as at the Beginning. His actions to me & others was about the same as the Major, who Had charge of us at Danville & I Beleive at Heart they were Both more Union than Confederate, but Nessesity or Circumstances Compelled them to Remain in the South & Be for the time Bein[g] a Rebel. Them two men I shall Ever Feel a Gratefull Remembrance of For their Kindness to us in our Direfull Nesesity.

About the first of November, some Rebel officer or Doctor Came through & told us that all the Irish, who were able to walk, to go out through the West Guards, that there was an officer there who wished to speak to us. That we would not be Guarded while out there & what none but Irishmen should go as none but them were wanted. I walked or Humped along as directed, got outside the Guard, who paid no attention to me.

I went on a short distance & in a little Clearing, I found about one Hundred & Fifty of my Country men Formed in a Circle & in their Center was a Rebel General all alone without a Rebel Guard or a Soul about Him but us. He was a man about 35 years of age Tall & as Fine a specimen of Manhood as I Ever saw, a Splendid Bold & Dashing Fearless look in His Eye & in Every appearance, A Gentleman & Brave Man. When He saw there was all there who were coming, He addressed us as Fellow Countrymen & introduced Himself as General Pat Claibourne [Cleburne][5] & His mission to us was to obtain Recruits from us for His Brigade, which was composed of Irishmen & He would take no others in it. The Brigade He Had Raised & organized Himself & it was then in His Devision for He was in Command of a Rebel Devision that was the substance of what He told us but He talked for about a Half Hour & talked Fluently, using Every argument the[y] could to induce us & using Principally our Nationality & that the South should be our Home & not the north, also using the non Exchange, of us & wilfull Carelessnes & Neglect of the Northern Government in leaving us so long in Prison.

He said He Had Visited the other Prisons & got some Recruits but wanted more. Yes, He talked smoothly and also Kindly & Had He been a Union officer I would Have Loved to Have fought under Him. I well Knew Him. There was not a word Spoken while He talked. We all Knew Him by Reputation & all Paid Him the Respect of Listening in Silence untill He ceased & waited for our answer when one old Grey Headed man Stepped out of the Ring & said, General, am I free to speak as I feel & think? Claibourne told Him He was Free to say Just what He pleased For Himself & Comrades that no one should Stop Him or Molest Him for what He should say.

I said Pat Claibourne was a Fluent Speaker & I will say that this Poor old Grey Headed Doubled up Prisoner of War, if not Quite as Fluent as Clairbourne was, He was Fully as Forcible a Speaker. He Had Followed the General in His remarks, & now took those Remarks up one by one, answered them & then Finished up strongly & Forcibly against Claibourne Himself. Irishman though He was & a Confederate General For Daring to come to us starved crippled Prisoners from their Irishman Treatment of us For Recruits for His Rotten Confederacy. He told Clairbourne that Himself & His Brigade as well as Every so called Irishman in their Ranks was a Disgrace to the Mother who Bore them, to the Country which gave them Birth & to the name of Irishman & when the old man Stopped, we in our weak Feebley Voice Cheered Him as Lustily as we could & that was our Answer to Pat Claibourne not a single man did He get from amongst us & when He saw us cheering, He turned & walked away & we Returned to our Prison Fare or rather Hospital Care.

While that old man was Raking Claibourne, I thought sure that His Hot Irish Blood would get the Better of His Promise & that He would have us Punished but no, He never Spoke & I beleive Really He thought more of that Poor old man For His plain Pointed Language then He would Had He Joined Him as a Recruit. I Heard He got only 17 Recruits out of all the Prisons, so He Found it Poor Recruiting amongst Starved, sick & crippled Irishmen in those southern Prisons.

Portrait of Major General Patrick R. Cleburne, ca. 1860–1870 (courtesy Library of Congress).

This same Pat Claibourne Commanded a Devision in Hardees Corps & that corp was always the Left of Braggs Army & therefore He was in the mob that cut our Devision up so bad at Stone River & many times Has my Devision Fought His but we always Found them Gallant Enemys. Pat Claibourne was Killed Leading His Devision about a month afterward at the Battle of Franklin, Tennessee.[6]

There was no change in my daily Life, but I was Gradual getting a little stronger. My Right Leg I could occasionally when standing Force or Stretch it so that it would touch the ground, but as soon as quit stretching, it would Spring Back. My left Leg remained nearly the same & take it all through I was pretty well. On the morning of about the 12th or 13th of November, there was a Rumour of a special Exchange of ten thousand of us but no man was to be taken I Heard but a wounded man & He would be supposed to be about as good as Dead before they would take Him. Well, I did not think they would Have Much Trouble in Finding that many men in all their Prisons & when the doctor came, I asked Him. He Said it was true but only wounded men would be taken.

After He left, I told Carter I was going to try & Play of[f] on them & get out if I Could. He Said that if I trick, He would to as He wanted to go with me. I asked Him if He was Wounded. He said no but that He was nearly Dead Any How & while we were talking, the three Rebel Doctors Composing the Board of Examiners accompanied by our little Doctor passed Right by us. Our doctor Knew He Had no wounded men there so He did not stop them but Kept right on East. Now there was I think three or Four other tents East of us & I Knew they would Keep on around them & then Come up the other side & Pass the north End of our tent so I Grabbed My Crutches & started for the north End & Carter followed me & we Just got there in time.

Carter standing on my right Hand, the Board Came along & I thought our Doctor would Call their attention to Carter & I standing there but no, He Knew neither of us was wounded & supposed we were Just standing there to see them Pass & they were Passing & Had got so far that I then Knew they were not going to stop & I Called, Doctors! The[y] stopped, turned around & one Fat Fellow said, well Sir, whats wanted? I said I want to be Examined. The[y] looked at our little doctor but He stepped Back & the[y] Came to me. This Fat [fellow] seemed to be the Principal of them & He asked me what was the matter? I told Him I was wounded & when I said that I caught our doctors Eye on me & He looked at me as much as to say your are caught now. The Fat one aske[d] me where? I told Him in the Knee. He asked to See it. I showed Him my left Knee. He then asked what Caused my leg to be drawn up so & I told Him the wound Caused it. He asked How the wound Caused My Leg to be so Contracted. I said I Supposed it was the Cord drawn up. As the Surgeon told me when tryeng to get the Ball out that it Laid between the Bone & Cord of my Leg & Supposed that was what Caused it. He asked where the Ball was Lodged & I showed Him where it was. He then looked to see where The Ball Came out & of Course not finding the place for it was Set there He Supposed I was telling truth then asked me what Battle I was wounded in? I told Him Chickamauga, Sept 20th 63. He looked at me a short time then asked my name, Company & Regiment. I told

Him & another one of them Put it down on a List. He Had & I felt solid on that Question.

They turned & again started away & I looked up at Carter & He was watching them with His mouth wide open. I Expected to Hear Him Call to them but no, they are going & I again Call Doctors. The[y] stopped again & asked me what I wanted now & I said Here is another men, I Fully Expected when the[y] Came Back that of Course Carter would Speak for Himself but no, the Doctors Came Back, Stood there in Front of Carter waiting for Him to tell where He was wounded & Carter Stood there Facing them His mouth wide open but not a word. Now I Knew from the looks of the Board they were mad because they Had to Come back & why Had not Carter spoken to them when they were there before. Our own Little doctor stood in the Back ground & telling me with His Eyes to Keep my mouth shut or I would get in to trouble, He looked as though that was the First time He Ever saw me & wondered what Kind of a Yank I was I Can see Him yet looking at me with Ankiety in His Eyes for Fear I should get into trouble.

Finally the Fat one sharply asked Carter, whats the matter with you? I Expected Carter would surely then answer but no & to save me, I could not Help it. It was an Impulse stronger than I could control, a some thing that seemed to Force the very words out of my mouth but when I saw the impatience of the Board & the Continued Silence of Carter, I answered them that He was Deaf & Dumb. The moments I Spoke I was then afraid that Carter would say He was not or by some movement or sign give me away & if so, I Knew My Doom was sealed & His too. The Board now turned their attention again to me & asked me How long He was Deaf & Dumb, where & How it Happened? I told them His Regiment Had Lain in Front of a Battery in Support of it at the Battle of Chicka-mauga & when they were Releived from there that Carter was Deaf & Dumb & Had been Ever since for I allways Since then Had to take Care of Him. But they Said the Firing of Artillery might make a man Deaf but would not make Him Dumb. I told them I Knew of no other Cause but that for His Dumbness that He was all right before the Battle & after it, He was as they then saw Him, They Looked at the Poor Long Devill of a Bean Pole standing there if not before, then He was now if not Dumb, at Least he was Dumb founded at Hearing for the first time that He was Deaf & Dumb & the cause of it & He Certainly stood there dumbfounded wild Eyed & scared. He was indeed a Pitifull Looking object & a good Subject For Exchange & they thought so too for they asked me, His name, Co., Regiment. Now Confound it I neither Know His Given name, His Co. or the number of His Regiment. I only Knew His name was Carter & He was From Indiana but then you Know as I Had taken Care of Him for the Last 14 months. I was supposed to Know Him well as He was a Particular Friend of mine & in answer to them, I Quickly gave them some given name & Carter, also some Co., Letter E, I think it was & also some Number of an Indiana Regiment. They Put down what I Had given them but only Carter & Indiana was true & to this day, I do not Know His true given name or Co. or number of His Regiment.

The Board Had not got out of Sight or Hearing when He Picked me up in His arms & Commenced Hollowing & carried me to our Bunk at the other End & we sat there talking or rather He was doing all the talking saying He Could never Forget me & so on when our doctor Came Suddenly on us & the first we Knew of Him being there. He said Hello, Carter, you can speak now can you? Your are not Deaf & Dumb — Eh — then He turned to me & said well, Glennan, what Kind of a Yankee Limb, are you any way? What Posses[s]ed you to act as you did? Tryeng to get yourself out was Bad Enough & when you succeeded, you ought to have been satisfied & let Carter talk for Him Self. But I said Carter, you saw your self, Could not Speak for Himself & I only answered for Him, the D[evi]l — He Could not speak. He said He can talk. I Said yes, but when the Board was there, He was Deaf & Dumb. The Doctor asked me How long I Knew Carter & I said about two weeks or since He was Brought to the Hospital that was the first time I Ever saw Him & that I Had given His wrong Given name & Co. & Number of Regiment. He then asked me How Long we Had been making our Plan up. I said we Had no Plan at all, the whole think Happened as He saw it Himself. What, He said, did not Carter agree to Play Deaf & Dumb while you answered For Him? I told no, the whole thing was accidental that we Had no understanding Whatever & the most scared one of the Lot was myself for fear Carter would <u>speak</u> after I said He was Deaf & Dumb. He then asked Carter How He felt during that time. Carter said He was so scared He could not speak & when I said He was Deaf & Dumb, He thought He would Burst. He was afraid the[y] would Hear Him Breathe & the whole thing seemed like a Dream & Hurrah, He was going Home. The Doctor said we were a Precious Pair of yanks & as He turned away, I asked Him if He was going to give us away & make trouble for us. He said no, He wished we were all going Home.

I then thought of Henry Lavelle. I Knew He was in the Hospital & where He was in it but How I Found out He was there, I do not Know but I thought of Him & that if I Could I would Help Him get out So I took my crutches & went to Him. He was in the other End of the Hospital in a Low Tight tent. I think there was 5 or 6 men all La[y]ing on the Floor & Henry was the furthest in from the Door or Flap that suited me for it was pretty dark there. His nurse was with me & I told Him what I wanted to do & asked Him to Remove Henry out of the tent. He done so. I told Henry that I would take His place & if I Passed would give His name, the Poor Fellow was nearly Dead But Realised what I was doing. He was taken out & I Lay down in His Place telling the nurse to be sure & Have the Board Brought in to me & I Lay there & studied How I could Play it on them. I Knew if the[y] saw My Face, the Chances were that the[y] would Recognize me or my voice my Leg & would be a sure shot to pass but it was so Remarkable that they would Know it Had been one before them & that would not Help Henry & Stop me from going out so I Concluded to play Sick, Keep my Face Covered as much as Possible & show nothing but My Eyes. That was the Best I Could think of. After a while, the Board came & I Heard the nurse say Doctors, there is a man in there wants to see you & a strange voice said who is it? The nurse answered, Lavelle. I supposed it was the doctor in charge of that Ward who asked who is it but in Came my fat Friend, the others Following almost Closed up the Entrance making it Quite dark.

The Boss Fat man asked well, my man, whats the matter with you & with the Lower Part of my Face under the Blanke[t], I told Him I was Sick & nearly Dead. It was a Filthy Hole & I did not think he would Examine Closely & He did not Remove the Covering but Said He Could not take a sick man. The doctor in charge said I was of Fit Subject to go through as it was impossible for me to Recover but the Fat man Said the Orders were strict one but wounded to be taken & the[y] walked out. Poor Henry when I Bid Him good By, He Cried. I tried to cheer Him with Hopes but He Had none & Said if He was with me, He would be all right. I often think of Him & wonder if He came out alive.[7]

Carter & I Prepared. I Had about a Blanket & a Half, one Cavalry Jacket & one old Blouse, a Pant with some or a little more Pretensions to the name than the ones Had I last described to you. I think I Had neither Shoes nor Cap & I Determined to take with me what I Had for Fear they might be again Fooling & put me in another Prison but Carter would not listen to such a thing. No, He was going through.

About three or Four Oclock, we were Ordered to the west Guard Line & there Found a Heavy Guard & Every man in Hospital, who was able to walk, was there not only those going out but those who Had to Remain.[8] An officer Called the names & as Each man was Called, He answered & stepped out. For Each man going out was able to walk by going slow. Carter stuck Close to me & on we went for the Station of Andersonville. When we got near it, they Halted us to see we were all Right & to be turned over to the officer under whose charge we were to be Placed. He Ranked as a major.

The Prisoners were all Right & it appeared there was to be so many nurses to go along to care for us & there seemed to be one more of them nurses than was required. The Extra nurse was a small wirey Country man of mine & the Major was almost directly in Front of me & about 10 feet from me when this Extra nurse Came up to Him & said, Major, I understand you Have Ordered me Back to Hospital. Yes sir, the Major said, we dont want you & you are not going with those Prisoners. The man answered He was going with those Prisoners whether He was wanted or not & Back to that Hospital, He was not going alive. The Major drew His Revolver & Presented it at His Breast within Four feet of it & Ordered Him Back. The man did not move a foot or Flinch an inch but threw up both His Hand to His Breast & tearing open the Bosom of His Shirt Bearing His Breast with 4 feet of a Navy Revolver. He Dared that Major to Fire Sayeng Here is a True Loyal Heart, that is Either going through with His Comrades or Dies right Here, so Fire for I tell you I am not going Back to Hospital. Fire, He Said, at the Fairest mark you Ever Had & the man Stood unflinching. It was speedy Death or Liberty for Him.

I could see that Major Quivering with Excitement & anger at being Defied by a Prisoner & before His own Men. The man for His Daring Bravery deserved Living & if shot for it, well deserved to be Revenged. For it would be a Cowardly act to place a Ball in that Brave Loyal Breast for its Endeavor to grasp Liberty when in its Reach. My own thought was Revenge on the Major if He fired & I looke along the Line of Poor

Starved Crippled Humanity but on Each face, I could read their thoughts & in Each Hand which Held a stick or crutch was grasped tight, yes, tight as those Poor weak fingers would allow & I Knew one word would start them if that Fatal shot was fired. It was the Majors Death if it was our death to avenge our Brave Companion.

There was about 250 of us & about 25 Guards, who stood aloof & seemed to think what to or Know what would Happen if the Major fired but no, He Controlled Himself, His Better nature saw the Cowardliness of the act if Perpetrated & I Beleive gave the man credit for His Daring act & words, so He turned away & the man Joined our Ranks where we Joyfully but Silently Received Him. We were then marched on to the Station, P[l]aced in Box Cars as before & the train started towards Macon or in the direction, we Had Come from East or towards Richmond.

So Good By, you Hell <u>Hole</u>, after me bein[g] in you nearly Eight months. Good By For myself & Comrades with me but God Help the Poor Yankee Boys Still within your Hated wooden walls. I may Here say that there was men confined in there untill the Following March 1865.

We travelled alon[g] all night, all next day & what we got to Eat if Any thing, I do not Remember but along in the Evening we were stopped, unloaded & marched a short distance & Put in to another Stockade, where I think there was seven or Eight thousand of our old Andersonville Comrades. They Had, since they Left Andersonville, been in several other Prisons & Kept moving around from one Pen to another.

The Stockade at this Place Millen,⁹ was Large & Clean. There was a Clear Stream of good water running through it. The Grass was yet green & a few trees, I Beleive, was still standing. We were ordered to Remain together near the Gate we Entered it on I Beleive it was on the south side & if so the stream ran from west to East. The grass felt good to Lay on & the whole appearance was cleanly Compared to Andersonville. It was late when we went in & the next morning, we Had lots of Visitors Amongst, which I Found Riley Beach,¹⁰ [a] Neighbour Boy of mine in 57 & 58 in KanKaKee county.

I do not Remember How long He Had been in Prison or His Regiment but He was always a Thin Featured Person & His Face in Prison did not improve His Looks in that Respect. He was the only one I Remember seeing there For I did not go around much & I Begun to think the Jonnies Had Played another one of those Exchange Jokes on us & I

Camp Lawton at Millen, Georgia, ca. 1865 (courtesy Hargrett Rare Book and Manuscript Library/University of Georgia Libraries).

Felt like I Had been Joked Enough that way & I Felt a Kind of I want to go Home Like. What we got there to Eat I Can not Remember but think we were there two days & nights & about dusk one Evening, we got Orders to get Ready. Riley was with me & I gave Him what Blankets I Had, also the Jacket for I thought I would Risk the Exchange & He Had a good Prospect of Remaining the winter & would need those things.

Carter still stuck to me Like a Brother. He seemed to think if He lost me, His chances was slim of getting through all right but if He Kept near me that all He would Have to do was to Follow me & I would Lead Him out. So we were taken out of Millan & away a short distance & after dark, we were again Piled in to Box Cars & after all were Loaded, they shook into Each Car out of a sack some sweet Potatoes. I Beleive I got one or two small ones & that is the first I Remember Eating that day or in fact since I came to Millan.

We Rolled along all night & in the morning, Found on waking or coming to my senses that the train was stopped in a Low Marshy swamp that we Had been there for an Hour or two waiting For day light to Come to be taken into Savanna a mile or two away. We Had Come about 80 or 90 Miles from Millan & from Millan to Andersonville was I think about 150 or 160 Miles or There abouts. <u>Gee</u> <u>Rusha</u>, <u>oh</u> no, I did not want something to Eat & I was not the only one For our Riding, Shaking & so long Fasting was telling Fearfully on our weak Sistems [systems] & men who Had walked from the Hospital to the station at Andersonville & who Had walked into & out of Millan, now Complained from our Crowded Condition in the Car & a good many of them Had not Even got a Potatoe the night before were now so weak they could Hardly speak & Laid there wishing For Death for it seemed as though we Had Reached the Limit of Human Endurance & that it would be Easier to die than try to Live For we Had not yet the certainty of Exchange.

We Had been Lied to so much that we could not Beleive the truth when told us. Who can tell the Conflicting agonies of our Minds between the thoughts of Hunger & weakness? The thoughts, Hopes of Exchange & the Possibility of it all Being another Rebel Lie to Decoy us Quietly into another Prison. All those thoughts are crossing Each other in our minds as we wait there for day light to come & not Knowing what it will Bring when it does come, our Guards tell us we are going to be Exchanged but can we Beleive them. If they would give us something to Eat, we could Beleive that but no, The[y] offer us what we Can not Beleive & can not or will not give us what we can Beleive & now while waiting For daylight, suppose we go Back to Andersonville & I will give three scenes that I Forgot while there. I would not now give them but I Have given none Like them & relating them will Help to while away the time untill daylight.

The First is the death of a Comrade by the Rebel Guard & By the verbal Command of Wirtz. There was amongst us Chickamauga Prisoners, a small old man, a Frenchman. He was about 40 or 45 years old in Comparison to what the most of us was at that time. Well this man, We Called, Chickamauga[11] or some Called Him Frenchy on account of His Nationality & He was as usual with French men, Lively & vivacious. He Had lost a Leg at Chickamauga & in Andersonville went around on two crutches. He seemed to be Previledged & could go outside when Ever He wanted. This was in the first month we were there & in about the Latter Part of April, the men inside got down on Him. Some way, they thought He was acting as spy on us & Reporting to Wirtz. The Cause of that suspicion was the Privi[l]edges He Enjoyed of going out when He pleased, but they got after Him & wanted to Kill Him.

He got over to the South Gate & Crawled in to the Dead Line & sat down. Wirtz was standing at the open Gate & He ordered Him out of there. The Guards made no attempt to shoot Him although Wirtz was there & in answer to Wirtz for Him to get out of the Dead Line, He said no, that He would Rather be shot By a Rebel than Killed by our own men & that they wanted to Kill Him, thinking that He was a spy on them & that Her[r] Wirtz Knew He was not. Wirtz then ordered the Guard to Kill Him, the Guard Fired & the Ball Entered His Jaw & Came out the opposite side of His Side under His arm, such was the death of Chicka-mauga.

The other incident is Preaching. During the time I was down Sick or during the months of June, July & August, I could Hear near me & on the main street, a man with a strong & Loud Voice Preaching or Hold-ing Forth to the Boys. This was always after Dark. He was called Reddy on account of His Red Hair, Red Whiskers & Red Complexion & I for years often thought How Hard & Faithfull that man Worked Exhorting His Fellow Prisoners & I Found Him Here a Member of this Home still Red Faced Red Header & as Lively in spirit as He was 27 years ago but Physically Broken down from exposure & suffering. He was 15 months & 20 days a Prisoner. His Name is Andrew C. Lloyed[12] & Belonged to Company F, 82nd Ohio Infantry & where He slept in Andersonville was next to that watch making or Repairing Establishment.

I showed you the day we took the stroll down the street & came so near Buy[ing] a cup of Bean soup out of that Fellows Boot Leg — & now let me show you a scene that I ought to Have shown you that day, namely a scene you may call amusing or Gambling. Call it as you Please, Here it is & alively one. It is too at least for some of the Participants in it. Some would call it Gambling Because there is Racing in it but for us outsiders & not intirested in the Race, it was Amusing & showed what time, Perseverance & Kind Treatment could do in o[b]taining a High Rate of speed & what activity could be obtained from those little Pets or Bosom Friends or Back Biting Enemys, which we agreed to Call Grey Backs.

Men are successfull in Business Generally only after years of Expe-rience or Practice & this applys Particularly to stock Raising & more Par-ticularly to Blooded Stock Raising. Now it took years in Civil Life to obtain the Experience that a Few Months Practice acco[m]plished Here in that Branch of Industry. Stock Raising, yes, we were all in it & but Few of us Devoted ourselves to Raising & training Blooded Racers, For it is a Racing scene you are about a witness.

We will Imagine two of those men out on that street for the Purpose of getting up A Race. One of them at Each End of the Street. It is about noon with the sun so Hot, it Feels Like it might be 198 in the shade but for all that the street is Crowded & those two men Have their Racing stock with them as also Each one of them Has His own Race Track. It is a Fact, those men Had got Every thing in the Race Line down so Fine that the[y] actually Carried with them their own Race Tracks. Well, they Each Have their Bloody Blooded Animal, I mean, Handy about their Persons as also their Race Track in this Hand & we will only Follow one of them.

He starts of[f] a yelling out. Heres your Racer, a Fame Brindle Bodied Bob Tailed Long Legged Racer & the Best Runner & Quickest Jumper in the stockade, For a Ration of Bread — or a Ration of meat — & along He goes Praising the Fine Proportions & Racing Propertys of His Stock & as soon as He comes near Enough so the other man Hears Him then He yells out Heres your man, Im your Mutton & Ive got the Racer that Can out run & out jump yours & a Ration of Bread to Back Him. They men meet & agree on the wager & in the meantime the lookers on take an intirest in the Race & make their Side Bets. Some may be Betting their Ration a day, two or three ahead. When Each of the two Principals Lay down Each a Half a Canteen that is their Race track & a good Lively one, it is too & Fully Large Enough, it not [—] Large for the stock that is going to Race on it.

As soon as they Place the two Race tracks side by side on the Baking sand & in the scorching sun, they Each then run their Hand into the Stable or stall or Place of Confinement where their animal usually Kept His Head Quarters or stomping Ground or Pasture, Call it what you Please but — Lo — He Has gone From His usual Haunt & the man searches Deligently for Him moving His Hand around to the diffirent pastures or Places where He thinks to find Him. One man is successfull & Holds His by the Ear. It is a good Hold for the vicious animal Cannot Bite Him but is Kicking viciously & switching His tail in anger & Pain, for it is a very tender spot of those animals is the Ear & in that Respect, they Resemble a mule, but there the Resemblance Ends between a Mule & one of them but the man Holding Him yells out, Hurry up & trot our your Racer. I cant Hold this Fellow all day. The other man is ankiously searching For His & it is useless for any of us to offer to Help Him Hunt for Him For it would not of course allows stranger to Cat[c]h Him. Oh no, none but His Keeper or Feeder Could Cat[c]h Him, they Knew Each other.

You Know the man finally gets His Cornered & Catching a Hold of Him, yells out Hurrah, Ive got Him! They then Examine the Race track to see the Condition of it For it Has to be in Prime Condition to make a Lively Race. Yes, it Has to be Hot, the Hotter the Better. The Hotter the track, the Quicker the Racer will get of[f] it & win. They Both meet, agree the track is Ready & now watch close & see the Fun. The men Both Hold their Racers over the center of the track, the man chosen umpire gives the word go & Both racers in Prime Condition & ankious to Escape from the Hands of their Keepers obtain their Freedom & drop in the Center of that mad Hot race track, So Hot that you Can Hardly Bear your Hand on it & the outer Edges are the Hottest for the[y] are the Farthest from the Earth & there for retain all the Heat of the Sun.

As soon as those wild Racing steeds touch the tin, it is too Hot there & off the[y] go as fast as the[y] Can Each tryeng to find a Cooler spot on it but no, of[f] the[y] Run around & Round, time after time some times one would get near the Edge but would Find it too Hot & Back it would go to the Center or away from the Edge. Now while it was near the Edge, the owner of it Would yell & cheer, Expecting it would run over the Edge & drop to the Ground for if so then He would win, for that was the Race.

The first one out of[f] the Half Canteen won the Race. That was the object in Heating them sometimes neither would get of[f] but Both Run themselves to death then the Race would be a draw & I Have seen as much actual Excitement at those Races as I have seen at Horse Races where there was Hundreds or thousands of dollars Bet, yes & I Have seen the whole crowd Fighting over Fanci[e]d Foul Play. One man would accuse another of shaking the canteen when His animal was near the Edge or winning or He would accuse Him of Blowing it Back to Keep it from Coming, but, so that any thing Fancied or Real, that was not Fair would Cause a Fight between the Principals & their Friends & Backers for as I said the Excitement was Just as High & Just as Real as if it was a Bona Fide Race & thousands of dollars was bet on it.

172

But Hello, I Declare it is Day Light & we can Hear the sound of Life in a large City. The Locomotive pulls us on a mile or two out of that swamp & we are Ordered out of the cars. Some are not able to move, there Limbs are cramped & their Stomacks are Empty so all who are able Help the others out. Who as soon as they feel the Fresh air, they Brace up Sufficient to move on & we move slowely, a Ragged Dirty Hungry & almost naked crowd, Poor Human Skeletons, Poor Human shadows of men, once Blist with Health Stren[g]th & a will to use it in the service of your country.

How many of you, My Poor Prison Friends, are now Living who that Sunday Morning Marched or Rather dragged ourselves along from them Prison Cars on through the streets of Savanah. Early, as it was about sunrise although the sun was Hid by a Heavy Fog from the Bay, so thick & it Remained so untill away in the afternoon that we could see but a short distance, but Early as it was the streets were Lined with People, Principally women, all seemed Kindly disposed to us & many, many of them with Baskets of Bread, Meat or Pies tried to get to us & give us something to Eat, but, no, the Inhuman Devils of Guards Pushed them Back at the Point of the Bayonet & would not allow them Kind Hearted Ladys to Hand us a mouthfull but they Ladies to tried to throw it to us over the Guards Heads, an[d] a little Came Amongst us that the men Caught & Eat thankfull for the Taste the[y] got. But the Guards Crowded them Further away & Hurried us along untill we Came to the Edge of the Bay or Water & there Amongst a Pile of Cotton Bales & on a Cotton Bale we signed the Parole to not again serve in the United States army against the South untill we were Regularly Exchanged.

Serve! From our appearance & actual condition, we were more Likely to serve Fattening a Grave Yard & that soon than to serve in the army. As we Signed the Parole,[13] we were put on Board a Rebel Steam Boat. It Looked Like a Ferry Boat for it was open all around with a Railing around it & we were all Packed on that deck so tight that I do not Remember Moving from the time we all got on it untill we were taken of[f] about Six Hours after we Had to Remain Standing. For if we Sat down, we were Liable to be Smothered or tramped on Like a Fat Steer in a Crowded Shipping Car. If one Lays down, the others will soon tramp it to death. The Cattle Can not Help it on account of their Crowded Condition & Neither Could our man on that Boat for I Can find nothing to Resemble our Position Better than the crowded Condition of a Cattle Car.

The Boat started from Savanah about 8 or 9 Oclock & Without a Morsel of Food of any Kind & in that Heavy Fog Steamed down Savanah Bay slowly. About noon, we Knew we were in the Vicinity of our Fleet of Transports For the Guards now told us were going near Fort Pulaski,[14] where our transports were waiting to Receive us & we were Watching Eager Ankious to again get a view of the Stars & Stripes, The Emblem of our Glorious Country, the Starry Banner, For which we Had Suffered Death Every Hour, Every Day, Every Week, Every Month For Fourteen Long Weary Months & I might with truth say, yes, Every Minute of that weary time Had we Suffered Death & Such a Death. God alone & those who Endured that Life Know & you, my Friend, may Have some Idea of what that Life was from my Feeble Description of it, <u>but</u> Mercifull God, Look, see. What is it? What is that there Floating — up — up — in the Sky, up, up above & over the Fog Flying Boldly, Bravely out from a slender Pole.

It is all we can see, it Looks as though that Pole is stuck in the Bank of Fog & that Flag is swinging from it. Look, what is it? What does it mean, Great & Mercifull Father in Heaven? Is it Possible? Can it be Possible that that is our Flag, that I again live to see it. No, it Cannot be Possible, My Eyes Deceive me & I will never see that Flag I Carried in Battle. That Flag I Suffered & Shed my Blood for, no, I was Deceived. It is gone. My Brain must be Wandering, I must be Dreaming but if so, I see others Looking Wild Excited, their Hearts Panting, their Poor Weak Exposed & Skinney chests Heaving & Eyes Wildly strained up above the Fog lookin to Heaven for again one Sight of that starry Emblem of our Deliverance. Give us, oh God, one more view, one more sight of it & then take us, let us Die if it is thy will in Sight of it that we can before we Die Say we Have seem The Flag of our Country once more.

There Look, some one Hoarsely cries, Look Boys! Look there it is again & we Look, yes, we are now nearer & see it Plainer. We see more of the Flag Staff & Know it Floates from an ocean — ste[a]mer & are Satisfied it is Real & no Dream & with a Sole of Joy & a Lump in My Throat, I Looked too Dumb with Joy to give a cheer or Speak a word. I Felt Like I Beleive a lost soul would if coming out of the Place of Darkness in to Heavenly Light, such my Friends was my own Feelings as I first saw the Stars & Stripes & about Noon of Sunday, the 20th of November 1864 & Such I Beli[e]ve was about the Feeling of all of us. We were too full of Joy to give a single Cheer. We Could not Even speak to Each other & if there was a dry Eye in that mass of Bones & Dried Smoked skin I do not Know it. I did not see it for we would watch that Flag as we Drew near, Brush the tears away & Look again, untill we got near Enough to see the Hull of the steamer then the moving Sailors in Blue Flannell & our Boat Anchored within about 15 or 20 rods of that Steamer *City of York* or *New York*[15] I Forget which.

Soon a small Boat put of[f] From our Boat to this vessell with the Stars & Stripes. The Fog would occasionally Settle & obscure the Body of the Boat but we Could always see the Flag & wer[e] Contented. Again the Fog would Raise so we could see the Hulls of several dark vessells other, or ocean Transports also waiting in this way, Each moment Expecting our Boat to close in to the steamer & Deliver or turn us over to them or that they would Close in to us & take us of[f] one.

Two Hours Passed & no Change of Positions, no move made to Remove us & we Begin to get uneasy. A Rumour Goes amongst us that they are not going to Exchange us, that the Commissioners Cannot agree & that they are going to take us Back. Back, no, we will never go, a Thousand times no, we will never live to go Back. We will sink the Rebel Craft the first move it makes to Head up Stream Back. No, we will die there in Sight of our Flag. We can now Die in Sight of it & will neve[r] go Back to die Like a Dog in a Rebel Hell Hole. There is we go Back, we are sure to Die & we can but die Here but die with our Eyes on the Stars & Stripes & if our men on those Boats will allow us all to die By Drowning So be it but Back, never, never, those are our Expressed Thoughts & given so the Rebel Guards may Hear us For we are Reckless, Wild & Care not. It is now Death or Freedom & we will Have nothing Else. The Guards Know we will do it for we care For nothing & speak out Freely what we think there is but Few Guards on the Boat & it would Have taken but very little with those thoughts in our minds to make us attack them. Nothing but the still weak Hopes we Had of an Exchange Hindered us from some Rash more, a Word from any one of us in our then Frame of mind & the men would accomplish any thing Proposed or Have Died For the Thoughts of Going Back was worse than Death to us in this state of mind.

We Remained For some time when soon the Boat we were on Commenced Drawing nearer & nearer to our Receiving Boat, the *City of New York* & we can not see a Body of Blue shirts standing By the Gang Plank & when the Boats are close together, the Plank is Pushed out Resting on the Rebel Boat & those Poor Skinny Creatures commence to drag themselves over it & as soon as they are in Reach of those strong willing waiting arms, they are Picked up if unable to walk Free or Fast Enough to make Room for the others Following.

My turn Came & I Crossed, two Pair of Yankee Arms are Reached out for me & I am again thanks be to God under the Protection of our old Flag after an absence of 14 Months to a day & almost to an Hour. I was Captured at Craw Fish Springs, Georgia on Sunday, September the 20th 1863 at about 3 or 4 Oclock in the afternoon & Paroled at Savanah, Georgia, November the 20th 1864 on a Sunday & turned over to the Hands of our men at or about 3 or Four Oclock in the afternoon & this Closes My Reminiscence or Experience of Prison Life So Fare Well Rebeldom. Farewell Rebel Hell Holes & Fare Well Rebel Percecutors, Farewell End.

My Dear Friends Since writing my Prison Life, I Have Found Some Records, which I wish to give Here as they apply to Andersonville & I will Write them before I Continue untill My Discharge and I Suppose as you Have been so Kind as to follow me in my Army Reminiscence & Prison Experience that you still wish to Follow me untill I finally get Discharged.

The First I give is the Sworn Testimony of the Rebel Surgeon, Joseph Jones[16] and given in the Trial of Wirtz for Cruelty & Murder of Prisoners at Andersonville. He was tried in the Spring of 1866 at Washington, D. C.

I give the surgeons own words–

This surgeon visited Andersonville in August 1864 & Says— From the want of Proper Police & Hygeinic Regulations alone, it is not Wonderfull that From Febuary 24th to September the 21st 1864, Nine Thousand Four Hundred and Seventy nine (9,479) Deaths should occur, nearly one Third of the Entire Number of Prisoners.

The Low grounds bordering the stream were Covered with Human Excrements & Filth of all Kinds, which in many Places seemed to be alive with working Maggots. An Indescribable Sickening stench arose from These Fermenting Masses of Human Filth From the Crowded Condition, Filthy Habits, Bad Diet & Dejected Depressed Condition of the Prisoners themselves. Their systems had become so disordered that the smal[l]est abration of the skin from the prick of a splinter From scratching or a Musquoto [Mosquito] Bite in some cases took on a Rapid & Frightful ulceration & Gangrene & the Long use of salt meat often imperfectly Cured as well as the most total Deprivation of vegetable & Fruit appeared to be the chief Cause of scurvey. I Carefully Examined the Bakery & Bread Furnished the Prisoners & Found that they were supplied at most Entirely with Corn Bread from which the Husk Had not been

Photograph of Dr. Joseph Jones, ca. 1861–65, Joseph Jones papers, Louisiana Research Collection, Tulane University.

Seperated. The Haggard Distressed Countenances of <u>these Miserable Dejected Living Skeletons & the Ghastly Corpses with their Glazed Eyes</u> Balls staring up into vacant space with the Flies swarming down their open Mouths & over the[i]r Ragged Clothes infested with Lice as they Lay Amongst the Sick & Dying Formed a Picture of Helpless, Hopeless Misery, it would be Impossible to Portray in words or Brush.

<u>In speaking of the Prison Hospital, He says</u> It was too often the case that the Patients were Received From the Stockade in a most Deplorable Condition. I Have seen Men Brought in From the Stockade in a Dying Condition Begrimmed From Head to Foot in their own Excrements & so Black from smok[e] & Filth that they Resembled Negroes Rather than White Men. The Following List was taken From the Prison & Hospital Records & gives the number of Prisoners Living at the End of Each month as also the number who Died for same Month.

Adjusting the rope for the execution of Henry Wirz in Washington, D.C., photograph by Alexander Gardner, 11 November 1865. Men on the scaffold from left to right: (1) Guards, (2) Captain G. R. Walbridge, commander of the Old Capitol Prison, (3) Father R. E. Boyle, pastor of St. Peter's R. C. Church, (4) Major Henry Wirz, (5) L. J. Richardson, military detective, (6) Father B. F. Wiget, pastor of St. Aloysius R. C. Church, (7) Major G. B. Russell, Provost Marshal of the District of Columbia and (8) Sylvester Ballou, military detective (courtesy Library of Congress).

at -	End -	of -	April -	1864	Living	10,427
‹›	‹›	‹›	‹›	‹›	Dead	576
‹›	‹›	‹›	May	‹›	Living	18,454
‹›	‹›	‹›	‹›	‹›	Dead	704
‹›	‹›	‹›	June	‹›	Living	26,367
‹›	‹›	‹›	‹›	‹›	Dead	1,201
‹›	‹›	‹›	July	‹›	Living	31,678
‹›	‹›	‹›	‹›	‹›	Dead	1,817
‹›	‹›	‹›	August	”	Living	31,693
‹›	‹›	‹›	‹›	‹›	Dead	3,076
‹›	‹›	‹›	September	‹›	Living	8,218
‹›	‹›	‹›	‹›	‹›	Dead	2,794

at -	End -	of -	October	‹›		Living	4,208
‹›	‹›	‹›	‹›	‹›		Dead	4,590
‹›	‹›	‹›	November	‹›		Living	1,359

The Greater Number of Deaths in September & October in Pro-portion to the number in Prison will be explained by the Fact that all the well men were Removed From Andersonville in these Months & none Remained but the sick & Wounded.

<u>Summary</u>

in	April	one	in	Every	Sixteen	Died
‹›	May	‹›	‹›	‹›	twenty-six	‹›
‹›	June	‹›	‹›	‹›	twenty-two	‹›
‹›	July	‹›	‹›	‹›	Eighteen	‹›
‹›	August	‹›	‹›	‹›	Eleven	‹›
‹›	September	‹›	‹›	‹›	Three	‹›
‹›	October	‹›	‹›	‹›	Two	‹›
‹›	November	‹›	‹›	‹›	Three	‹›

Day and Date of the greatest number of Prisoners in Andersonville

August 8th 1864 — 33,114.
Day and Date of the greatest number of Deaths in Andersonville
August 23rd 1864 — 127.
Number of Prisoners during its occupation — 45,615.
Daily Average Deaths — 29¾.
Ratio of mortality Per 1,000, mean stren[g]th — 24.
Mortality of 18 thousand.
Registered Patients — 75 Per Cent.

<u>As that Closes my Prison Life & Record, I will now Continue</u> & Help to again be under the Folds of our Glorious old. As soon as I reach the inside of our Boat, A Jolly Tar on Each Side Hands me a Cup of Coffee & some Hard tack. I Hump along past them to Leave Room for others, who are treated the same way For as soon as one of us touches our Deck, a sailor on one Hand H[a]nds a Tin Cup of Coffee & a Sailor on the other Side gives some Crackers to Each man as He Passes untill all are on Board.

I Hear some cheering from our Tars & Learn that the man, who waved the Stars & Stripes in Andersonville on the morning of the Fourth of July is amongst the Batch I Came with & as soon as He got on our Boat, He went up on the Hurricane Deck, took the Flag from around His Body & waved it over the Rail in the Face of the Rebels & that Caused the Gallant Boys in Blue Flannel to cheer Him. As soon as we Eat & Drank what was given to us, we Crawled to the Barrell of Coffee of which there were a good many of them scattered around the Deck, Helped ourselves to Yankee Coffee. There was also Plenty of Hard Tack Boxes opened & also scattered around & also Plenty of <u>Pork</u> but that I do not Remember Eating any of. Thank you, the Coffee & B Cs are good Enough for me & I Knew the Danger to our weak stomachs of Fat Pork. No, I am much oblidged not any, thank you.

<u>As soon as the men Had Eaten Enough they were taken to the stern of the Boat</u> & soon I went in that direction. Two sailors took me in Hand — & zip, Rip, Gee Whizz, <u>splush</u> ch chi chuck Im scalded, Oh Thunder, Help! Murder! Murder! Im <u>Ruined</u>! {Whats the Matter you say?} Why would you Beleive it them two great Big Flannel Jackets Jumped right square on to me, a little Fellow like <u>me</u>. {Its a shame I Hear

Serving out rations to our exchanged prisoners on board the "New York," sketched by William Waud, 1864 (courtesy Library of Congress).

you say to treat you that way for nothing.} Yes, I agree with you but that's not the worst. For as soon as they got their Big Paws on me, zip, Rip went my Prison Uniform & over Board it went to get drowned & all them nice Fat Ring Tailed Bob Tailed Line Backed Brindled Blue Speckled Lop Eared one Eyed sons of — Sons — of — well, I will say it for once now, that I am on our own Boat, yes, all them sons of the Southern Confederacy there now that I Had Fed from my own Back & Bosom Friend of my nights dreams & Daily Skirmishing Bosom Friends & Friends that stuck to me closer than A Brother — My Pets, Farewell you are gone & the only Harm I wish you is that you may never Return. Yes, youre gone & I am Loused Like a Rat in a Tub of Sea Water & them two fellows scrubbed on me untill I thought they were going to scrub all the outside of[f] me so they could see what was inside but if they did they would Have been Badly Fooled for there was nothing there that they Could see but Coffee & Hard Tack.

They Found me I suppose too Tough so they turned me out of the Tub & over to two more men who soon Had me in a Uncle Sames Uniform & now as I am again, O Boy & though still Low in Statue about 4 feet High when I Stood on one Leg Like a Duck but I am not that Kind of a Duck. Oh no, Im a — Im — a — Boy in Blue & now make my Bow to you, this is the first time I dare Present my self to you for Before I got those nice Clothes, I Really was not Fit to be —- Oh — Please dont ask me — for you may see I am Bashfull but now I Hold my Head & Left Leg up & salute you as your very Humble Servant Ed.

That Evening a Missionary Came & gave Each of us a sheet of Paper & Envelope telling us to write Home — Home — Home, Oh God, I thank thee that it is again Possible with thy Help for me to again see Home after those Long weary months. Yes, I write Home to my Father not Knowing He was Dead.[17] I write telling them of my Parole but not of my Condition for I was not yet out of Danger. No, there was now danger in over Eating & many Lost their Lives by doing so. Poor, Poor Comrades, you at Least Had the Pleasure of Dying with your appetite satisfied, clean clothing on you, your Bodys clean & with Kind sympathising Friends around you. Oh How Many — Many — times in the months Past would I not Cheerfully, Willingly & Gladly Have given any man the Previlege to Have taken my Life in Exchange For Enough to Eat once so that I would Have at Least Died with a Full Stomach & not with the Pangs of

Hunger in me. Yes, oh yes, Friends its truth. I would Have given my Life Joyfully for Enough Food Many times—Many—Many times.

We were placed that Evening on Board an ocean Transport, a steamer. The Hold or Between Decks was fitted for us by Strewing the Floor of it with 6 or 8 inches of clean Straw on which we all Layed Helping ourselves from a Pile of Blankets. The covering was all done by Steam & Before I Layed down, I noticed Just outside the Cook House 4 or 5 Barrells of Mess Pork. The Barrells were opened & intended for our Breakfast next mornin[g] but that Pork never was Cooked, that or any other night. In Fact, it never saw day Light for the Fellows got up in the night, in their sleep I suppose & Eat it out of them Barrells. There was nothing said but other Barrells opened.

That day we remained as we were in Savanah Bay & under the Guns of Fort Pulaski over which the Stars & Stripes Floated. I think we were about 20 or 25 miles Below the City of Savannah. Next Morning we steamed out for the open Sea. I Remained on Deck near all day. I wanted all the Fresh Free air I could get & was not afraid of sea Sickness but others were & Remained Below between Decks.

In the afternoon, I stood by the side of the Vessell Looking over when a Big Long Hoosier Came & stood along side of me. I looked up at Him & saw He Had never been on sea & therefore did not know what was the matter with Him. I suspected He Had been one of the Fellows that Had been Fishing in them Pork Barrells & if so, I Knew what ailed Him & the Remidy for it. Oh yes, I took Quite an Intirest in that Poor Hoosier & His Constitutional Troubles & I Considered it My Duty to Releive Him of a Part of it & in order to apply the Remedy I Kept Him in Conversation, Keeping Sharp Look out on Him. I watched the changing of His Features untill I saw His Face turning a Sickly white & Large Beads of Sweat gather on His Face. I Knew the time was near & I said, Oh Look! Look at that Big Fish Running by the Vessel & He stooped over the Side but Could See no Fish. Now a well Person looking at Running water & Particularly sea water from the side & close to the vessell, it will make them Dizzy any How So as I Had Him intirested in a Fish story, I Kept His attention on the water Looking For what He Could not see a Live Shark or Porpoise, For I Had to vary the Fish For the occasion untill I got Him Just Ripe for the operation then I said, Oh, Look— Look—I Beleive thats a Whale. See Him, He reached over the side to

Look for a Whale & I Commenced to <u>Reesh</u> Like I was sick to my — Oh under my <u>West Cut</u> — & dont you Beleive that Hoosier in which I took so much intirest on account of His Sickly appearance — Him, too.

A total st[r]anger to me, Ill be Blamed if He did not Commence mocking <u>me</u> in that Reeching — & I could Hear the splash, splash — swish — swish — P — chuck — chuck of Big Hunks of Pork — that He was a drawing out from under His Waist Cut some way & Dropping them in the sea — sea — to feed that whale I Had been showing Him in my <u>Eye</u> when I got His Pump in good working Order.

I thought it time for me to go as I might be wanted some other place so I skipped along like a Lame duck on one <u>Leg</u>. I Had Thrown my Crutches away & as I got near the steps to go down Between Decks, I Looked Back — & that Hoosier Had turned two or three steps after me but changed His mind as He Had not Fed that Whale Enough yet & felt a Sudden Call to go Back & give Him some more So He shook His Fist at me & I went down Between decks, Layed down in the straw & covered up good with Blankets to Meditate on the ingratitude of Some Human Natures & to wonder what that Hoosier meant by shaking His Bunch of Bones at me in the manner He Had. Im sure I done the very best I Could for Him & Still He did not appear to be satisfied. I Beleive He was mad at Himself for Having to throw all that nice Mess Pork over Board & if so, I Forgive Him. But if that man is Living yet, He thinks it was me that made Him <u>Sick</u>.

In a short time He came down & Looked around as though He was ankiously looking for a Particular Friend. I did not Suppose it was me He was Looking For as I was a stranger to Him but indeed He Looked angry & very Friendless Like He Had just Parted for Ever with the only Friend He Had & for the next day or two when I would meet Him, I would turn my Head away from Him for I did not Like the way He treated me when I tried to Show Him the Monsters of the Deep.

On we steamed on the Bosom of old ocean, on Past Fortress Monroe[18] — & when we came in Sight of Land we could see snow on the sides of the mountain. Ouch, is it not getting Cold but for all that I would not Leave the Deck. No, it Put me in mind of years & years ago when I Enlisted to Fight for our Glorious old Flag, of the Pleasant times I Had in 61 while in Missouri & would wake up in the morning after sleeping all night on the Hard Frozen ground with only one small Thin Blue Blanket under me & one of the same Kind over <u>me</u> — & three or Four inches of snow over that. Yes, this snow on the Mountains of North Carolina Reminds me of those Early scenes of my Army Life but now I am Coming Back & How, in what Condition Am I, Poor Crippled & at present Deformed, one Leg — my Left drawn up I was going to say under my Arm but no, it might as well be Carried on my Shoulder for all the Practical use it was to me. So those Early thoughts are useless For me the[y] Can never Come.

Again we sail on & Come to the Shores of Maryland, My Maryland — we Have Past a Winter scene of Frost & snow. The scene now is not so wintry & Bleak Looking. No, the atmosphere is more wild & on the night of the 25th, we Come to Annapolis, Maryland. It was dark & I Remember but little of the City. As we Passed through there was Conveyances there waiting for us & we were taken to the Parole Camp. I was placed under treatment in a Hospital Barrack. Carter remained still with me as He Had done all the time from Andersonville & Helped me a Great deal by doing for me what he Could. The next Morning after our Arrival,

Painting of Fort Monroe, Point Comfort, Virginia, by Clara Gunby Huffington, ca. 1864 (Gunby Family Collection, Edward H. Nabb Research Center for Delmarva History and Culture, Salisbury University, Salisbury, Maryland).

Camp Parole, Annapolis, Maryland, 1865 (courtesy Library of Congress).

we again Received a Complete new Uniform & those we wore on Board were Burnt. We were now clear of all Wild <u>animals</u>—clean in <u>Body</u> & am a Number one Appetite you Bet durin[g] this time. From my Release I Had Continued to be as Carefull as Possible of my Food For several Had <u>Died</u> while on sea & there were a good many of us let to go from the same Cause, over Eating.

That Day, we all Received two months <u>Pay</u>. I Received 48 Dollars. I then Lived Principaly on Oysters which Could be Bought there in Camp at 10 Cent Per quart. Oysters & Crackers were my Diet with an occasional visit to the Sutlers to obtain some Kind of a Liquod to Preserve the Oysters & give an Appetite for more.

After 4 or 5 days, the doctor told me I would Have to Quit using strong Drink or if not, He Could not save me For then Even it would be a close shave to do it, as there was only, He said, the Thickness of His nail of sound Flesh between the Running sore on my neck & my Wind Pipe & that if the Scurvey got into my Wind Pipe neither He or all the Doctors in the U. S. Could save me. I told Him I was not using it only 3 or 4 times a day to stren[g]then me & that I did not use it as a stimulant & would not & would Quit it if He Said So as it was Injuring me. He said to Come & stay with Him & He would give me all the Porter I could Drink as that was stren[g]thening & good for me & I agreed with Him Right there on that Question & went with Him. He Fixed a Lounge up in His office for me & Had a Box of Porter placed there in a corner telling me to drink all I wanted no matter How much & He would see I had Plenty of it.

I could go out when I wanted to & now its Porter Oysters & Crackers. In about a weeks time, I Could Feel myself getting Better Fast. My right Leg was now nearly all Right & my Left one getting ashamed of itself tried to Follow Suit. It was slow in doing it but was doing very well Considering, Hmmm, the man it was under.

I about this time went down to the Sutlers & weighed myself. I weighed seventy nine Pounds & suppose that when I was Paroled about 10 or 12 days before at Savanah, I would not weigh Seventy Pounds & now my Friends, you may Have Some Idea of what I Looked Like when a Prisoner & I Beleive there was men amongst us that was worse than that. My Average weight befor I Enlisted was about 155 or 160 Pounds so you see, I left in those Southern Hell Holes about 90 Pounds of Flesh.

For the Bones I Brought out with me as I Could not well spare them although I came very near Leaving them too & coming out without them so you see as I though[t] Enough of My Bones as to Bring them with me, it is my Duty to try & Replace that Lost Ninety Pounds on them & I do the Best I Can but Have never yet & never will get it all together again. I Suppose it is scattered over too much of the then so called Confederacy, Richmond, Va., Danville, Va., Andersonville, Ga. You all three Have a Portion of it & you all owe me a Debt that you with all you Past, Present & Future Wealth, Could not Repay me what I Left in your Citys & Pens.

Time Passed & I Improved Fast. I am now able to get around with a Perseptible Limp in my Left Leg — & on the 16th of December by Order of the Secretary of War, all Paroled Prisoners were allowed a 30 day Furlough. I got mine on that day With transportation to Leavensworth, Ks. Hurrah For Home, I am going to try & Eat my Christmas Dinner at Home. Home — Dear Sweet Name — Home — not Long ago, I Had Forgotten that I Ever Had a Home — but now, yes, now I Know I Had a Home in Kansas. Yes, I Had written to them then away, away For that Home to surprise them by once more Eating My Christmas Dinner there & away I went on through Baltimore, through Harpers Fer[r]y, & Wheeling, Va. on through Crestline, Ohio. There Carter Left me for His Home then on through Richmond, Indiana & on to Chicago, Ills.

There I Found my Brother, who Had a letter For me. My Dear Father was Dead, Had died the August before & I, I in Prison at that time myself Playing with Death Each minute, Each Hour, Each day of that weary month of August 1864. Yes, I Played & Slept With Him & He Left me A Miserable creature as Familiar as I was with Him, He Left me & took my Kind Loving Father, So the Letter Said, Well Gods Will be Done. Home, Where are you? What Are you without my Kind <u>Father</u>? Father, May You Rest in Peace, For give me Friends For giving way to my Feelings. I Have only Paid a Just Tribute to a Kind Loving Parent, who I Have sadly missed then & <u>Ever</u> <u>Since</u>.

I Hunted up William Best Brother in Law, John Gallagher & Found Him on the Lake Shore. He told me Bests Wife Had Died in October about the same time Bill Died. There was only two days diffirense in their Deaths. She died about the 8 or 9th in Chicago & He Died on the 11th in my arms in Prison & though seperated at the time of Death, United them in Heaven. Gallagher told me their Gran[d]father in Pen[n]sy[l]vania took the children a Boy & Girl about 8 & 10 years of age with Him — & I gave Bills message with the scapular to Him for them Making an affidavit of His Death so the children could get His Pay & Bounty.

In the Letter sent stating My Fathers Death was also Directions How I should reach Home by stopping at the End of my stage, look & getting a Horse from a Neighbour to bring me Home. I staid I think two or three not more, days with my Brother then away From Chicago— on through St. Louis, Mo. & at St. Charles, Mo., on Account of Ice in the River, we were delayed from some few Hours before we got across & when we did get across the Missouri River at that place, we were too Late For the train & Had to wait.

I Finally got to Macon City on Sunday morning, the 25th of December, Christmas Day & Found there would be no train For St. Joe, Missouri until 4 oclock in the afternoon. So I was oblidged to Eat my Christmas Dinner in a Hotel & amongst strangers but the Landlord was very Kind — & it was not His Fault if I did not Enjoy My Christmas & dinner. At 4 oclock we again started for St. Joe. The next morning Early, we were Running very slow for the R. R. track was in very bad Condition.

There was two men in the Seat in Front of me Eating Breakfast. They Had a Bottle of Lyquor, some Buiscuits & Ham & were Having a good time. After Riding all night, I was Hungry myself for I Had Brought no Lunch thinking as usual the train would stop for Breakfast but no, the train would not stop untill it got to St. Joe about 20 miles yet to go— & I was wishing those men would invite me to Breakfast when Crash — Rip — Tare [Tear] — & Swear — the People in the Car yell, the Women scream & out the[y] Rush at Both doors & Jump of[f]. The train was going very <u>slow</u> — & I alone am in that <u>Car</u>.[19]

{Why dont I go too?} Why you see, I Can't I am Fast Pinned tight between the Broken Boards of the Car Floor & the Back of the Seat in Front of me with a Long Strip of R. R. Iron sticking straight up 4 or 5 inches from my Left Hand & Running up about 4 feet above my Head. My Left Leg is Caught & squeesed tight & Held as though in a vise. This unfortunate Left Leg the Rebs Had tried to shoot it of me & Left an ounce of Lead in it. The Surgeon Had wanted to Cut it of[f] as a useless Limb. The scurvey Had Doubled it up Like a Jack Knife & now the Hannibal & St. Joe R. Road Company[20] wanted to make Sausage meat of it, Bones & all & it Felt to me that way.

Already wedged in as it was, I tried to Pull it out but I would Have to teare it from my Body. By this time, the train Had Come to a stop & as I said there was not a soul in the Car but myself. The others Had Jumped of[f] away Back & Ill be Dog gone if that Lunch is not still all Right, Even the Bottle is Hunk-a-Dory. So I Reach over the Back of the seat took a Long strong Look at that Bottle now in my Hand, set the Bottle down & then Pitched in to the Grub.

I was very Busy when the Conducter & Passengers Came up. The town men that Had occupied the Seat Came in, I told them they were very Careless in not taking their <u>Grub</u> with them. The[y] Looked at the Bottle. I told them all gone. The conducter asked why I Had not gone out with the others. I said I Could not go & Leave that Food & Bottle but that now I was Ready. They soon Liberated me from my Limbo & I Found my Leg Badly Squeesed but it was used to that & a Lot of the <u>Bark</u> was Peeled of[f] the north side of the Shin Bone & Left in the wreck.

The Car was Pitched over the Bank of the track & we all Piled in the other two Coaches. The Car I was in was the last one & the Rail Had split & one End Happened to Come up through the Floor right at my Feet so Quick that it Caught me as I Have Described. It was a close Call for Death after all I Had gone through for if that Peice of a Rail Had

Come 6 inches nearer it would Have Impaled me on it & then I Could not Have Eaten them Fellows Lunch.

Without any other accident we got to St. Joe, there I took the R. Road to Weston a few miles down the River & there took the stage to Leavenworth. There again took the Stage for Lawrence & stopped an Hour or so while waiting for the southern stage at Thomas McEllroys.[21] They were strangers to me then but treated me very Kindly. In the Letter I got at Chicago, I was told to stop there & as I am giving details & little Incidents, I must give one Here that At the time surprised me.

I Had Come by Stage from Leavenworth through the night & it was Early morning when I got to Mr McEllroy's. In opening gate to go in the yard, there was a little Child, a Girl of about three years old. When She saw me opening the Gate, She Called out as Loud as Her Voice would allow. Oh, Mama! Mama!—Heres Ed Glennan, Heres Ed Glennan! Gee Whizz, what Little Bird Has Been telling this Child who I am? Why, she was not Born when I was in Laurence last in 1860. This child is not over three years of age & Knows one at First sight like an old acquaintance besides this Family are Entire Strangers to me & I was wondering How I should Introduce myself when Here is a three year old Child, who never saw me Before, Knows me on Sight & is Calling to Her Mother to Come out & be Introduced to me by Herself.

Yes she Has allready introduced me before Her mother Sees me at all For before I got to the Door, Mrs. McEllroy Meets me & says youre Welcome. We Have been Expecting you For several days. But I asked How do you Know me? How does your Child Know me so well by name? You are Strangers to me & she cannot be over three years old. Oh, she say your Folks often Come up Here & they told us to be on the look out for you & <u>Mary Ann</u> Has heard us speak of you & Knew you were a <u>soldier</u>, so she Knew it was you. Well, Dog Bite my Buttons—{But say dont you} think it is a good thing for me that I was, oh, was not a Horse Thief. I do.

In a few Minutes, the stage Came along. It Had to Pass the House I got in & on to Ottawa then a Place of about a Dozen Houses with Hardly Lumber Enough in all of them to Build one good House, then on to Ohio City about 8 or 9 miles South of Ottawa. There my stage Riding Ended & I asked the Driver where a Mr. McGlinn[22] Lived & He Pointed to the Left & East of the Road to a House a short distance away.

I Had been told to stop at Mr. McGlinns & get a Horse to take me Home as the Rest of my Journey Had to be made the Best I Could & there was no Public Conveyance, any nearer Home than the Place I Had now Stopped. I was now about 18 or 20 Miles from Home.

I went to the House Pointed out to me & Enquired for Mr. McGlinn. The Lady of the House I suspected Knew who I was or Else took me For a chicken Thief or something For she asked me if I was not Ed Glennan. Gee Whizz, my name must be written on My Face For it seems Every Stranger I speak to Knows my name & this Lady is a stranger to me, still she Knows me & I Know this is the first time She Has Ever seen me but she seems a Pleasant Good Natured Lady & Received me Kindly & warmly by the Fire. I said yes, I am Ed Glennan & Beleive if she saw me to day that she would say I was Ed Glennan yet.

I told Mrs. McGlinn that I Received a Letter in Chicago telling me to stop at Her House & I would get a Horse to take me Home as I was on my way there From Prison. She Regretted very Much that there was not a Horse there as Her Husband Had gone south a Few days before with all their Horses as He Had taken Cattle south & Required the Horses to use in driving them —& I may Here State that that Ladys Kindness to me then by Kind words to me & afterwards by Kind actions of Herself & Family to me when I Realy needed a Kind Friend, she Has Ever Proved one to me & From any Heard I say God Bless Her & Her Family For all their Kindness Bestowed on a stranger as I was to them is my Cincere Wish.

When I Found I Could not get a Horse as there was none there, I Concluded to start a Foot to Mr. Jerry Sullivans[23] about 6 or 7 Miles Distant & Nearer Home Expecting there to get one. I was Determined to reach Home that night if I Possibly Could for I Had been absent from there for Four years. Mrs. McGlinn wished me to stay and Have some thing to Eat. I suppose I Looked Hungry Enough but I Excused myself, it was getting Late I think about 4 Oclock in the afternoon —& if I Failed in getting a Horse at Mr. Sullivans, I would Have to walk Home. For if Living, I was Determined to get there that night. Bidding this Kind Lady Good By, I Arrived at Mr. Sullivans about Dusk. He Knew me slightly as He Has seen me in the Fall of 60 where I First came to Kansas. He soon Had a Poney saddled & Just at Dark, I started across the Pra[i]rie.

I Knew the Direction to take —& Dark though it was, I Let that

Indian Poney go, it with all sails set & we made splendid Time against a Head Wind. I got to Hugh McEvoys[24] Dwelling. I was acquainted with Him & when I Left in 60, I Left my Family there. But they Had Removed & I did not Know where to or in what direction. Mr. McEvoy was Glad to see me as also His Kind wife — & He got a Horse & came with me to Mr. Dan Doolin[25] about a mile from there across the Pra[i]rie. It was very Dark & no one saw us until Hugh McEvoy opened Door & Walked in & I after Him.

The first one near the Door was Mr. Doolin & Mr. McEvoy Introduced me to Him. Mr. Doolin, I wil[l] make you acquainted with Mr. Glennan — & Poor <u>Dan</u> said How do you do, Mr. Doolin. He though[t] Mr. McEvoy was Introducing Himself To Himself but He wasn't. No, He was Introducing Him to me but in the Hurry & Excitement, Mr. Dan Doolin totaly Ignored my name & acknowliged the introduction of Himself to Himself as I Have said. Now there is a good deal of Diffirence in the appearance of Mr. Doolin & myself, still on that occasion He thought I was He — & He was Himself.

My Brother Mike[26] was Married & Living with or in the same House so My Brother got a Horse & Rode Home with me about 2½ miles Further. We got there about 9 oclock of this night of Wednesday, the 28th of December & after an absence of a Little over Four years, I am again Home. I Found My Mother, oldest Sister Ann & two Brothers, Thomas & Christopher,[27] there. My other sister, Mary, who I Have Mentioned so often in my Reminiscence is married & not there & my two younger Sisters, Bridget & Ellen, are at sc[h]ool at the Osage Mission[28] about 85 miles south.

In January, I sl[i]pt on the Ice & Injured my Hip, the Left one of Course as usual. It Had to be that unfortunate Left Leg, its always in the way — & Just where it ought not to be that Hindered me from Returning at the Expiration of my Furlough. I went down to the Mission saw my sisters & they came Back with me — & I Returned in March by the same Route I Came without any incident worth Relating.

I Reported at Parole Camp & in a day or two, I Had to go to Hospital there with Diptheria[29] that Came near Croking me & while there, my nurse seeing my Face full of Black specks asked what they were. I told Him Rebel Powder Put in there at Island No. 10. He said I ought to Have them out so I told Him go ahead. He took His Pen Knife & Darning

Needle & worked away untill He was tired & I looked like a Butcher shop. I Remained in Hospital near three <u>weeks</u> then was Ordered to Chicago to be mustered out. I got Transportation & a Loaf of Bread for the Journey. I Had no Money & that Loaf of Bread was Supposed to do me for about 60 Hours & travel a Distance of 1,500 miles.

I started from Aninopolis & got to Baltimore. There I Had to remain 4 or 5 Hours For my train & in Loafing around the City, I found a Recruited Rendezvou[s]. The Recruiting officer, a Captain, wanted me to Enlist in Hancocks veteran Corp.[30] I told Him I was on my way to Chicago to be mustered out & could not Enlist in the East untill I was Discharged from the West but that if He could obtain my Discharge there without me going to Chicago I would give Him three Hundred Dollars & Join Hancocks Corp.

Three Hundred Dollars was a Big Bait For Him to make in a Hour or two for I was going when my train would be Due & told Him so. Remember my Friends, I was Homeless, Friendless & Amongst strangers without a Cent of Money, Physically Broken <u>down</u> — & Careless of what Became of me. Yes, I would Have given Him Five Hundred Dollars for my Discharge then & gone Back to the Front & given the Jonnies another chance to Finish what was Left of me — & I would not Have Had far to go.

Things were very Lively around Richmond that April 1865. That Captain Telegraphed to the Secretary of War to find out if I Could be Discharged there — & my Reason for Desiring it. The answer Came no, I Had to be mustered out the same Place I was mustered in, so that Failed — & I away from Baltimore on a night train. In the coach was a Company of Soldiers going to Harpers Ferry. I was Sitting Amongst them, my Loaf of Bread all gone & about 9 or 10 oclock, those soldiers got out their Lunches & Bottles & were Having a good time. I, myself, was Feeling Hungry. Now I dont want you, my Friends, to think that I was Hungry all the time although I Beleive I Look that way.

Those Fellows were all Enjoying themselves & seeing me sitting there without Eating, one asked me if I Had Brought nothing to Eat & drink with me. I said no, that I Had none & was a stranger amongst them going west to be Discharged. Gee, you ought to have seen the Bread, Chicken, Ham & Bottles Passed to me when them fellows Found a strange Hungry Western Galoot about my sise amongst them. Each one

wanted me to Eat & Drink with Him & I felt Real sorry that I Had not
a two Bushel sack along to Hold the Grub offered me & a City Corporation to Hold the Liquod <u>Refresh</u> but Beleive me I done Justice to it for
I did not Know where or how I would get the next.

Along in the night, they got of[f] the train & next morning was
Sunday. About 6 Six oclock, we got into Bellair, Ohio[31] & Found it being
Sunday, there would be no train untill afternoon. Pl[e]asant Prospect to
Loaf around all day without a cent, no Breakfast & no Dinner. There
was a Lot of other soldiers on the train. They also were going Home to
diffirent Parts of the West but I Knew none of them & I now See them
all Rush together to a Large Hotel for Breakfast & I see them dive down
the Basement. Why? Whats the matter with me getting Breakfast too? I
am a Soldier <u>yet</u> & if that Hotel Keeper is giving a Soldier Breakfast, I
want one too.

So in I go with the crowd, seat myself & Lay in a good supply of
Steak. I was always Fond of Steak for Sunday Mornings Breakfast when
I am travelling & in a Strange Place amongst strangers & without the
money to pay for it so you may be certain I Laid in a supply but my
Blame waist — D[evi]l waist Cut, I mean was too small for me. I was
Feeling Pretty well, I thank you. The men were going out.

The Proprietor standing in the Door Rec[e]iving from Each man
the 25 cts for His Breakfast. I Had no Small Change Loose about me so
I Crowded in amongst them, Hid my Forage cap under my arm, got
close to the Door & when He was making change for one of the men, I
Crowde[d] through between them & Hollowed but to an Imaginary Man
going up the steps & give it to me. The Proprietors Had a lot of loose
change in His Hand as I made the Rush, He made a grate to stop me,
missed me & dropped some of the change stooped to Pick it up & when
He Looked I was not there. No, my Cap was on my Head. I Stood on the
top of the steps Looking at Him. It was not me, oh no, I'd lost no Hat
& the Rest of the men seeing their opportunity were Coming out in a
Rush, some Half a Dozen Had already Passed by Him while He was
stopped — & He stepped into the door again & Collected His Quarter
from those yet inside.

The loss of my Hat Cost Him about a Dollar & a Half or two dollars.
The Price of a new Hat & He might as well Have given me a new Hat in
the first place as to make all that Fuss about it for nothing. I felt satisfied

& if He grumbled there was no one to Blame but Himself. If He Had attended to His own Business & leave me alone to attend to mine, Every thing would be all Right.

I walked around the town. It was at that time but a small town about 12 miles from Wheeling, Va. About nine Oclock in Passing a Jews Clothing Store, a Soldier in it saw me Passing & called to me to stop. He Came out & said you Lost your Hat this morning. I told Him no, but I took that way to get my Breakfast as I Had no money.

We got in conversation. I told Him where I was going & Dead Broke. He was from Ohio—& Discharged & on His way Home. He said there was a lot of the Boys there Just as He was & some were then iside Buying Clothing for all were yet in Uniform. He gave me two dollars & Fifty Cents. He said that much will take you to Chicago but dont spend a Cent while you are with us, He said & to stay with Him & He would see I wanted for nothing that as we Had to wait untill afternoon, the Boys were goin[g] to Enjoy them selves. It being Sunday made no diffrence, the stores were all open.

I Had not asked Him for any money but I was thanKfull for it Coming so Freely & I went inside the store with Him. There were 5 or 6 other Boys in there Buying. Now this Buying Clothing by 6 or 7 Soldiers when they intend to Have a good time is quite Amusing as Least it is to the Boys Buying, if not to the man Selling—& it is only from Jews that they would Buy in this way from they all seemed good Fellows & Bent on Enjoying them selves. They told the Jew they were all Discharged & all wanted to Buy a Full suit of clothing. That tickled Isaac as only one man could Buy at a time. So one man asked to see a vest He done so & agreed on the Price, about 2 dollars but before He Paid the Jew, He made Him Promise to treat all Hands. This the Jew Readily agreed to & out we all went. I think with myself, there was seven or Eight of us & Each one took a ten Cent drink.

We all went Back & another man Bought a Hat but Before He Paid for it the Jew Had to Promise to set them up & out we went & again a ten Cent Drink all around—& so the Boys Kept on For 6 or 7 times always Some one of them Buying some low Prised article & Each time Making that Jew Bring us all out & treat untill that Jew got wild. It was taking Half & over Half the Price of the Articles Sold to treat the Crowd & he Began to tumble to the Joke & all this time they were Picking out the other clothing to match what they Had Bought, making the Poor Jew Beleive the[y] would Buy all from Him. The Poor Israelite did not what to do if He Kept on treating the Boys both Profit & Principal was going into the Hands or Pockets of the Saloon Keeper instead of into His own So He Finally tried to Persuade the Boys that they Had Enough & to Buy all their Clothing at once. They told Him go to the Bucket & take a drink — & out they went to another Jew & Played the same on Him.

We all Had Dinner. They would not allow me to Either Pay or Play Loosing my Hat. About 4 oclock, the train Came & off for Chicago — & at some station on the Road at midnight the next night I Heard that President Lincoln Had been assasinated. Nex[t] Morning, I arrived in Chicago & again stopped with my Brother.[32] I was there & saw Lincolns

Funeral procession entering Cook County Courthouse in Chicago where President Abraham Lincoln's body lay in state, photograph by S. M. Fassett, 1865 (courtesy Library of Congress).

Body when the[y] took it to His Home For interment.[33] I Had a good time Generally while there & nothing of any Consequence occurred to me while there.

Only one night at a Public Ball, I was yet in Uniform & a smart City chap Thinking I was Greener than I Looked tried to take Precedence of me in the <u>Monee</u> <u>Musk</u> <u>Dance</u>.[34] I was in the Head Couple & Had to Lead of[f] & I Suppose He Hated being in Broad cloth to Follow the Union Blue & Just as the Music struck up, He swung in with His Partner to Lead of[f] — & I swing in on Him & Lead Him of[f] to the Full Satisfaction of my Partner, who said I Had done Just Right & only what she would Expect of me. I spoiled that Fellow Broad Cloth & night Dance & for a short time, there was musick without the Band but Every thing soon Quieted & the Ball went on with your Humble Servant in His Position.

I Began My Army Life in war in Chicago August 1861 — & I End it in June 1865 in Chicago with this my Last Trouble with Fellow man, For I was Discharged June 4th 1865 — & now Kind Friends Farewell with many thanks For your Kindness in Following me through my Pleasures & Trails of three years & nine months of a Soldiers Life — Farewell. The End.

Chapter Notes

Abbreviations

ACWS   Historical Data Systems, comp. American Civil War Soldiers [database on-line]

AGIL   Report of the Adjutant General of the State of Illinois, Containing Reports for the Years 1861–66

APW   Ancestry.com. Andersonville Prisoners of War [database on-line].

BDFJ   Biographical Directory of Federal Judges

CWSS   National Park Service. Civil War Soldiers and Sailors System

DANFS   Dictionary of American Naval Fighting Ships

DARE   Dictionary of American Regional English

DNB   Dictionary of National Biography

ICWMDR   The Illinois Civil War Muster and Descriptive Rolls database

OAR   Official Army Register of the Volunteer Force of the United States Army for the years 1861, '62, '63, '64, '65

OCWVB   Oklahoma Civil War Veteran Burials

OR   The War of the Rebellion: a compilation of the official records of the Union and Confederate armies

ORUCA   Supplement to the Official Records of the Union and Confederate Armies

OROC   Official Register of the Officers and Cadets of the U.S. Military Academy

Introduction

1. Ancestry.com. *1851 England Census* [database on-line]. Provo, UT: Ancestry.com Operations, 2005. http://www.ancestry.com.

2. Ancestry.com. *1860 United States Federal Census* [database on-line]. Provo, UT: Ancestry.com Operations, 2009. http://www.ancestry.com.

3. Anna Marie Wilson. "Edward Glennan Family." http://trees.ancestry.com/tree/22028030.

4. Camp Douglas was situated on a tract of land at 31st Street and Cottage Grove Avenue that was owned by Henry Graves. In early 1862, the camp became a Union prisoner-of-war camp. [William Bross, *Biographical Sketch of the late Gen. B. J. Sweet — History of Camp Douglas* (Chicago: Jansen, McClurg & Co., 1878), 11–12; Dennis Kelly, *The History Of Camp*

Douglas, Illinois, Union Prison, 1861–1865. (1961, reprint. Atlanta, GA: U.S. Dept. of the Interior, National Park Service, Southeast Region, 1989), 5; Kelly Pucci, *Camp Douglas: Chicago's Civil War Prison* (Charleston, SC: Arcadia, 2007), 7.]

5. Edward Glennan, *Reminiscence of the War of 1861 to 1865 By a Member of 42nd Ills*, Rose Embry Carey Collection, Edward H. Nabb Research Center for Delmarva History and Culture at Salisbury University (hereafter cited as Glennan reminiscence), I: 12.

6. Glennan reminiscence, I: 58.

7. Glennan reminiscence, II: 180.

8. Glennan reminiscence, I: 126.

9. Glennan reminiscence, I: 156–157.

10. Glennan reminiscence, I: 167–168.

11. Glennan reminiscence, I: 188–189.

12. Glennan reminiscence, II: 108.

13. Glennan reminiscence, II: 118.

14. Glennan reminiscence, III: 177.

15. In the U.S. National Home for Disabled Volunteer Soldiers record for Glennan, his discharge date was 5 May 1865. [Ancestry.com. *U.S. National Homes for Disabled Volunteer Soldiers, 1866–1938* [database on-line]. Provo, UT: Ancestry.com Operations, 2007. http://www.ancestry.com; Wilson, "Edward Glennan Family."]

16. Ancestry.com. *Kansas State Census Collection, 1855–1925* [database on-line]. Provo, UT: Ancestry.com Operations, 2009. http://www.ancestry.com; Ancestry.com. *1870 United States Federal Census* [database on-line]. Provo, UT: Ancestry.com Operations, 2009. http://www.ancestry.com; Irma Ward, *Douglas County, Kansas Marriages, 1870.* http://skyways.lib.ks.us/genweb/archives/douglas/marriage/marr1870.htm.

17. According to the U.S. National Home for Disabled Volunteer Soldiers records, Glennan was a patient from 24 January 1889 to 5 April 1893, 14 May 1912 to 8 July 1913, 3 October 1913 to 6 April

1914, 4 May 1916 to 18 April 1918, 11 August 1919 to 5 January 1920, 23 December 1920 to 18 September 1922, and 12 December 1922 to 22 December 1923. [*U.S. National Homes for Disabled Volunteer Soldiers.*]

18. Debra Graden, *Leavenworth, Kansas Deaths, 1923–30* [database on-line]. Provo, UT: Generations Network, 1998. http://www.ancestry.com; Wilson, "Edward Glennan Family."

Chapter One

1. The 8th Texas Cavalry or Terry's Texas Rangers were organized by Benjamin Franklin Terry, a sugar planter, and Thomas S. Lubbock and mustered into Confederate service in Houston in September 1861. [Jones, *Historical Dictionary of the Civil War*, 1420.]

2. An Irish immigrant, William Best (b. ca. 1833), a resident of Chicago, Illinois, enlisted on 5 August 1862 as a private in Co. E of the 88th Illinois Infantry Regiment at Chicago, Illinois. He was captured on 20 September 1863 at Chickamauga, Georgia, and died as a prisoner on 11 October 1864 at Andersonville, Georgia, of scorbutus or scurvy. His military record indicated he was married and had dark hair, grey eyes and stood 5' 7¾". [*ICWMDR; APW.*]

3. Unable to identify.

4. The "widow" Eliza Glenn was a young woman whose husband, John, had died of illness while fighting for the Confederacy. Located a mile and a half west of La Fayette Road, her home, a little log cabin, was used as General Rosecrans' headquarters as it was perfectly positioned on a high hill. The house was later destroyed by Confederate artillery during the Battle of Chickamauga. [Glenn Tucker, *Chickamauga: Bloody Battle in the West* (New York: Bobbs-Merrill, 1961), 119, 139; Peter Cozzens, *This Terrible Sound: The Battle of Chickamauga* (Urbana: University of Illinois Press, 1992), 139–140, 392.]

5. James F. Hewitt or Frank James Hewitt (b. ca. 1843), a native of Hillsdale, Michigan, enlisted as a private on 10 August 1861 in Co. F of the 42nd Illinois Infantry Regiment at Camp Douglas in Chicago. A farmer before the war, he would later be promoted to corporal. He died on 20 November 1863 of wounds received at Chickamauga, Georgia. His military record indicated he had dark hair, dark eyes and stood 5'5". [*ICW MDR.*]

6. Jacob "Jake" Dingman (b. ca. 1840), resided in North Buffalo, Michigan, when he enlisted as a private on 30 July 1861 in Co. F of the 42nd Illinois Infantry Regiment at Camp Douglas, Chicago, Illinois, by Captain Webb. He was killed on 20 Sept 1863 at Chickamauga, Georgia. His military record stated he was married and had light hair and blue eyes and stood 5'11". [*ICWMDR.*]

7. Glennan might have meant Company K where there was a First Sergeant Sherwin W. King who died at Chickamauga. [*ICWMDR.*]

8. Known as the Savannah Campaign, Sherman left the captured city of Atlanta, Georgia on 15 November 1864 and ended his march with the capture of the port of Savannah on 21 December 1864. The campaign is remembered for inflicting significant property damage, particularly to industry and infrastructure as well as to civilian property. [Boatner, *The Civil War Dictionary*, 722.]

9. Hardtack or hard tack is a simple type of cracker or biscuit, made from flour, water, and salt. [John D. Billings, *Hardtack and Coffee or The Unwritten Story of Army Life* (Lincoln: University of Nebraska Press, 1993), 113.]

10. Located in Richmond, Virginia, the Libby prison, erected in 1845 by John Enders, was located in a three-story brick warehouse on Tobacco Row, a collection of tobacco warehouses and cigarette factories, adjacent to the James River and Kanawha Canal near its eastern

terminus at the head of navigation of the James River. [Boatner, *The Civil War Dictionary*, 482; Wagner, *Civil War Desk Reference*, 611; "Major Turner's Escape'" *New York Times*, 7 July 1895, p. 28.]

11. Located on the westside of 21st Street between Main and Cary Streets, about mid-block, just north of General Hospital #16, the Smith Building, the tobacco factory of Smith and McCurdey, opened on 19 May 1862 and was destroyed in evacuation. [Robert W. Waitt, Jr., *Confederate Military Hospitals in Richmond*, Official Publication #22. (Richmond, VA: Richmond Civil War Centennial committee, 1964).]

12. Colonel Abel D. Streight, after being captured with 322 men by General N. B. Forrest on 3 May 1863, tunneled out of Libby Prison with 108 other officers on 9 February 1864. [J. T. Chalfant, "LIBBY TUNNEL: Who is Entitled to the Honor of Planning and Digging It?," *National Tribune*, 29 January 1885; Thomas C. Mays, "Col. Streight's Escape," *National Tribune*, 28 February 1907; "Gen. Butler's Department," *New York Times*, 16 February 1864, p. 1.]

13. John Hunt Morgan (1825–1864), an Alabamian, organized the Lexington Rifles in 1857 and led them to Bowling Green to join the forces of General Buckner when the Civil War began. He was promoted to colonel of the 2nd Kentucky Cavalry on 4 April 1862 and brigadier general on 11 December 1862. His raids in the summer of 1863 into Kentucky, Indiana and Ohio were the farthest north any uniformed Confederate troops penetrated during the war. In April 1864, he was placed in command of the Department of Southwestern Virginia and while in Greenville, Tennessee, he was killed in the garden of the house where he had been sleeping. [Warner, *Generals in Gray*, 220–221.]

14. Unable to identify.

15. Unable to identify.

16. Glennan wrote "that you Know I

Had to a Kind of you Know a Keep watch of them."

17. Born in County Roscommon, Ireland, Mary Glennan (1836–1914) married Daniel McManus (1832–1897) and resided in Reeder Township, Anderson County, Kansas. She died in Osawatomie, Miami County, Kansas, and was buried alongside her husband in St. Patrick's Cemetery in Emerald-Williamsburg, Kansas. [Sue Henner, "Sue Henner's Family Pages," http://awt c.ancestry.com; Wilson. "Edward Glennan Family."]

18. Intended to hold 3,700 prisoners, the Danville prison of six tobacco and cotton warehouses was overcrowded within weeks. More than 1,300 Union soldiers died from illness and malnutrition and the prison was infested with vermin and the smallpox epidemic. [Wagner, *Civil War Desk Reference*, 611; Patricia B. Mitchell, "'Truly Horrible' Danville Civil War Prisons." http://www .victorianvilla.com/sims-mitchell/local /articles/phsp/008.]

19. From the Code of Hammurabi, the phrase means equal retribution of an offensive act.

20. Dropsy is the swelling of soft tissues due to the accumulation of excess water. [*Webster's Dictionary*, 1466.]

21. Residing in Ashkum, Iroquois County, Illinois, before the war, James Brett (b. ca 1837) enlisted on 14 August 1862 in Co. K of the 88th Illinois Infantry Regiment at Chicago. An English immigrant, he was captured on 20 September 1863 at Chickamauga, GA and died as a prisoner on 25 July 1864 at Andersonville, Georgia of scurvy. His military record indicated that he was a married farmer with light hair, blue eyes and stood 5' 4½". [*ICWMDR; APW.*]

22. Born in Whitehall, New York, Henry Levoy (b. ca 1843), a farmer from Aurora, Kane Co, Illinois, enlisted on 23 September 1861 in Co. B of the 36th Illinois Infantry Regiment. He was captured on 20 September 1863 at Chickamauga, Georgia, held at Andersonville and survived. He was exchanged on 1 April 1865 and later mustered out on 15 July 1865 at Springfield, Illinois as a paroled prisoner. His military record indicates he had light hair, hazel eyes, and stood 5' 5". [*ICW MDR; APW.*]

23. Ben McCulloch (1811–1862) was a surveyor and Indian Fighter who fought in the Mexican War under Zachary Taylor. On 11 May 1861, he was commissioned brigadier general in the Provisional Confederate Army and assigned to the command of troops in Arkansas. He won the battle of Wilson's Creek but lost his life during the Battle of Elkhorn with a fatally wound in the breast by a Federal sharpshooter. [Warner, *Generals in Gray*, 200–201.]

24. An acceptable behavior for one person should be acceptable for another person. [John Ray, *A Collection of English Proverbs, Digested into a Convenient Method for the Speedy Finding Anyone Upon Occasion; with Short Annotations. Whereunto Are Added Local Proverbs with Their Explications, Old Proverbial Rhythmes, Less Known or Exotic Proverbial Sentences, and Scottish Proverbs* (Cambridge: J. Hayes, 1670), 98.]

25. Resident of Lafayette, Indiana, James Glennan enlisted on 14 December 1861 in Co. E of the 35th Indiana Infantry Regiment and deserted on 23 July 1862. [*ICWMDR.*]

26. Samson was a biblical figure from the Book of Judges, who was given Herculean strength by God.

27. Referencing someone weakened by ill health or whose vitality is spent. The last run of shad appeared in John Burroughs's 1876 novel *Winter Sunshine*. The last rose of summer appeared in Mark Twain's 1872 novel *Roughing It*. *The Last of the Mohicans* was an 1826 novel of James Fenimore Cooper. [*DARE*, III: 296, 416.]

28. George S. Stuart (b. ca. 1843) en-

listed as a private on 28 June 1861 in Co. A of the 21st Illinois Infantry Regiment at Springfield. Born in Kent, Litchfield County, Connecticut, he was a farmer residing at Decatur, Macon County, Illinois, before the war. As a paroled prisoner, he died in Annapolis, MD on 18 November 1864 of typhoid fever. He had brown hair, blue eyes and stood 5'8". [*ICWMDR.*]

29. A coffee extract mixed with sugar and milk. [George Washington Cable, *Famous Adventures and Prison Escapes of the Civil War.* (New York: Century, 1911), 45.]

30. Jefferson Finis Davis (1808–1889) graduated from West Point in 1828 and fought in the Mexican War as a colonel of a volunteer regi-ment. He served as the United States Secretary of War under the Pierce Administration and as a U.S. senator from Mississippi. Although against secession, he believed each state was sovereign and had an unquestionable right to secede from the Union and when Mississippi seceded from the Union, he resigned from the Senate in January 1861. The following month, he was appointed president of the Confederate States of America. On 10 May 1865, Davis was captured in Irwinville, Georgia, by Federal troops. [Jones, *Historical Dictionary of the Civil War,* 376–380.]

Chapter Two

1. Unable to identify.

2. One of the first official black regiments, the 54th Massachusetts Colored Troops was authorized in March 1863 with Colonel Robert Gould Shaw as their commander. The regiment gained recognition with the skirmish on James Island, South Carolina, and the assault on Fort Wagner near Charleston, South Carolina. [Dyer, *A Compendium of the War of the Rebellion,* 1266.]

3. Heinrich Hartmann Wirz (1823–1865), a Swiss immigrant, became director of Camp Sumter, located near Andersonville, Georgia, in March 1864. The prison suffered an extreme lack of food, tools and medical supplies, severe overcrowding, poor sanitary conditions and a lack of potable water. Approximately 45,000 prisoners were incarcerated during the camp's fourteen-month existence, and 13,000 died. Wirz was arrested in May 1865 by a contingent of federal cavalry and taken by rail to Washington, D.C., where the federal government intended to place him on trial for conspiring to impair the lives of Union prisoners of war. He was the only man tried, convicted and executed for war crimes during the Civil War. [Jones, *Historical Dictionary of the Civil War,* 1597–1598.]

4. The expression came from an old Irish ballad entitled "Mush, Mush, Mush, Tu-ra-li-ad-dy." [Earl J. Stout, *Folklore from Iowa* (New York: American Folk-Lore Society, G.E. Stechert and Co., agents, 1937), 136.]

5. From 17th to 20th April 1864, the battle of Plymouth was a Confederate assault that combined army forces under Major General Robert Hoke and two ironclads, the CSS *Albemarle* and CSS *Cotton Plant*, against the union forces at Plymouth, North Carolina. The two Confederate ironclads forced the wooden hulled Union warships to abandon the garrison at Plymouth and the army pushed the defenders out of one fort and into the other. With the navy gone and the forces surrounded, the Union garrison surrendered. [David A. Norris, "Battle of Plymouth," *Encyclopedia of the American Civil War,* 1533–1534.]

6. In 1891, John Jacob Astor IV, Cornelius Vanderbilt II and Jay Gould were among the richest and most powerful men in the United States.

7. Chucker-luck was a gambling game of English origins and played with three dice tumbled in a cup and a board

with squares numbered from one to six. In placing stakes on any square, the player bets the bank even money that one of the dice will show the number chosen. [*DARE*, I: 659.]

8. Glennan was referring to the phrase "the early bird catcheth the worm," a seventeenth century proverb. [Ray, *A Complete Collection of English Proverbs*, 103.]

9. Could be Harmon Scramlin, who was held at Andersonville for ten months and exchanged on 14 November 1864. He was also imprisoned at Belle Isle for two months and in Libby prison for two months. Born 11 May 1841 in Charleston, Michigan, he joined on 10 August 1861. His record stated he was a six-foot farmer with light hair and blue eyes. He was seriously wounded in the head in the battle of Stone's River. [*AWP; ICWMDR;* Lake City Publishing Co., *Portrait and Biographical Record of Kankakee County, Illinois* (Chicago: Lake City Publishing Co., 1893), 673.]

10. Transmitted by mosquitoes, yellow fever is a viral infection that if it enters the second phrase can be fatal with bleeding in the mouth, eyes and gastrointestinal tract and with liver damage. [*Webster's Dictionary*, 2649.]

11. Moon blind is the inability to see clearly in dim light due to a deficiency of vitamin A. [*Webster's Dictionary*, 1466.]

12. On 11 July 1864, six prisoners were found guilty of murdering other inmates and were sentenced to death by hanging. Their names were William Collins, a private in Co. K of the 88th Pennsylvania Infantry Regiment, who was born in England in 1835; Charles F. Curtis, a private in Co. A of the 5th Rhode Island Heavy Artillery, who was born in Canada; Patrick Delaney, a private in Co. E of the 83rd Pennsyvania Infantry Regiment, born in Ireland; Andrew Muir or Munn of the United States Navy, who was born in Dublin, Ireland; John Sarsfield, a pri-

vate of the 144th New York Infantry Regiment, who was born in Ireland in 1841; and John Sullivan, a private of the 76th New York Infantry Regiment, who was born in Ireland in 1836. Sullivan was also known as W. R. Rickson of the U.S. Army. The Andersonville hospital register listed all the condemned correctly except Delany, whose first initial is mistakenly recorded as "J.," and Curtis, who gave his name as Seaman W. R. Rickson of the U.S. Navy. For some reason the headstone for "Rickson" at Andersonville National Cemetery is placed over Sullivan's grave, instead of Curtis's, and Curtis has a stone of his own. [Ovid L. Futch, *History of Andersonville Prison* (Gainesville: University of Florida Press, 1968), 64, 71; William Marvel, *Andersonville: the Last Depot* (Chapel Hill: University of North Carolina Press, 1994), 69–71.]

13. Native of Londonderry, Ireland, Father William John Hamilton (1832–1900) was the head of the southeast missions and pastor of the Church of the Assumption in Macon, Georgia, who alerted Bishop Verot in May 1864 about the inhumane treatment of the prisoners at Andersonville. Verot immediately sent Father Peter Whelan, the vicar general of the Diocese of Savannah, to attend to the spiritual care of the prisoners from June through October 1864. Father Henry Peter Clavreul, Father John Kirby and Father Anselm Usannez, a bilinqual Jesuit, also assisted. Many sources have Father Peter Whelan as the principal priest at Andersonville, not Father Hamilton. [Robert Scott Davis, *Ghosts and shadows of Andersonville: essays on the secret social histories of America's deadliest prison* (Macon, GA: Mercer University Press, 2006), 25, 130–132; Futch, *History of Andersonville Prison*, 59–61; Marvel, *Andersonville: The Last Depot*, 14; Rita H. DeLorme, "Andersonville and Beyond: Reviewing the Career of Very Reverend Henry Peter Clavreul," *Southern Cross*

(22 January 2004): 3, http://www.diosa v.org/files/archives/S8404p03.pdf; Rita H. DeLorme, "Scanning the High-Profile Priesthood of Father William J. Hamilton," *Southern Cross* (20 March 2008): 3, http://www.diosav.org/files/archives/S 8812p03.pdf.]

14. The man that fell during the hanging was William Collins. [Futch, *History of Andersonville Prison*, 71.]

15. In the morning of 4 July 1864, soldiers of the 5th New Hampshire Volunteers flew a makeshift flag made out of cotton cloth with red and blue ink and sang patriotic songs. Jared M. Davis, sergeant of the 5th New Hampshire Volunteers, donated the flag to the New Hampshire Historical Society. ["The Small Flag with a Huge Story," *New Hampshire Historical Society*, http://www.nhhistory. org/news.html.]

16. Harvey Perry "Ped" Weir (ca. 1843–1918) joined Co. B of the 42nd Illinois Infantry Regiment on 28 July 1861 in Red Oak as a musician. A native of Henry County, Illinois, he deserted on 1 April 1862 at Murfreesboro, Tennessee. On 3 October 1862, he was transferred to Co. A of the 111th Illinois Infantry Regiment as a drum major. He was a prisoner of war at Andersonville and survived, later exchanged at Atlanta, Georgia, on 19 September 1864. According to his military records, he had light hair, blue eyes and stood 5' 4". After the war, he lived in Weir City, Cherokee County, Kansas, which was named after his father, Thomas McCardy Weir. In 1913, he was admitted into the Leavenworth National Home for Disabled Volunteer Soldiers. He died in 1918 and was interred at Los Angeles National Cemetery. [*ICWMDR; APW; U.S. National Homes for Disabled Volunteer Soldiers, 1866–1938*; Ancestry.com. *U.S., Burial Registers, Military Posts and National Cemeteries, 1862–1960* [database on-line]. Provo, UT: Ancestry.com Operations, 2012; http://www.an-cestry.com.]

17. Richard Thatcher (1846–1909) enlisted on 25 July 1862 at Salem, Illinois as a musician in Co. H of the 111th Illinois Infantry Regiment and mustered in on 18 September 1862 at Camp Marshall. Born in Pike County, Illinois, he was attending school before the war and mustered out on 6 June 1865 at Washington, D.C. On 22 July 1864, he was captured and sent to Andersonville and survived, being sent to Atlanta on 19 September 1864. Later in life, he became the first president of the Territorial Normal School of Oklahoma (now the University of Central Oklahoma) from 1891 to 1893. [*ICWMDR; APW; OCWVB*; January Mattingly, *Edmond Oklahoma: Always Growing* (Chicago: Arcadia, 2002), 9; University of Central Oklahoma. Archives and Special Collections, "Presidents of the University of Central Oklahoma," http://library.uco.edu/archives/ ucohistory/university-presidents.cfm; Jonathan Shipley, "Assassinology," *Lost Magazine*, no. 21 (February 2008), ht tp://www.lostmag.com/issue21/assassi-nology.php.]

18. Born in Ohio, James Birdseye McPherson (1828–1864) graduated from West Point first in his class of 1853. After the outbreak of the Civil War, he rose from a first lieutenant of engineers in August 1861 to a major general of volunteers with a command of a division of the XIII Corps in 8 October 1862. He served as aide-de-camp to Henry W. Halleck and as chief engineer to U. S. Grant. In January 1863, he was given command of XVII Corps during the Vicksburg campaign and was promoted to major general of the Regular Army on 1 August 1863. McPherson died while returning to his command from Sherman's headquarters near Atlanta. [Warner, *Generals in Blue*, 306–308.]

19. The 111th Illinois Infantry was organized by Colonel James S. Martin at Salem, and mustered in 18 September 1862 at Camp Marshall. It was comprised

of men from the counties of Marion, Clay, Washington, Clinton, and Wayne. [Dyer, *A Compendium of the War of the Rebellion*, 1093; *AGIL*, VI: 144.]

20. Starting at high noon on 22 April 1889, the Oklahoma Land Run of 1889 was the first land run into the Unassigned Lands. An estimated 50,000 people lined up for their piece of the available two million acres and within hours the cities of Oklahoma City and Guthrie were formed, with populations of at least 10,000. [Roy Gittinger, *The Formation of the State of Oklahoma (1803–1906)* (Berkeley: University of California Press, 1917), 152–157.]

21. The town of Neodesha is located in Wilson County in southeast Kansas. On 26 May 1888, Boston Corbett, John Wilkes Booth's killer, escaped from an asylum and stayed briefly with Richard Thatcher. They met during their imprisonment at Andersonville in the Civil War. [Shipley, "Assassinology."]

22. Originated in the seventeenth century, "tar" was a nickname for sailors. The term referred to their tarpaulin hats as well as the tar worn on hands and in the hair from the days when tar was used everywhere on ships to preserve rigging and seal seams. In the eighteenth century, it was combined with "Jack," creating "Jack Tar," to mean a working mariner. [*Webster's Dictionary*, 2340.]

23. The Dix-Hill Cartel Prisoner Exchange System was put into effect on 22 July 1862 to handle the general exchange of prisoners of war between the Federal government and the Confederacy. [Wagner, *Civil War Desk Reference*, 603.]

24. As a result from a severe rainstorm, a spring opened up on 10 August 1864, just inside the west deadline north of the creek. Believing it was an answer to their prayers, the prisoners named it Providence Spring. [Futch, *History of Andersonville Prison*, 62; William Best Hesseltine, *Civil War Prisons: A Study in War Psychology* (New York: Frederick Ungar, 1964), 153.]

25. Official records have Glennan being transferred to the hospital on 4 October 1864. [Ancestry.com. *Selected Records Relating to Federal Prisoners of War Confined at Andersonville, GA, 1864–65* [database on-line]. Provo, UT: Ancestry.com Operations, 2007; http://www.ancestry.com.]

Chapter Three

1. One who is employed in the loading or unloading of ships. [*Webster's Dictionary*, 2239.]

2. Sumac berries are rich in vitamin C, which helps fight off the onset of scurvy.

3. John Anderson enlisted as a private on 16 September 1861 at Monongahela City, Pennsylvania, in Co. D of the 79th Pennsylvania Infantry Regiment. He later became a corporal in Co. I. He was captured and died of dysentery at Andersonville, Georgia on 27 July 1864. [*APW.*]

4. Could be Isaiah Carter of the 38th Indiana Infantry. [*ICWMDR.*]

5. Nicknamed Stonewall of the West, Patrick Ronayne Cleburne (1828–1864) enlisted as a colonel at the age of 33 in the 15th Arkansas Infantry Regiment. On 4 March 1862, he was promoted full brigadier general with a commission in Confederate States Regiment and later promoted on 13 December 1862 to full major general. He was killed on 20 November 1864 at Franklin, Tennessee. [Clement A. Evans, ed., *Confederate Military History: A Library of Confederate States History*, 12 vols. (New York: A.S. Barnes, 1962), XIV: 396.]

6. The battle at Franklin on 30 November 1864 was a disastrous defeat of General Hood's Army of the Tennessee. Union Major General Schofield had withdrawn his army north toward Nashville after the engagement at Spring Hill the previous day. When the Union forces reached Franklin they found the bridges

over the Harpeth River destroyed or unusable and decided to fortify in the entrenchments left over from the first battle of Franklin while the bridges were repaired. General Hood pursued the Union forces to Franklin and decided to attack the entrenched troops in order to prevent them from joining the forces holding Nashville. The only avenue available for the assault was a frontal one across nearly two miles of open ground in full view of the enemy. The attack was a disaster with the Confederacy losing fifteen generals, fifty-three regimental commanders and nearly a quarter of the Army of Tennessee. The Confederate army did not recover from this battle and was decimated at Nashville a couple of weeks later. [James Lee McDonough, "Battle of Franklin," *Encyclopedia of the American Civil War*, 771–772; *The Union Army*, V: 440–442.]

7. Henry Levoy was exchanged on 1 April 1865. [*APW.*]

8. Glennan left Andersonville prison on 14 November 1864. [Ancestry.com. *Selected Records Relating to Federal Prisoners of War Confined at Andersonville, GA, 1864–65* [database on-line]. Provo, UT: Ancestry.com Operations, 2007. http://www.ancestry.com.]

9. Located five miles north of Millen, Georgia, Camp Lawton, a square stockade enclosing forty acres, was built in the summer of 1864 to relieve the congestion of prisoners at Andersonville. [Boatner, *The Civil War Dictionary*, 118, Wagner, *Civil War Desk Reference*, 610.]

10. Riley V. Beach (b. 1842), a native of Delaware County, Ohio, resided in Limestone, Kankakee County, Illinois, before enlisting as a private on 6 August 1862 in Co. B of the 113rd Illinois Infantry Regiment. A farmer by trade, he stood 5' 8½", had brown hair and hazel eyes. He was captured at the battle of Guntown, Mississippi, and was a prisoner of war for nine months. After the war, he moved to David City, Ne-

braska, in the fall of 1870 and became the first schoolteacher in that town, later the principal. In 1879, he was elected as County Superintendant of Public Schools and in 1882, he was the local preacher for the David City M. E. Church. [*ICWMDR*; A. T. Andreas, *History of the state of Nebraska* (Chicago: Western Historical Co., 1882), http://www.kancoll.org/books/andreas_ne/butler/butler-p4.html.]

11. Thomas W. Herburt (b. ca. 1827), a native of Quebec, Canada, resided in Quincy, Adams County, Illinois before enlisting as a private on 8 August 1862 in Co. C of the 84th Illinois Infantry Regiment. A farmer before the war, he stood 5' 2", had light hair and blue eyes. He was wounded and captured at Chickamauga on 20 September 1863. A rebel sentinel killed him on 15 May 1864 at Andersonville, GA. [*ICWMDR.*]

12. Andrew C. Lloyd served as a private in Co. F of the 82th Ohio Infantry. After the war, he spent time at the National Military Home in Kansas and died on 18 May 1904. [Ancestry.com. *Headstones Provided for Deceased Union Civil War Veterans, 1879–1903* [database on-line]. Provo, UT: The Generations Network, 2007. http://www.ancestry.com.]

13. The prisoners would sign a statement or an oath of honor stating they would not take up arms or perform any duty that soldiers normally performed until they were properly exchanged. Parole camps were established to house the paroled soldiers while they awaited exchange, but in other cases the parolee was allowed to return home until exchanged. [Boatner, *The Civil War Dictionary*, 619–620; Francis T. Miller, ed., *The Photographic History of the Civil War In Ten Volumes: Prisons and Hospitals* (New York: Castle, 1957), VII: 32.]

14. Part of a system of coastal fortifications to protect the United States against foreign invasion, Fort Pulaski was located on Cockspur Island at the mouth

of the Savannah River and constructed under the direction of General Babcock and Second Lieutenant Robert E. Lee. Named in honor of Kazimierz Pulaski, the Polish commander who fought in the American Revolution. [Boatner, *The Civil War Dictionary*, 296–297.]

15. Unable to identify.

16. Joseph Jones was a professor of medical chemistry in the Medical College of Georgia at Augusta. He received his degree in 1858 from University of Pennsylvania and served for six months as a private before moving to the medical department under the supervision of Dr. S. P. Moore, surgeon general. [McElroy, *Andersonville*, 298–299.]

17. Born in 1808, Edward Glennan died on 1 August 1864 in Anderson County, Kansas, and interred in St. Patrick Church, Emerald-Williamsburg, Kansas. [Wilson, "Edward Glennan Family."]

18. Fort Monroe is located on the tip of the Virginia Peninsula, known as Old Point Comfort. The fort guarded the approach the navigational shipping channel between the Chesapeake Bay and the entrance to the harbor of Hampton Roads, which itself is formed by the confluence of the Elizabeth River, the Nansemond River, and the James River. During the Civil War, the fortification never fell into the Confederate possession. [Jones, *Historical Dictionary of the Civil War*, 508.]

19. If the crash occurred twenty miles from St. Joseph, Missouri, it would have happened between the towns of Easton and Hemple.

20. Charted in 1847, the Hannibal and St. Joseph Railroad was completed in February 1859, becoming the first railroad to cross northern Missouri starting in Hannibal (adjacent to the Mississippi River) in the northeast and going to St. Joseph (adjacent to the Missouri River) in the northwest. [S. S. Brown, "Railroads of St. Joseph." in *The Encyclopedia of the History of Missouri*, 1901 ed., V: 287–288.]

21. In 1864, Thomas McElroy, born ca. 1830, was an Irish farmer residing in Lawrence, Douglas County, Kansas. He has a wife named Catherine, born ca. 1840, and daughter Mary Ann, born ca. 1861. [Ancestry.com. *1870 United States Federal Census* [database on-line]. Provo, UT: Ancestry.com Operations, 2009. http://www.ancestry.com.]

22. Irishman Thomas McGlinn and his wife Eleanor, both born ca. 1830, resided in Ohio City, Franklin County, Kansas. [*Kansas State Census.*]

23. Jeremiah Sullivan, born ca. 1810, was an Irish immigrant farmer who resided in Ohio City, Kansas. [*Kansas State Census.*]

24. Hugh McEvoy, an Irishman born ca. 1831, married a New Yorker named Margaret and they had three children, Henry, Mary and John. They resided in Reeder Township, Anderson County, Kansas. [*Kansas State Census.*]

25. Daniel Doolin (b. ca. 1835) was an unmarried Canadian living "next door" to Michael Glennan, Edward's brother, in Reeder Township, Anderson, Kansas. [*Kansas State Census.*]

26. In 1863, Michael Glennan (1833–1913) married Mary Grant (1843–1875) and had six children (Edward, Mary Bridget, Helena, Johannes, and Anna Elizabeth). On 1 February 1877, he married for the second time to Catherine Leydon (1848–1907) and they had one child, Catherine. A farmer in Reeder Township, Anderson County, Kansas, he died in Pottawatomie, Coffey County, Kansas, and was interred in St. Patrick Church, Emerald-Williamsburg, Kansas. [Cindy Lawson, "Cindy Lawson's Family," http://worldconnect.rootsweb.ancestry.com/cgi-bin/igm.cgi?op=GET&db=celawson&id=I1233; Wilson, "Edward Glennan Family."]

27. The Glennan family moved from Kankakee County, Illinois, to Reeder Township, Anderson County, Kansas. When Edward visited home, his father

had already died, leaving his mother, Aileen Alice (Slyman) Glennan (1812–1888), his sister, Ann (1840–1875), and his two brothers, Thomas, (1847–1901), and Christopher (1856–1939). Aileen Alice died in Anderson County, Kansas. Ann married Irishman John Christy (1822–1892) and had three children, Noreen (b. 1867), Alice (b. 1871) and John E. (b. 1875). Thomas would later marry Bridget Therese Cashman in 1877 and had a family of twelve. He resided in Anderson County, Kansas, until ca. 1891, where he resided in the town of Purcell, McClain County, Oklahoma, in the Chickasaw Indian Territory. Thomas was interred in Hillside Cemetery in Purcell, Oklahoma. Christopher died in Norman, Oklahoma, and was interred in Blessed Sacrament Church, Lawton, Oklahoma. [Lawson, "Cindy Lawson's Family"; Sharon Burnett-Crawford, "Bridget Therese Glennon," *OKBits: An OKGen-Web Project*, http://www.rootsweb.ances-try.com/~okbits/lawton.html; Sharon Burnett-Crawford, "Chris Glennon," *OKBits: An OKGenWeb Project*, http ://www.rootsweb.ancestry.com/~okbits/u nindex4.html; Wilson, "Edward Glennan Family."]

28. Bridget (1849–1918) and Ellen Anna (1850–1927) attended Osage Mission, located in present-day St. Paul, Kansas. Under government sponsorship, Jesuit missionaries from the Missouri Province, St. Louis, Missouri, and the Sisters of Loretto from Nerinx, Kentucky, taught Osage and Quapaw Indian boys and girls at the Osage Mission and Manual Labor School on the Osage Reservation from 1847 to 1872. Bridget married farmer-turned-railroad contractor Lincoln Ellis Clarke (1843–1928) in 1869 and had eleven children. They resided in Franklin County, Kansas (1869–1878), St. Louis, Missouri (1879–1889) and Evanston and Chicago, Illinois (1890–1910) and back to Franklin County, Kansas (1915), and both died in Los Angeles County, California, and were interred in Forest Lawn Memorial Park, Glendale, California. Ellen Anna married Charles Walker Embry (1850–1916) in 1875 and had six children. They resided in Franklin County, Kansas, and were interred in St. John's Catholic Cemetery, Homewood Township, Franklin County, Kansas. [Lawson, "Cindy Lawson's Family;" Marquette University, Department of Special Collections and University Archives, "Osage Mission and School Records finding aid," http://www.mar-quette.edu/library/collections/archives/ Mss/OMS/OMS-sc.html; Wilson, "Edward Glennan Family."]

29. Diphtheria is a potentially fatal contagious disease that usually involves the nose, throat, and air passages, but may also infect the skin. Its most striking feature is the formation of a grayish membrane covering the tonsils and upper part of the throat. [*Webster's Dictionary*, 637–638.]

30. Hancock's Veteran Corps, commanded by Winfield Scott Hancock, was organized in December of 1864 in Washington. The Corps was composed of veterans who had served full terms and therefore not subject to the draft. Consisted of no less than twenty thousand infantry, the recruits would enlist for no less than one year. They were assigned in the spring of 1865 to the 2nd Brigade, Provisional Army of the Shenandoah, and served until June of 1865. The recruits were paid a special bounty of $300 and if they preserved their arms to end of their term, would retain them as their own upon being honorably discharged from service. ["A Veteran Army Corps," *New York Times*, 29 November 1864, p. 1; "A New Army Corps— Hancock's Veterans," *New York Times*, 29 November 1864, p. 4.]

31. Bellaire, Ohio, located along the Ohio River in Belmont County, was known in the Reconstruction Era as the Glass City for the numerous glass-mak-

ing facilities from 1870 to 1885. Both the Baltimore & Ohio Railroad and the Central Ohio Railroad went through the town. [Saul B. Cohen, *The Columbia Gazetteer of the World* (New York: Columbia University Press, 1998), I: 308; A. T. McKelvey, ed., *Centennial History of Belmont County, Ohio, and Representative Citizens* (Chicago: Biographical, 1903), 170–171.]

32. Residing in Chicago by 1860, Patrick Glennan (ca. 1832–1873) married Irish-born Margaret Sloan (ca. 1830–1914) and they had two children, Alice F. (1859–1920) and Edward Patrick (1860–1941). Employed as a teamster, Patrick died in Chicago and was interred in Calvary Cemetery. [*1860 United States Federal Census;* Wilson, "Edward Glennan Family."]

33. The funeral train of President Abraham Lincoln arrived in Chicago on 1 May and his body was placed in state at the Cook County Courthouse. The viewing was open to the general public from 5 p.m. until 8 p.m. the next day.

The funeral train left the next day for Springfield, Illinois. ["The President's Obsequies: From Chicago to Mr. Lincoln's Home," *New York Times*, 3 May 1865, p. 5; William T. Coggeshall, *Lincoln Memorial. The Journeys of Abraham Lincoln from Springfield to Washington, 1861, as President Elect; and from Washington to Springfield, 1865, as President Martyred; comprising an account of public ceremonies on the entire route and full details of both journeys* (Columbus, OH: The Ohio State Journal, 1865), 268–282.]

34. "Money Musk" is a classic American contra dance, one of a group of dances frequently referred to as the "chestnuts." It was composed and given the title "Sir Archibald Grant of Moniemusk's Reel" by the Scottish violin tune composer Daniel Dow, ca. 1775. [Francis O'Neill, *Irish Folk Music: A Fascinating Hobby, with Some Account of Allied Subjects, Incl. O'Farrell's Treatise on the Irish or Union Pipes and Touchey's Hints to Amateur Pipers* (Chicago: Regan, 1910), 204.]

Bibliography

Print

Boatner, Mark Mayo, III. *The Civil War Dictionary.* New York: David McKay, 1959.

Bross, William. *Biographical Sketch of the Late Gen. B. J. Sweet — History of Camp Douglas.* Chicago: Jansen, McClurg, 1878.

Brown, S. S. "Railroads of St. Joseph." *The Encyclopedia of the History of Missouri.* 6 vols. Conard, Howard L., ed. New York, Louisville, St. Louis: Southern History, 1901.

Cable, George Washington. *Famous Adventures and Prison Escapes of the Civil War.* New York: Century, 1911.

Cassidy, Frederic G., and John Houston Hall. *Dictionary of American Regional English,* 4 Vols. Cambridge, MA: Belknap Press of Harvard University Press, 1985.

Cist, Henry M. *The Army of the Cumberland.* 1882, reprint. Wilmington, NC: Broadfoot, 1989.

Coggeshall, William T. *Lincoln Memorial. The Journeys of Abraham Lincoln from Springfield to Washington, 1861, as President Elect; and from Washington to Springfield, 1865, as President Martyred; Comprising an Account of Public Ceremonies on the Entire Route and Full Details of Both Journeys.* Columbus: Ohio State Journal, 1865.

Cohen, Saul B. *The Columbia Gazetteer of the World.* New York: Columbia University Press, 1998.

Connelly, Thomas Lawrence. *Autumn of Glory: The Army of Tennessee, 1862–1865.* Baton Rouge: Louisiana State University Press, 1971.

Cozzens, Peter. *No Better Place to Die: The Battle of Stones River.* Urbana: University of Illinois Press, 1990.

Daniel, Larry J. *Days of Glory: The Army of the Cumberland 1861–1865.* Baton Rouge: Louisiana State University Press, 2004.

Davis, Robert Scott. *Ghosts and Shadows of Andersonville: Essays on the Secret Social Histories of America's Deadliest Prison.* Macon, GA: Mercer University Press, 2006.

Dupuy, Richard Ernest, and Trevor N. Dupuy. *The Compact History of the Civil War.* New York: Hawthorn, 1960.

Dyer, Frederick H. *A Compendium of the War of the Rebellion.* 3 vols. New York: Thomas Yoseloff, 1959.

Evans, Clement A., ed. *Confederate Military History: A Library of Confederate States History.* 12 vols. New York: A.S. Barnes, 1962.

Foote, Shelby. *The Civil War: A Narrative — Fort Sumter to Perryville.* Vol. I. New York: Random House, 1958.

Force, M.F. *Campaigns of the Civil War. Vol I: From Fort Henry to Corinth.* Wilmington, NC: Broadfoot, 1989.

Fox, William F. *Regimental Losses in the American Civil War, 1861–1865: A Treatise on the Extent and Nature of the Mortuary Losses in the Union Regiments, with Full and Exhaustive Statis-*

tics Compiled from the Official Records on File in the State Military Bureaus and at Washington. Dayton, OH: Morningside, 1974.

Futch, Ovid L. *History of Andersonville Prison.* Gainesville: University of Florida Press, 1968.

Gittinger, Roy. *The Formation of the State of Oklahoma (1803–1906).* Berkeley: University of California Press, 1917.

Hesseltine, William Best. *Civil War Prisons: A Study in War Psychology.* New York: Frederick Ungar, 1964.

Hewett, Janet B., ed. *Supplement to the Official Records of the Union and Confederate Armies.* 80 vols. Wilmington, NC: Broadfoot, 1995.

Illinois. Military and Naval Department. Report of the Adjutant General of the State of Illinois, Containing Reports for the Years 1861–66, rev. ed. 9 vols. Springfield: Phillips Bros., 1900–1901.

Jones, Terry L. *Historical Dictionary of the Civil War.* Lanham: Scarecrow, 2002.

Kelly, Dennis. *The History Of Camp Douglas, Illinois, Union Prison, 1861–1865.* 1961, reprint. Atlanta, GA: U.S. Department of the Interior, National Park Service, Southeast Region, 1989.

Lake City Publishing Co. *Portrait and Biographical Record of Kankakee County, Illinois.* Chicago: Lake City Publishing Co., 1893.

Marvel, William. *Andersonville: The Last Depot.* Chapel Hill: University of North Carolina Press, 1994.

Mattingly, Jan. *Edmond, Oklahoma: Always Growing.* Chicago: Arcadia, 2002.

McDonough, James Lee. "Battle of Stone's River." *Encyclopedia of the American Civil War: A Political, Social, and Military History.* Heidler, David S., and Jeanne T. Heidler, eds. New York: W.W. Norton, 2000.

_____. "Battle of Franklin." *Encyclopedia of the American Civil War: A Political, Social, and Military History.* Heidler, David S., and Jeanne T. Heidler, eds. New York: W.W. Norton, 2000.

_____. *Stones River: Bloody Winter in Tennessee.* Knoxville: The University of Tennessee Press, 1980.

McElroy, John. *Andersonville: A Story of Rebel Military Prisons.* Greenwich, CT: Fawcett, 1962.

McKelvey, A. T., ed. *Centennial History of Belmont County, Ohio, and Representative Citizens.* Chicago: Biographical, 1903.

Miller, Francis T., ed. *The Photographic History of the Civil War In Ten Volumes: Prisons and Hospitals.* New York: Castle, 1957.

Norris, David A. "Battle of Plymouth." *Encyclopedia of the American Civil War: A Political, Social, and Military History.* Heidler, David S. and Jeanne T. Heidler, eds. New York: W.W. Norton, 2000.

O'Neill, Francis. *Irish Folk Music: A Fascinating Hobby, with Some Account of Allied Subjects, Incl. O'Farrell's Treatise on the Irish or Union Pipes and Touchey's Hints to Amateur Pipers.* Chicago: Regan, 1910.

Powell, Dave. "Battle of Chickamauga." *Encyclopedia of the American Civil War: A Political, Social, and Military History.* Heidler, David S., and Jeanne T. Heidler, eds. New York: W.W. Norton, 2000.

Pucci, Kelly. *Camp Douglas: Chicago's Civil War prison.* Charleston, SC: Arcadia Publishing, 2007.

Ray, John. *A Collection of English Proverbs, Digested into a Convenient Method for the Speedy Finding Anyone Upon Occasion; with Short Annotations. Whereunto Are Added Local Proverbs with Their Explications, Old Proverbial Rhythmes, Less Known or Exotic Proverbial Sentences, and Scottish Proverbs.* Cambridge: J. Hayes, 1670.

_____. *A Complete Collection of English Proverbs,* 5th ed., John Belfour, ed. London: George Cowie, 1813.

Scott, Robert N. *The War of the Rebellion:*

Bibliography

A Compilation of the Official Records of the Union and Confederate Armies. 128 vols. Harrisburg, PA: National Historical Society, 1985.

Stout, Earl J. *Folklore from Iowa.* New York: American Folk-Lore Society, G.E. Stechert, agents, 1937.

Tucker, Glenn. *Chickamauga: Bloody Battle in the West.* New York: The Bobbs-Merrill Co., 1961.

Tucker, Spencer C. "Battle of Island No. 10." *Encyclopedia of the American Civil War: A Political, Social, and Military History.* Heidler, David S., and Jeanne T. Heidler, eds. New York: W.W. Norton, 2000.

The Union Army: A History of Military Affairs in the Loyal States 1861–65 — Records of the Regiments in the Union Army — Cyclopedia of Battles — Memoirs of Commanders and Soldiers. 8 vols. 1908, reprint. Wilmington, NC: Broadfoot, 1998.

Wagner, Margaret E., Gary W. Gallagher and Paul Finkelman. *The Library of Congress Civil War Desk Reference.* New York: Simon & Schuster, 2002.

Waitt, Robert W. Jr. *Confederate Military Hospitals in Richmond.* Official Publication #22. Richmond, VA: Richmond Civil War Centennial Committee, 1964.

Warner, Ezra J. *Generals in Blue: Lives of the Union Commanders.* Baton Rouge: Louisiana State University Press, 1964.

_____. *Generals in Gray: Lives of the Confederate Commanders.* Baton Rouge: Louisiana State University Press, 1959.

Webster's Third New International Dictionary of the English Language Unabridged. Springfield, MA: Merriam-Webster, 1986.

White, Kristy Armstrong. "Battle of Corinth." *Encyclopedia of the American Civil War: A Political, Social, and Military History.* Heidler, David S., and Jeanne T. Heidler, eds. New York: W.W. Norton, 2000.

Newspapers

National Tribune
New York Times

Online Resources

Ancestry.com. *Andersonville Prisoners of War* [database on-line]. Provo, UT: Ancestry.com Operations Inc, 1999. http://www.ancestry.com.

_____. *1870 United States Federal Census* [database on-line]. Provo, UT: Ancestry.com Operations, 2009. http://www.ancestry.com.

_____. *Headstones Provided for Deceased Union Civil War Veterans, 1879–1903* [database on-line]. Provo, UT: The Generations Network, 2007. http://www.ancestry.com.

_____. *Kansas State Census Collection, 1855–1925* [database on-line]. Provo, UT: Ancestry.com Operations, 2009. http://www.ancestry.com.

_____. *Selected Records Relating to Federal Prisoners of War Confined at Andersonville, GA, 1864–65* [database on-line]. Provo, UT: Ancestry.com Operations, 2007. http://www.ancestry.com.

_____. *U.S., Burial Registers, Military Posts and National Cemeteries, 1862–1960* [database on-line]. Provo, UT: Ancestry.com Operations, 2012. http://www.ancestry.com.

Andreas, A. T. *History of the state of Nebraska.* Chicago: Western Historical Co., 1882. http://www.kancoll.org/books/andreas_ne/butler/butler-p4.html.

Burnett-Crawford, Sharon. "Chris Glennon." OKBits: An OKGenWeb Project. http://www.rootsweb.ancestry.com/~okbits/unindex4.html.

DeLorme, Rita H. "Andersonville and Beyond: Reviewing the Career of Very Reverend Henry Peter Clavreul." *Southern Cross.* (22 January 2004), 3. http://www.diosav.org/files/archives/S8404p03.pdf.

Bibliography

_____. "Scanning the high-profile priest-hood of Father William J. Hamilton." *Southern Cross.* (20 March 2008), 3. http://www.diosav.org/files/archives/S8812p03.pdf.

Erickson, Mahlon, and John Erickson. "Oklahoma Civil War Veteran Buri-als—Tabor through Thurston." http://www.geocities.com/Heartland/Forest/7014/okcwvetsta.htm.

Illinois State Archives. "The Illinois Civil War Muster and Descriptive Rolls database." http://www.sos.state.il.us/departments/archives/datcivil.html.

Lawson, Cindy. "Cindy Lawson's Family." http://worldconnect.rootsweb.ancestry.com/cgi-bin/igm.cgi?op=GET&db=celawson&id=I1233.

Marquette University, Department of Special Collections and University Archives. "Osage Mission and School Records finding aid." http://www.marquette.edu/library/collections/archives/Mss/OMS/OMS-sc.html.

Mitchell, Patricia B. "'Truly Horrible' Danville Civil War Prisons." http://www.victorianvilla.com/sims-mitchell/local/articles/phsp/008.

Shipley, Jonathan. "Assassinology." *Lost Magazine,* no. 21 (February 2008), http://www.lostmag.com/issue21/assassinology.php.

"The Small Flag with a Huge Story." *New Hampshire Historical Society.* http://www.nhhistory.org/news.html.

University of Central Oklahoma. Archives and Special Collections. "Presidents of the University of Central Oklahoma." http://library.uco.edu/archives/ucohistory/university-presidents.cfm.

Ward, Irma. *Douglas County, Kansas Marriages, 1870.* http://skyways.lib.ks.us/genweb/archives/douglas/marriage/marr1870.htm.

Wilson, Anna Marie. "Edward Glennan Family." http://trees.ancestry.com/tree/22028030.

Index

Numbers in **bold italics** indicate pages with photographs.

Index